Falconer Madan

Rough List of Manuscript Materials

Relating to the History of Oxford

Falconer Madan

Rough List of Manuscript Materials
Relating to the History of Oxford

ISBN/EAN: 9783337338305

Printed in Europe, USA, Canada, Australia, Japan

Cover: Foto ©ninafisch / pixelio.de

More available books at **www.hansebooks.com**

ROUGH LIST

OF

MANUSCRIPT MATERIALS

RELATING TO THE

HISTORY OF OXFORD

CONTAINED IN

THE PRINTED CATALOGUES OF THE BODLEIAN
AND COLLEGE LIBRARIES

*ARRANGED ACCORDING TO SUBJECT
WITH AN INDEX*

BY

F. MADAN, M.A.

Fredk York Powell

Oxford

AT THE CLARENDON PRESS

1887

PREFACE.

The following list has been compiled between April 14, 1886, and the present date, from the printed catalogues of Bodleian MSS. and of MSS. in the College Libraries of Oxford, for the use of students of the history of the University and City.

The collections here included are the following, the subjoined date being that of the index used :—

Ashmole, 1866.
Barlow, 1697.
Barocci, 1853.
Bernard, 1697.
Bodley, 1697.
Boreales codices, 1832.
Canonici, 1854, 1864.
Casaubon, 1853.
Charters and Rolls, 1878.
Clarendon papers, Catal. vols. 1–3, 1869–76.
Clarke, E. D., 1853.
Classici codices (so far as indexed in 1697 and 1853).
Digby, 1883.
Dodsworth, 1697.
D'Orville, 1853.
Douce, 1840.
Dugdale, 1697.
Fairfax, 1697.
Fell, 1697, 1853.
Gough, 1814.
Grabe, 1853.

Hatton, Charles, 1697.
— Christopher, 1697.
James, 1697.
Jones, 1697.
Junius, 1697.
Langbaine, 1853.
Laud, 1853, 1885.
Leland, 1697.
Malone, 1836.
e Musaeo, 1697.
Rawlinson, A, B, C, 1878.
Roe, 1853.
Saibante, 1853.
St. Amand, 1853.
Selden, 1697.
Tanner, 1860.
Topographical MSS. (recent).
Wood, 1697.

College MSS., except Ch. Ch., 1852.
Ch. Ch. MSS., 1867.

Some Bodley Additional MSS. are included, so far as they are entered in the Bodleian interleaved copy of the Index of 1697. The Oriental catalogues have also been consulted. The compiler has not felt himself bound to verify the entries in the printed indexes referred to.

The arrangement by subjects, which is original, is an experiment, on a larger scale than has yet been attempted for any place, to bring into convenient order the literature of Oxford. Personal names have been almost entirely omitted. Where the subdivision of a subject is more elaborate under the heading of the University than under the City, it must be remembered that the smaller divisions are supposed to be implicit in the larger, when not expressly drawn out. Thus *Boating* (see 863) is, for the City, 353.

It is hoped that the order of subjects and the notation used may be of some independent value to those who are likely to use this list. If they will arrange their own Oxford notes on uniform slips of paper (say $5 \times 2\frac{1}{2}$ in.) in accordance with the present scheme, much additional information might be made available for reference. The notation is specially adapted to allow of an expansion based on the principle that each unit indicates a subdivision of the *preceding* unit. Thus 631–639 are capable of infinite subdivision by such forms as 6311–6319, 6321–6329, etc. The numbers in the present list do not exceed (or fall short of) three digits, so that between any two there may be inserted nine additional divisions without exceeding four digits.

The List formed part of the compiler's Library work, and is printed by the desire of Bodley's Librarian.

BODLEIAN LIBRARY, OXFORD.
July, 1887.

CONTENTS.

	PAGE
Analysis of Subject Headings	1
PART I.—MS. Materials in order of Subjects General 101–115 . . City 121–390	5 Univ. 401–970
PART II.—Alphabetical Index of Subject Headings . .	143

OXFORD.

ANALYSIS OF SUBJECT HEADINGS.

OXFORD.
    GENERAL NOTES, 101.
        Name, 102.
        Natural history, 103.
        External appearance, 115.

CITY.
    GENERAL NOTES, 121.
    LOCAL DIVISIONS, 130.
        Parishes, 131.
        Cathedral, 154.
        Suburbs, 155.
        Public Institutions and Buildings, 163.
        Streets, quarters, etc., 215.
        Old Institutions, 240.

GOVERNMENT, 270.
    Public Officers and Offices, 280.

CITY:—CLASSES OF THE COMMUNITY, 300.
    Nobility, 301.
    Gentry, 302.
    Professional men (middle classes), 303.
    Manufacturers, 304.
    Tradesmen, 305.
    Common people, 308.
    Religious orders, 315.

LIFE AND MANNERS, 330.
    Religious, 333.
    Intellectual and literary, 337.
    Commercial, 339.
    Political, 343.
    Scientific, 345.
    Artistic, 347.
    Social, 352.
    Personal, 357.

EXTERNAL RELATIONS, 360.
    To the country at large, 361.
    To the Crown, 362.
    To Church and Dissent, 366.
    To Parliament, 368.
    To the neighbourhood, 370.
    (To the University.)
    To other cities, 371.

HISTORY AND ANTIQUITIES IN GENERAL, 380.
    (At different periods.)
    Incidents, 387.
    Personal history, 388.

DOCUMENTS, RECORDS and MISCELLANEA, 390.

UNIVERSITY.

GENERAL NOTES, 401.
External appearance, 406.

LOCAL DIVISIONS, 410.
University Institutions and Buildings, 411.
Collegiate   ,,   ,,   ,,   444.
Halls, 477.
Private Halls, 482.
Old Institutions, 483.

GOVERNMENT, 500.
Officers and Offices, 513.

CLASSES OF MEMBERS, 530.
Graduates (Professors, etc.), 531.
Undergraduates, 620.
Members of Colleges or Halls, 630.
Religious Orders, 660.

COURSE OF STUDIES, 701.
General conditions, 701.
Special studies, acc. to faculty, 726.
University Scholarships, 795.
    ,, Prizes, 813.

LIFE AND MANNERS, 830.
Religious, 835.
Intellectual and literary, 840.
Political, 844.
Scientific, 847.
Artistic, 849.
Social, 855.
Personal, 900.

UNIVERSITY:—EXTERNAL RELATIONS, 911.
    To foreign lands, 912.
    To the country, 918.
    To the Crown, 925.
    To Church and Dissent, 932.
    To Parliament, 933.
    To the neighbourhood, 937.
    To the city, 938.
    To other universities, 939.
    To schools, 946.
    To colleges, etc. within itself, 948.

HISTORY AND ANTIQUITIES IN GENERAL, 950.
    (At different periods.)
    Incidents, 961.
    Personal history, 962.

DOCUMENTS, RECORDS, AND MISCELLANEA, 970.

OXFORD.

PART I.

LIST, IN ORDER OF SUBJECTS.

OXFORD.
  GENERAL NOTES, 101.
    General Account of Oxford, by John Leland in his Itinerary, A.D. 1542.
      Leland Itin. 2, *fol.* 17 (*O. C.* 5108).

  Name, 102.
    The various names of Oxford.
      Wood F. 29^a, *fol.* 2^v (*O. C.* 8491).

  Natural History, 103.
    Site and Position, 104.
      Longitude and Latitude.
        Ashm. 339, *fol.* 164^v; 396, *fol.* 68^v; 789, *fol.* 369^v; 1796, *fol.* 90^v.
      The situation of Oxford.
        Wood F. 29^a, *fol.* 3 (*O. C.* 8491).
      The altitude of Oxford.
        Ibid., fol. 7.
    Air, Sky (Astronomy), and **Weather** (Meteorology), 105.
      (Several sets of old astronomical tables and observations made at or for Oxford 1310, 1316, 1437, 1438–40).
        Laud Misc. 674, *foll.* 67, 75, 43^v, 99^v.
      Ditto (no date, but 14th or 15th cent.).
        Laud Misc. 594, *fol.* 84.
      Tabula radicum mediorum motuum solis, lunae, etc. ad meridiem Oxon., 1340–1600.
        Digb. 17, *fol.* 15^v.

(Oxford—General Notes.)

Tabula conjunctionum et oppositionum solis et lunae, etc. super meridiem Oxon., 1341–6.
Digb. 176, *foll.* 94–119.

Nota de tempestate anno 1361.
Digb. 57, *fol.* 28^v.

Tabula eclipsium super meridiem Oxoniensem, 1376–89.
Digb. 57, *fol.* 119^v.

Canon Almanack de locis planetarum, in usum Oxoniensium, 1440.
Magd. Coll. 182, *fol.* 36.

Liber quadrantis, cum tabulis ad meridiem Oxon.
Digb. 98, *fol.* 162.

Tabulae variae astronomicae ad meridiem Toleti London. et Oxon.
Digb. 114, *fol.* 22–32.

Tabulae variae planetarum super meridiem Oxon.
Ibid., 57, *fol.* 119^v–126.

Calendarium de mediis motibus planetarum super meridiem Oxon.
Ibid., 57, *fol.* 9.

(See also *Incidents*, 387.)

Earth (Geology), 106.

Water, 107.

Floods, 108.

Water-supply, 109.

Plants (Botany), 111.

Animals (Zoology), 112.

Health (diseases, pestilence, plague, cholera, etc.), 113.

Notice of such as died of the infection, 1577.
Tann. 79, *fol.* 182.

Notes of the practice of a physician chiefly in and near Oxford, 1589–1614.
Rawl. A. 370.

Letter of Tho. Tanner about small pox in Oxford, 30 Aug. 1695.
Tann. 24, *fol.* 56.

Drainage, 114.

(**Oxford—General Notes.**)
External appearance (descriptions, guides, plans, views), 115.
 Transcript of Ant. à Wood's Description of Oxford.
  Gough Oxf. 5.
 Patent to D. Loggan for publishing engravings of Oxford, 17 Mar. 167$\frac{2}{3}$.
  All S. Coll. 241, *fol.* 372.
 Notes of a tour round Oxford, 1785, by an artist.
  Top. Oxf. c. 33.
 28 Indian-ink drawings of old gates, halls, parish churches, etc. in Oxford, by B. Green. *c.*
  Gough Oxf. 50.
 Indian-ink drawings of churches, the Town Hall and antiquities in Oxford. *c.*
  Top. Oxf. b. 14.
 81 drawings chiefly of Oxford, by J. C. Nattes, 1804.
  Top. Oxf. b. 3.
Buildings (architecture), 116.
Oxford Historical Society, 118.

CITY.

GENERAL NOTES, 121: (see also *History, &c.*, 380).
 Deeds affecting the City of Oxford as a corporation.
  Charters Cal., pp. 13, 116, 281–292, 338, 359, 372, 375, 378, 586, 662.
 Rentale monast. Osneyensis de reditu in burgo villae Oxoniae, 1453–1479.
  Wood F. 10 (*O. C.* 8472).
 —1463.
  C. C. C. 280, *fol.* 96.
 —1498.
  Wood F. 10 (*O. C.* 8472).
 Papers concerning the history and antiquities of the City of Oxford.
  Wood F. 29^a (*O. C.* 8491).
 Description of the city by Wards: (see also *Rawl. B.* 400^a).
 N.E. Ward.
  Wood F. 29^a, *fol.* 10 (*O. C.* 8491).

(City—General Notes.)
S.E. Ward. *Ibid., fol.* 23.
S.W. Ward. *Ibid., fol.* 43.
N.W. Ward. *Ibid., fol.* 53.

Population, census, lists of citizens, etc., 122.
Names of some inhabitants, 1606.
Ashm. 181, *fol.* 126.
List of debtors to the King, chiefly in Oxford and the neighbourhood, 1643.
Clar. i. 1739.

Size and bounds, 123.
Description of the ancient bounds of the City, in French (Henry VI's time).
Charters Cal., p. 311.

Character and importance, 124.

Military, 125.

Commercial, 126.
Papers on opening trade between Oxford and London in the Civil War, 5 and 19 Aug. 1644.
Clar. i. 1780, 1786.

As a resort, 127.

Domesday survey (1086), Hundred rolls (c. 1279), and other ancient public records, 128.
The state of the City at the time of the Conquest.
Wood F. 29ᵃ, *fol.* 8 (*O. C.* 8491).

Arms, motto, etc., 129.

LOCAL DIVISIONS, 130.

Charter affecting La Lavandrie.
Charters Cal., p. 290.

Parishes, 131.
Collections concerning St. Frideswide's property in the parishes of Oxford, from the Cartulary (?) of St. Frideswide.
Wood C. 4 (*O. C.* 8526).
Miscellanea de antiquis ecclesiis et parochiis in Civ. Oxon. per Brianum Twyne.
Wood F. 29ᵃ, *fol.* 372 (*O. C.* 8491).

(City—Local Divisions.)

Churches, 132.
    Ecclesiarum Catalogus etc., per M. Windesore.
        C. C. C. 280, *fol.* 12.
    Monuments, Inscriptions and Arms in the parish churches, 1659.
        Rawl. B. 397 (in *foll.* 1–217).
    — 1660 (?) to 1736 and 1750, supplementing Wood's History of the City.
        Ibid., B. 400^d, *foll.* 36–108.
    Collections of monumental inscriptions in Oxford, Bristol, etc., by R. Rawlinson.
        Rawl. B. 400^d.
    Arms in Carfax Church etc., tricked.
        Wood D. 19, *fol.* 132 (*O. C.* 8564).
    Curious inscription in one of the churches.
        Tann. 23, *fol.* 80.

All Saints, parish and church, 133.
    Charters affecting the parish.
        Charters Cal., pp. 284, 290, 291, 297, 304, 349–51, 374, 662.
    Arms in the church, 1574.
        Wood D. 14 (*O. C.* 8548).
    Extracts from the Registers: Bur. 1564–1673, Marr. 1560–1647, Bapt. 1560–1611.
        Wood D. 5 (*O. C.* 8524).
    Extracts from the Registers, 1565–1669.
        Tann. 454, *fol.* 144.
    Of All Saints'.
        Wood F. 29^a, *foll.* 318, 337 (*O. C.* 8491).
    Extracts from the muniments.
        Wood D. 2, p. 323 (*O. C.* 8513).
    Notes of Arms in the Church.
        Wood B. 14 (*O. C.* 8585).
    Subscriptions for rebuilding the church.
        Rawl. C. 805, *fol.* 5.

Carfax, parish and church, see *St. Martin*, 143.

(City—Local Divisions.)

Holy Trinity, parish and church, 134.

Holywell (St. Cross), parish and church, 135.
   Charters affecting the parish.
      Charters Cal., pp. 290, 304, 350.
   Extracts out of the Registers, Bur. 1583–1676.
      Wood D. 5 (*O. C.* 8524).
   Of St. Cross (Holywell).
      Wood F. 29^a, *foll.* 302^v, 355 (*O.C.* 8491).

St. Aldate, parish and church, 136.
   Charters affecting the church or parish.
      Charters Cal., pp. 304, 305, 308, 350.
   Judgement in a suit about the tithes of St. Aldate's (time of Edw. VI).
      Rawl. C. 712, *fol.* 33^v.
   Extracts from the Registers, Bur. 1538–1676, Bapt. 1538–1678, Marr. 1538–1670.
      Wood. D. 5 (*O. C.* 8524).
   Carta Ric. Jones concedens messuagia in usum ecclesiae S. Aldati 27 July, 9 Eliz. (1567).
      C. C. C. 280, *fol.* 28.
   Arms in the church, 1574.
      Wood D. 14 (*O. C.* 8548).
   Of St. Aldate's.
      Wood F. 29^a, *fol.* 329 (*O. C.* 8491).
   Of St. Aldate's church.
      Ibid., fol. 298 (*O. C.* 8491).
   Extracts from the muniments.
      Wood D. 2, p. 67 (*O. C.* 8513).
   Anecdote about a stone house in St. Aldate's, built by a cook of Ch. Ch.
      Tann. 466, *fol.* 67^v.

St. Barnabas, parish and church, 137.

St. Clement, parish and church, 138.
   Charters affecting the parish.
      Charters Cal., pp. 281, 305.

(City—Local Divisions.)

Extracts from the Registers, Bur. 1643–1644, Marr. 1626.
 Wood D. 5 (*O. C.* 8524).

Of St. Clement's.
 Wood F. 29ᵃ, *fol.* 302.

Notice of the parsonage.
 Tann. 305, *fol.* 141.

St. Cross, parish and church, see *Holywell*, 135.

St. Ebbe, parish and church, 139.

Arms in the church, 1574.
 Wood D. 14 (*O. C.* 8548).

Extracts from the Registers, 1575–1646.
 Tann. 456*, *fol.* 58.

— 1575–1672.
 Wood D. 5 (*O. C.* 8524).

Extracts from the muniments.
 Wood D. 2, p. 342 (*O. C.* 8513).

Of St. Ebbe's.
 Wood F. 29ᵃ, *fol.* 303ᵛ (*O. C.* 8491).

St. Giles, parish and church, 141 (see 232).

Charters affecting St. Giles's.
 Charters Cal., pp. 290, 312.

Extracts from the Register: Bur. 1609–74, Marr. 1612–62, Bapt. 1577–1635.
 Wood D. 5 (*O. C.* 8524).

Of St. Giles's.
 Wood F. 29ᵃ, *fol.* 306ᵛ (*O. C.* 8491).

Extracts from the muniments.
 Wood D. 2, p. 348 (*O. C.* 8513).

Coin and seal found in St. Giles's parish.
 Rawl. C. 867, *foll.* 57ᵛ, 76.

St. John Baptist, parish, 142.
 (*Church*, see *Merton College*, 467).

Charters affecting St. John Baptist parish.
 Charters Cal., pp. 290, 351, 352.

(City—Local Divisions.)

Parish Register, 1617–90, in Ant. à Wood's hand.
  Rawl. B. 402ᵃ.

Register of the parish (17th cent.), transcribed by Ant. à Wood.
  Rawl. B. 402ᵃ.

Account of beating the bounds of the parish, 1682: by Ant. à Wood.
  Rawl. B. 402ᵃ (at beginning).

Of St. John's.
  Wood F. 29ᵃ, fol. 308 (O. C. 8491).

St. Martin, parish and church (Carfax), 143.
  (See also Carfax, 222.)

Charters affecting St. Martin's parish.
  Charters Cal., pp. 284, 290, 291, 305, 306, 352.

Extracts from the Registers, 1562–1667.
  Tann. 456*, fol. 46.

Extracts from the Registers: Bur. 1562–1671, Marr. 1565–1640, Bapt. 1583–1643.
  Wood D. 5 (O. C. 8524).

Arms in the church, 1574.
  Wood F. 14. (O. C. 8548).

Of St. Martin's (Carfax).
  Wood F. 29ᵃ, foll. 310, 344 (O. C. 8491).

Extracts from the muniments.
  Wood D. 2, p. 48 (O. C. 8513).

Note of Arms in Carfax church.
  Wood B. 14 (O. C. 8585).

Epitaph in church.
  Rawl. B. 400ᶜ, fol. 389.

Description of Carfax conduit.
  Top. Oxf. e. 6.

St. Mary Magdalen, parish and church, 144.

Narratio de Radulpho quodam ad altare B. Mariae Magdalenae apud Oxon.
  Laud. Misc. 524 (sec. xv), fol. 10ᵛ (O. C. 1049).

Charters affecting the parish.
  Charters Cal., pp. 283, 284, 353.

(City—Local Divisions.)

Extracts from the Registers : Bur. 1574–1677, Marr. 1574–1580, Bapt. 1579–1633.
   Wood D. 5 (*O. C.* 8524).

Extracts from the Registers, 1574–1677.
   Tann. 456*, *fol.* 66.

Of St. Mary Magdalene.
   Wood F. 29ᵃ, *foll.* 309, 332 (*O. C.* 8491).

Extracts from the muniments.
   Wood D. 2, p. 298 (*O. C.* 8513).

Note of Arms in St. Mary Magdalene church.
   Wood B. 14 (*O. C.* 8585).

St. Mary the Virgin, parish and church, 145 (see 146).

Charters affecting the church and parish.
   Charters Cal., pp. 281, 284, 286, 306, 307, 351, 353.

Letter about the clock and church of St. Mary, by N. Ormanet, in Latin, 23 Feb. 155$\frac{7}{8}$.
   Tann. 456, *fol.* 1.

Arms in the church, 1574.
   Wood D. 14 (*O. C.* 8548).
   Wood F. 33, *fol.* 125 (*O. C.* 8495).

Extracts from the Registers : Bur. 1599–1677, Marr. 1602–44, Bapt. 1599–1666.
   Wood D. 5 (*O. C.* 8524).

Of St. Maries church.
   Wood F. 29ᵃ, *fol.* 294 (*O. C.* 8491).

Extracts from the muniments.
   Wood D. 3, p. 250 (*O. C.* 8514).

Epitaphs in St. Maries church.
   Wood F. 29ᵃ, *fol.* 321 (*O.C.* 8491).

Epitaph in the church.
   Rawl. B. 400ᶜ, *fol.* 391.

St. Mary the Virgin, Church, as University Church, 146.

St. Michael, parish and church, 147.

Charters affecting the parish.
   Charters Cal., pp. 296, 353–55.

(City—Local Divisions.)

Extracts from Registers: Bur. 1582–1645, Marr. 1569–1631, Bapt. 1559–1627.
Wood D. 5 (*O. C.* 8524).

Extracts from the Registers, 1559–1679.
Tann. 456*, *fol.* 64.

Of St. Michael's.
Wood F. 29ᵃ, *foll.* 312, 341 (*O. C.* 8491).

Excerpts from the muniments of St. Michael's.
Wood D. 2, p. 35 (*O. C.* 8513).

Benefactions of Mr. Tho. Fawkener, out of the parish Register.
Wood D. 5 (*O. C.* 8524).

St. Paul, parish and church, 148.

St. Peter le Bailey, parish and church, 149.

Charters affecting the parish.
Charters Cal. pp. 290, 310.

Arms in the Church, 1574.
Wood D. 14 (*O. C.* 8548).

Extracts from the Registers, 1587–1645.
Tann. 456*, *fol.* 57.

Extracts from the Registers: Bur. 1587–1660.
Wood D. 5 (*O. C.* 8524).

Of St. Peter's in the Bayly.
Wood F. 29ᵃ, *fol.* 317 (*O. C.* 8491).

Extracts from the muniments.
Wood C. 1, p. 75 (*O. C.* 8515).

St. Peter in the East, parish and church, 151.

Charters affecting the church and parish.
Charters Cal., pp. 287, 288, 290, 302, 355, 356.

Extracts from the Registers: Bur. 1562–1652, Marr. 1569–1616, Bapt. 1604–05.
Wood D. 5 (*O. C.* 8524).

Extracts from the Registers, 1562–1652.
Tann. 456*, *fol.* 59ᵛ.

Arms in the Church, 1574.
Wood D. 14 (*O. C.* 8548).

(City—Local Divisions.)

Arms in a private house in St. Peter's parish, 1574.
  Wood D. 14 (*O. C.* 8548).
Of St. Peter's in the East.
  Wood F. 29ᵃ, *foll.* 315ᵛ, 347 (*O. C.* 8491).
Dispute about entering St. Alban hall to certify parish bounds (17th cent.): by Ant. à Wood.
  Rawl. B. 402ᵃ (at beginning).
Short account of the foundation of St. Peter's in the East: by Tho. Hearne.
  Rawl. C. 851, *fol.* 42.
Extracts from the muniments of St. Peter's in the East.
  Wood D. 2, p. 44 (*O. C.* 8513).
Epitaphs, parish records, etc.
  Rawl. C. 867, *foll.* 38ᵛ, 41, 60.

St. Philip and St. James, parish and church, 152.

St. Thomas, parish and church, 153.
  Charters affecting the parish.
    Charters Cal., pp. 290, 356, 359, 662.
  Extracts from the Registers: Bur. 1561-1650, Marr. 1583-1620, Bapt. 1562-96.
    Wood D. 5 (*O. C.* 8524).
  Extracts from the Registers, 1561-1652.
    Tann. 456*, *fol.* 52.
  Arms in the Church, 1574.
    Wood D. 14 (*O. C.* 8548).
  Of St. Thomas's.
    Wood F. 29ᵃ, *fol.* 319ᵛ (*O. C.* 8491).
  Extracts from the muniments.
    Wood D. 2, p. 348 (*O. C.* 8513).
  Some benefactors to the parish.
    Wood F. 28, at end (*O. C.* 8490).

Trinity, see *Holy Trinity*, 134.

Cathedral, 154 (see also *Christ Church*, 459, and *St. Frideswide's*, 262).
  Charter of foundation of the episcopal See and of the Dean and Chapter of the Cathedral Church of Christ in Oxford, 4 Nov. 1546.
    Ch. Ch. 344, *fol.* 48.

(City—Local Divisions.)

Arms in the cloister, 1574.
Wood D. 14 (*O. C.* 8548).

Arms in "St. Frideswide's," 1574.
Ibid. (*O. C.* 8548).

Lowe's lamentation, verses on the services of the Cathedral, by Thomas Smith, 1660.
Tann. 306, *fol.* 373.

Of the Cathedral Church.
Wood F. 29ª, *fol.* 291 (*O. C.* 8491).

Weekly Communion at the Cathedral in Will. III's time.
Rawl. C. 983, *fol.* 46.

A poem in defence of the decency of the Cathedral, occasioned by a Banbury brother.
Tann. 466, *fol.* 68.

Suburbs, 155.

The suburbs.
Wood F. 29ª, *fol.* 70 (*O. C.* 8491).

Binsey, 156.

Of Binsey.
Wood F. 29ª, *fol.* 300ᵛ (*O. C.* 8491).

Botley, 157.

Cowley St. John's, 158.

Medley, 159.

New Hincksey, 161.

Oseney Town, 162.

(Public) Institutions and Buildings, 163.

Founders, benefactors, endowments, estates, 164.

Ancient rent-rolls of the City.
Charters Cal., pp. 381–83.

Archb. Laud's benefaction to the poor of Oxford, in his will, Jan. 164¾.
Clar. i. 1816.

Banks, 165.

Canals, 166.

(City—Local Divisions.)

Castle, 167.
  The Castle.
    Wood F. 29ᵃ, *fol.* 65 (*O. C.* 8491).
  See also *St. George's College, etc.*, 494.

Cemeteries, 168.

Funerals, 169.

Dissenting Chapels, 171.

Hospitals, 172.
  Almshouses, 173.

Inns (Alehouses, Hotels, Public-houses, Taverns), 174.
  Arms of Sir W. Petre in the window of the Crown Inn (17th cent.).
    Ashm. 1137, *fol.* 142.
  Lines on the "Fleur de Luce."
    Tann. 466, *fol.* 66ᵛ.
  Charter affecting the Maidenhead inn.
    Charters Cal., p. 284.

Ladies' Halls (Lady Margaret and Somerville), 175.

Lunatic Asylums, 176.

Mansfield College, 177.

Market, 178.
  Writs of 8 Edw. II (1314–15) about price of Victuals in Oxford.
    Wood F. 27, *art.* 20 (*O. C.* 8489).
  Information given to the Clerks of the Market, 16 Aug. 1662.
    Tann. 338, *fol.* 148.
  The Market.
    Wood F. 29ᵃ, *fol.* 95 (*O. C.* 8491).

Assay of weights and measures, 179.

Assize of bread and ale, 180.

Clerks of the market, 181.
  Perambulation of the Clerks of the Market, 1808–28.
    Top. Oxf. f. 2.

Forestallers, 182.

Regrators, 183.

Supervisors, 184.

(City—Local Divisions.)

Martyrs' Memorial, 185.

Mills, 186.
    Charters affecting the Castle Mills.
        Charters Cal., pp. 347, 348.
    — Holywell Mill.
        Ibid., p. 350.
    — Templars' Mill.
        Ibid., p. 350.
    Mills, old and new.
        Wood F. 29^a, *fol.* 5 (*O.C.* 8491).

Mint (tokens and coins), 187.

Music room (Holywell), 188.

Post office, 189.

Prisons, 191.

Pusey House, 192.

Radcliffe Observatory, 193.

Railways and Stations, 194.

Roman Catholic Churches, 195.

St. Stephen's House, 196.

Schools, 197.
    Blue Coat School, 198.
        Records of the Blue Coat School, by Hen. Hughes.
            Top. Oxf., e. 15.
    Cathedral School, 199.
    High School for Boys, 201.
    High School for Girls, 202.
    Magdalen School, 203.
        Collections relating to Magd. school, by the rev. Rob. Brine.
            Gough Oxf. 9.
        Ex oratione pro puero in schola Magdalenensi
            Rawl. C. 753, *fol.* 45.
    New College School, 204.
    Nixon's School, 205.

(City—Local Divisions.)

Theatres, 206.

Town Hall, Corn Exchange, etc., 207.

Tramways, 208.

Vehicles (cabs, carriers, flys, etc.), 209.
> Petition of Thomas Egerly, carrier of the Univ. to and from London (to K. Charles I).
> *Wood F.* 27, *art.* 4 (*O. C.* 8489).

Coaching, 211.

Volunteers, 212.

Workhouse, 213.

Wycliffe hall, 214.

Streets (215), quarters and wards (216), rivers (217), bridges (218), walks (219).
> Orders for improving and cleaning the streets of Oxford (17th cent.).
> *Wood F.* 31 (*not O. C.* 8493).
> Charter affecting Northgate hundred.
> *Charters Cal.*, p. 353.
> The division of the City by Wards.
> *Wood F.* 29ª, *fol.* 8ᵛ (*O. C.* 8491).
> Topographical description of the wards, by Ant. à Wood (a copy).
> *Rawl. B.* 400ª.
> The rivers about Oxford.
> *Wood F.* 29ª, *fol.* 4 (*O. C.* 8491).
> Charter affecting Pettypont.
> *Charters Cal.*, p. 312.
> The Bridges.
> *Wood F.* 29ª, *fol.* 108 (*O. C.* 8491).

Broad St., 221.

Carfax (quarter and conduit and Penniless bench), 222.
> Charter affecting Carfax.
> *Charters Cal.*, p. 306.
> Waterpipes from Carfax conduit.
> *Rawl. C.* 421, *fol.* 1.

(City—Local Divisions.)

Cherwell, 223.
    Charter affecting the Attye in the Cherwell.
        Charters Cal., p. 306.
    Course of the Cherwell, by M. Windesore.
        C.C.C. 280, *fol.* 34.

Cornmarket St., 224.

Folly Bridge (Grandpont), 225.
    Charter affecting Grandpont.
        Charters Cal., p. 290.
    See also *Bacon's Study*, 241.

High St., 226.
    Charters affecting the High St.
        Charters Cal., pp. 290, 307, 308.

Hithe Bridge, 227.
    Charters affecting "Hyde" bridge.
        Charters Cal., pp. 347, 348.
    Order for the repair of the highway to Hithe Bridge, 1634.
        Rawl. C. 421, *fol.* 9.

Magdalen Bridge (East Bridge), 228.
    Charter affecting "East Bridge."
        Charters Cal., p. 306.

Park Town, 229.

Port Meadow and other meadows, 231.
    Of the meadows about the City.
        Wood F. 29^a, *fol.* 119 (*O. C.* 8491).
    Charters affecting King's Mead.
        Charters Cal., pp. 347-49.
    Depositions of witnesses about Port Mead, A.D. 1533.
        Wood D. 18, *fol.* 40 (*O. C.* 8563).
    Charter affecting Stockwell mede.
        Charters Cal., p. 310.

St. Giles's, 232 (see 141).

Thames or Isis, 233.
    The course of the Isis, by M. Windesore.
        C.C.C. 280, *fol.* 34.

(City—Local Divisions.)
Order of the Vice-Chancellor for levying tolls on the Thames, 15 June 1638.
Tann. 338, *fol.* 63.

Turl, 234.

Walton manor, 235.
Charter affecting Walton manor.
Charters Cal., p. 359.

Old Institutions and buildings (which have ceased to exist or are chiefly of historical interest) (monasteries, etc.), 240.
Excerpts from Twyne's collections concerning the monasteries in Oxford.
Wood   (*O. C.* 8562). (Lost.)
Miscellanea de antiquis ecclesiis et parochiis in Civ. Oxon. per Brianum Twyne.
Wood F. 29ᵃ, *fol.* 372 (*O. C.* 8491).

Bacon's Study on Folly Bridge, 241.

Beaumont (palace, etc.), 242.
Charters affecting Beaumont.
Charters Cal., pp. 282, 290.

Coffee Houses, 243.

Conversorum Domus, 244.
Of several Houses of Converts.
Wood F. 29ᵃ, *fol.* 277 (*O. C.* 8491).

Dantesburne church, 245.
Of Dantesburne or Danesbourne church.
Wood F. 29ᵃ, *fol.* 302 (*O. C.* 8491).

Gates (Bocardo, etc.), 246.
Charter affecting Northgate.
Charters Catal., p. 209.
Charter affecting Smith Gate
Ibid., p. 290.

Godstow (Bened. nunnery), 247.
Nota e carta fundationis.
Rawl. B. 103, *fol.* 259.

(City—Local Divisions.)
Excerpta ex cartulario de Godstow.
Dodsw. 10, *fol.* 202 (*O. C.* 4152).
„   59, *fol.* 185 (*O. C.* 5001).
„   66, *fol.* 84 (*O. C.* 5008).

Chartulary in English.
Rawl. B. 408.

Charters of Godstow, translated into English.
Rawl. B. 408, *foll.* 92–147^v, 153^v–155^v, 192–93.

Abstract of the Register, in English.
Qu. Coll. 88, *fol.* 261.

Dedicatio ecclesiae per Alex. episc. Linc., donatio Regis Stephani, carta Rich. I.
Wood F. 21, *art.* 10 (*O. C.* 8474).

Carta Hen. II concessa abbatiae S. Joh. Bapt. de Godestow.
Dodsw. 25, *fol.* 116 (*O. C.* 4167).

Adam Abbot of Evesham's Address to the Nuns of Godstow mentioned.
Leland Coll. 4, p. 177 (*O. C.* 5105).

Notes of Dorset and Oxford lands formerly belonging to the nunnery surrendered in 1611 and sold in 1609–18.
Rawl. B. 253, *fol.* 86^v–7, 121^v–2.

Pen-and-ink sketch of Godstow nunnery, 1666, by Ant. à Wood.
Rawl. B. 408, *init.*

Sketch of the ruins in 1666.
Rawl. B. 408, *init.*

Drawing of the remains by M. Burghers.
Rawl. B. 206, *fol.* 5.

De Godstow.
Leland Coll. 1, p. 73 (*O. C.* 5102).

Notes concerning Godstow.
Wood D. 11, p. 38 (*O. C.* 8517).

Notes, epitaphs, etc. at Godstow.
Wood E. 1, *fol.*   (*O. C.* 8505).

Note of a stone found at the nunnery.
Rawl. C. 867, *fol.* 52^v.

(City—Local Divisions.)

Lands of the nunnery.
Ashm. 860, *fol.* 362.

Account of the nunnery.
Rawl. B. 400e, *fol.* 3-15.

Collections relating to Godstow nunnery, by E. R. Mores.
Gough Oxf. 18.

Extracts by Gough from Wood's MSS. about Ewelme, Godstow and Harpenden.
Ibid., 59.

Hermitages and Cells, 248.

Of several old Hermitages.
Wood F. 29^a, *fol.* 277 (*O. C.* 8491).

Hospitals, 249.

Of several old Hospitals.
Wood F. 29^a, *fol.* 277 (*O. C.* 8491).

Hospital of St. Bartholomew, 251.

Charters affecting the hospital.
Charters Cal., pp. 281, 307.

Collectanea ex archivis Coll. Oriel. praecipue de Hosp. S. Barth^{maei}.
Wood F. 28, *fol.* 57 (*O. C.* 8490).

Of St. Bartholomew's Hospital.
Wood F. 29^a, *fol.* 280 (*O. C.* 8491).

Inscriptions etc. there to 1736 or 1750, supplementing Wood's History of the City.
Rawl. B. 400, (*in foll.* 36-180).

Notice of it.
Rawl. C. 867, *fol.* 56^v, 58.

Hospital of St. John, 252.

Charters affecting the hospital.
Charters Catal., pp. 287, 312.

Statutes of St. John's Hospital.
Top. Oxf. d. 8.

Of. St. John Baptist's Hospital.
Wood F. 29^a, *fol.* 288 (*O. C.* 8491).

(City—Local Divisions.)
Excerpts from the records.
Wood D. 2, pp. 161, 228, 230 (*O. C.* 8513).
Notes concerning it from the muniments of Magdalen.
Wood D. 11, p. 1 (*O. C.* 8517).

Houses, etc., old private, 253.
Notes of houses in Oxford belonging to Godstow, surrendered in 1611 and sold in 1609-18.
Rawl. B. 253, *fol.* 121^v-2.
Arms in " Mr. Freer's house and the next house to it," 1574.
Wood D. 14 (*O. C.* 8548).
Arms in a house in St. Peter's in the East, 1574.
Ibid. (*O. C.* 8548).

Jewry, see *Jews* (326, 687).

Lanes, old, 254.
Cheney Lane : Charter affecting Cheney Lane.
Charters Cal., p. 662.
Grope Lane : Charters affecting Grope Lane.
Charters Cal., pp. 307, 353.
Hamile Lane : Charter affecting Hamile Lane.
Charters Cal., p. 305.
Jewry Lane : Charter affecting Jury Lane.
Charters Cal., p. 350.
Keepharm Lane : Charter affecting Kepharme Lane.
Charters Cal., p. 350.
Overhe Lane : Charter affecting Overhe Lane.
Charters Cal., p. 309.
St. Edward's Lane : Charter affecting St. Edward's Lane.
Charters Cal., p. 297.

Oseney Abbey (Austin Canons) and **St. Nicholas' Church,** 255.
Cartularium monasterii de Oseney, about 1275.
Ch. Ch. 343.
Notae paucae ex registro de Oseney, olim cod. Cotton. Vitell. E. xvi, hodie desiderato.
Rawl. B. 484, *fol.* 37.

(City—Local Divisions.)
Excerpta de Registro abbatiae de Oseney.
    Dodsw. 39, *fol.* 95 (*O. C.* 4181).
    James 6, p. 53 (*O. C.* 3843).
Excerpta ex cartulario monast. de Oseneia.
    Dodsw. 78, *fol.* 117 (*O. C.* 5019).
Excerpta ex Registro.
    Tann. 12, *fol.* 72^v.
Excerpts from Oseney records at Ch. Ch.
    Wood D. 2, pp. 360, 417, 587 (*O. C.* 8513).
Excerpta "ex libro rationali Osneiæ."
    James 26, p. 160 (*O. C.* 3863).
Excerpta ex libro rationali de Oseney.
    Wood D. 18, *fol.* 125 (*O. C.* 8563).
Excerpta ex Chronicis et Registris de Oseney.
    Ibid., foll. 135, 155.
Officia varia abbatis.
    Rawl. C. 739.
Obituarium.
    Ibid., fol. 8.
Nomina abbatum.
    Ibid., fol. 164^v.
Carta fundationis abbatiae de Oseney.
    Dodsw. 10, *fol.* 180 (*O. C.* 4152).
Charters affecting Oseney abbey.
    Charters Catal. pp. 1, 2, 134, 135, 284, 300, 315–384, 660, 661.
Translation of Oseney Charter 13 Edw. II, in English.
    Top. Oxf. b. 17.
Deeds between Oseney abbey and Godstow abbey, translated into English.
    Rawl. B. 408, *foll.* 93–4.
Libri in bibl. Canonicorum de Oseney.
    Leland Coll. 3, p. 56 (*O. C.* 5104).
Conventio inter Abbatem de Oseney et Ricardum fil. Johannis de secta curiae apud Steple Claydon.
    Dodsw. 33, *fol.* 36 (*O. C.* 4175).

(City—Local Divisions.)

Acta capituli generalis, 1443.
Rawl. B. 401.

Acta etc. Capituli ord. Augustin. celebrati apud Monast. de Oseney, A. D. 1449.
Wood (2) 21 (O. C. 8609).

Rentale monast. Osneyensis de redditu in burgo Villae Oxoniae, et computus Collectorum ejusdem redditus, 1453-1479.
Wood F. 10 (O. C. 8472).

Rental of Oseney abbey of revenues from land in the city, 1463.
C.C.C. 280, fol. 96.

— 1498.
Wood F. 10 (O. C. 8477).

Letters, bonds etc. relating to Christ Church, Oseney, etc., 1519-1631.
Top. Oxf. c. 22.

Valor ecclesiasticus monasterii, 26 Hen. VIII (O.C. 1534-5).
Tann. 342, fol. 80.

Oseney surrender accounts, Hen. VIII's time.
Top. Oxf. b. 16.

Petition of the abbey to the King about charges out of the abbey funds.
Tann. 342, fol. 97.

Account by J. Leland, A. D. 1542.
Leland Itin. 2, fol. 18 (O..C. 5108).

Prospect of the N. side of the ruins of Oseney Church, 1574, a copy by Ant. à Wood.
Wood 276b, fol. 117.

Owned MS. Digb. 23, art. 1.

Collectanea Willelmi Wyrley de monasterio Osneiae.
Wood F. 16 (O. C. 8478).

Fragmentum e chronico Walteri de Hemingford, 1264-1297, cum additamentis abbatiam de Osneia spectantibus.
Digb. 168, fol. 147.

Notae de Oseney.
Leland Coll. 1, p. 81 (O. C. 5102).

(**City—Local Divisions.**)
Notes concerning Oseney abbey.
Wood D. 11, p. 89 (*O. C.* 8517).

Of Osney Abbey.
Wood F. 29ª, *fol.* 214 (*O. C.* 8491).

Of St. Nicholas' church in Oseney abbey.
Wood F. 29ª, *fol.* 315ᵛ (*O. C.* 8491).

Rewley Abbey (Cisterc.), 256.

Notae de Rewley.
Leland Coll. 1, p. 81 (*O. C.* 5102).

Of Rewley Abbey.
Wood F. 29ª, *fol.* 221 (*O. C.* 8491).

Short account, by Ant. à Wood.
Wood F. 21, *art.* 5 (*O. C.* 8474).

Coins found at Rewley: remains of the abbey.
Rawl. C. 867, *foll.* 40, 43ᵛ, 44ᵛ.

St. Andrew (parish and church), 257.

Of St. Andrew's Church in Oxford [?].
Wood F. 29ª, *fol.* 300 (*O. C.* 8491).

St. Benedict (parish and church), 258.

Of St. Benedict's.
Wood F. 29ª, *fol.* 300 (*O. C.* 8491).

St. Budoc (parish and church), 259.

Of St. Budoc's.
Wood F. 29ª, *fol.* 301 (*O. C.* 8491).

St. Edward (parish and church), 261.

Charters affecting the parish or church.
Charters Cal., pp. 290, 305, 307, 351.

Of St. Edward's.
Wood F. 29ª, *fol.* 304 (*O. C.* 8491).

St. Frideswide's (nuns, Sec. can., Austin can.), 262.
(See also *Cathedral*, 154; *Christ Church*, 459.)
Cartularium monasterii S. Frideswyde.
Ch. Ch. 340: *C. C. C.* 160.

(City—Local Divisions.)

Collectanea Willelmi Wyrley de monast. S. Frideswidae (Registrum cartarum monast. S. Frideswidae, etc.): imperfect.
    Wood F. 16 (*O. C.* 8478).

Excerpta ex Registro monast. S. Frideswidae, in bibl. Ædis Christi.
    James 6, p. 38 (*O. C.* 3843).

"Ex libro B. Frideswidae in manibus Br. Twyne," (now at Corpus).
    James 26, p. 137 (*O. C.* 3863).
    James 30, p. 66 (*O. C.* 3867).

Excerpta ex Registro monast. S. Frideswidae in bibl. coll. Corporis Christi, A.D. 1644.
    Dodsw. 55, *fol.* 17 (*O. C.* 4197).

Collections from registers, papers, deeds etc. relating to St. Frideswide's, at Ch. Ch. and in the Cartulary at Corpus, with a list of Priors.
    Wood C. 2 (*O. C.* 8516).

Excerpts from the records of St. Frideswide's.
    Wood D. 2, p. 480 (*O. C.* 8513).

Collections about property belonging to St. Frideswide's, in Oxford parishes from the Cartulary (?) of St. Frideswide's.
    Wood C. 4 (*O. C.* 8526).

Charter of Ethelred to St. Frideswide's, Lat. and Old English.
    Wood D. 18, *fol.* 6 (*O. C.* 8563).

Charta Johannis Regis ecclesiae S. Frideswidae Oxon.
    Dodsw. 25, *fol.* 110 (*O. C.* 4167).

Charters affecting St. Frideswide's.
    Charters Cal., pp. 127, 273, 300–14, 338, 345, 351, 374.

Petitio prioris et conventus S. Frideswidae Oxon., in Parliam. 4 Edw. III (A.D. 1330).
    Dodsw. 115, *fol.* 83 (*O. C.* 5056).

St. Frideswide's surrender accounts, Hen. VIII's time.
    Top. Oxf. b. 16.

(City—Local Divisions.)

St. Frideswide's priory and nunnery.
> Wood F. 29ª, fol. 230 (O. C. 8491).

Of St. Frideswide's.
> Ibid., fol. 304ᵛ (O. C. 8491).

Notes concerning St. Frideswide's.
> Wood D. 11, p. 91 (O. C. 8517).

Short account, by Ant. à Wood.
> Wood F. 21, art. 4 (O. C. 8474).

Note about it.
> Ashm. 854, fol. 297.

Account of a crucifix found in St. Frideswide's, now in the Bodleian.
> Rawl. C. 867, fol. 52.

St. George (parish and church), see *St. George's college*, 494.

St. Michael at South Gate (parish and church), 263.
Charters affecting the church and parish.
> Charters Cal., 283, 309–10.

Of St. Michael's at Southgate.
> Wood F. 29ª, fol. 313 (O. C. 8491).

St. Mildred (parish and church), 264.
Charters affecting the church and parish.
> Charters Cal., pp. 288–90, 292, 309, 310, 355, 662.

Of St. Mildred's.
> Wood F. 29ª, fol. 313ᵛ (O. C. 8491).

St. Nicholas, see *Oseney abbey*, 255.

Streets, old, 265.
Bridge St.: Charters affecting Bruggestrete.
> Charters Cal., pp. 281, 305.

Cat St.: Charters affecting Cat St.
> Charters Cal., pp. 353, 355, 356.

Eastbridge St.: Charter affecting Astbrugestrete.
> Charters Cal., p. 281.

Fish St.: Charter affecting Fish St.
> Charters Cal., p. 350.

(City—Local Divisions.)

Horsemonger St.: Charter affecting Horsemonger St.
Charters Cal., p. 282.

Irishman St.: Charter affecting Irishman St.
Charters Cal., p. 359.

Kibald St.: Charter affecting Kibold St.
Charters Cal., p. 308.

Pennyfarthing St.: Charter affecting Pynferthynge.
Charters Cal., p. 350.

St. John's St.: Charters affecting St. John's St.
Charters Cal., pp. 307–8.

Schidyard St.: Charters affecting Shidyerde St.
Charters Cal., pp. 306–8, 353.

Stockwell St.: Charters affecting Stockwell St.
Charters Cal., pp. 356–7, 586.

Walls of the City (Canditch, etc.), 266.

The antiquity of the City Wall with its reparations.
Wood F. 29^a, *fol.* 57 (*O. C.* 8491).

GOVERNMENT (Incorporation and constitution), 270.

Doubts of the Univ. concerning the City Charter (1635?),
Tann. 338, *fol.* 35.

Town Council, as a body, 271.

Regulations, proclamations, petitions, letters, etc., 272.

Petition of the City to Will. III about the election of a town-clerk, 1688.
Rawl. C. 865, *fol.* 23.

Law Courts (trials of all kinds, coroners' inquests, etc.), 273.

Ancient coroners' inquests in Oxford.
Charters Cal., p. 292.

Placita assisarum, 1380.
Rawl. C. 188, *fol.* 3.

Calendar of prisoners at the Assizes, July 1730.
Rawl. C. 452, *fol.* 133.

Calendar of prisoners at the Assizes, Aug. 1736.
Rawl. C. 452, *fol.* 170.

(City—Government.)

Brief of the Prosecution in the King *v.* J. Williams for murder, 1828.
Top. Oxf. b. 4.

Local Board, 274.

Police, 275.

 Criminals, 276.

School board, 277.

Magistracy, 278.

Procedure, public, 279.

Public Officers and Offices, 280.

Burgesses, 281.

 Elections (poll-books, etc.), 282.

Mayor, 284.

Notes relating to the Mayoralty, with a catalogue of Mayors and Bailiffs to 1626: by Brian Twyne.
Wood F. 26 (*O. C.* 8502).

List of Mayors of Oxford, 1122–1695.
Wood D. 7(5) (*O. C.* 8523).

Bailiffs, 285.

Catalogue of Bailiffs, to 1626, by Brian Twyne.
Wood F. 26 (*O. C.* 8502).

List of Bailiffs of Oxford, 1122 (?)–1695.
Wood D. 7(5) (*O. C.* 8523).

Excerpts from the Computus Bailivorum, etc.
Wood D. 2, p. 280 (*O. C.* 8513).

Aldermen, 286.

Town-Councillors, 287.

Town-Clerk, 288.

Petition of the City to Will. III about the election of a town-clerk, 1688.
Rawl. C. 865, *fol.* 23.

Notice of election of town-clerk, 1697.
Tann. 23, *fol.* 50.

Finance (rates, revenues, tolls, taxes, etc.), 289.

(City—Classes.)
CLASSES OF THE COMMUNITY, 300.
  Nobility, 301.
    An account of the Nobility buried in and about Oxford 1643–(1680?), by Ant. à Wood (list in Catalogue).
      Wood F. 4 (*O. C.* 8466).
  Gentry (old families, heralds' visitations, etc.), 302.
    Concerning several old families in Oxford (Kepeharme, Torald, Stockwell, Halegod, Bodyn, Burewald).
      Wood F. 29^a, *fol.* 360 (*O. C.* 8491).
    Heralds' visitations of the county and city of Oxford, 1575 and 1597.
      Qu. Coll. 132.
    — 1634.
      Ibid., 129.
    An account of the gentry buried in and about Oxford, 1643–(1680?), by Ant. à Wood (list in Catalogue).
      Wood F. 4 (*O. C.* 8466).
  Professional men (middle classes), 303.
  Manufacturers, 304.
  Tradesmen, 305 (see also *Privileged persons*, 654).
    Charter affecting "Bocheria" in All Saints parish.
      Charters Cal., p. 291.
    Papers relating to orders of the Chancellor to butchers etc. not to kill meat in Lent, 1578–1630.
      Rawl. C. 421, *foll.* 78–112.
    Charter affecting the Cordwainers in Carfax parish.
      Charters Cal., p. 352.
    Charter affecting goldsmiths in All Saints parish.
      Charters Cal., p. 297.
    License from the Vice-chancellor to H. Smith butcher to kill flesh in Lent 1662.
      Top. Oxf. e. 8.
  Trade Guilds, 306.
    Papers about the Ensham estate of the Cooks' Company in the University of Oxford, about 1720.
      Top. Oxf. d. 3.

(City—Classes.)

Note of the Mercers' feast.
Rawl. C. 867, *fol.* 80.

The incorporation of the company of shoemakers.
Wood F. 29ª, *fol.* 368 (*O.C.* 8491).

(Lost).

(See also *Life, Commercial, Clubs,* 342.)

Freemen, 307.

Common people, 308.

    Labour, 309.

    Pauperism, 311.

    Thrift, 312.

Religious orders, 315.

    Roman Catholics (see *Univ., Rel. Orders, Roman Catholics,* 661).

    Protestants, 318.
        Church of England, 319.

        Dissenters (Nonconformists), 320.
            Baptists, 321.
            Congregationalists, 322.
            Methodists (Wesleyans, etc.), 323.
        Puritans, 324.

    Jews and the Jewry, 326.

        Charter affecting the little Jewry.
            Charters Cal., p. 351.

        Collections concerning the Jews in Oxford.
            Wood F. 29ª, *fol.* 358 (*O.C.* 8491.)

(Lost).

(See *Conversorum Domus,* 244).

    Other (Quakers, etc.), 328.
    Meeting of Quakers at Oxford, 1662.
        Tann. 338, *foll.* 133, 135.

    Other (Socialists, etc.), 329.

(City—Life and Manners.)

LIFE AND MANNERS, General Notes, 331.

    Morals and discipline, 332.

  Religious, 333.

    Sermons, 334.

    Missions, 335.

    Clubs and Societies, 336.

  Intellectual and literary, 337.

    Clubs and Societies, 338.

  Commercial, 339.

    Fairs, 341.

      Of the Fairs.

        Wood F. 29ª, *fol.* 104 (*O. C.* 8491).

    Clubs and Societies, 342.

    (See also *Trade guilds*, 306.)

  Political, 343.

    Clubs and Societies, 344.

  Scientific, 345.

    Clubs and Societies, 346.

  Artistic, 347.

    Music, 348.

    Dramatic, 349.

      The Vice-chancellor and strolling players (letter from A. Charlett), 1698.

        Tann. 22, *fol.* 54.

    Clubs and Societies, 351.

  Social, 352.

    Amusements, 353.

    Clubs and Societies, 355.

      Freemasons, 356.

  Personal, 357.

    Dress, 358.

(City—External Relations.)
EXTERNAL RELATIONS, 360.
  To the country at large, 361.
  To the Crown, 362.
    Petition of the City to Will. III about the election of a town-clerk, 1688.
      Rawl. C. 865, *fol.* 23.
  Royal charters, letters, mandamuses, etc., 363 (see also *Archives*, 394).
    City charters.
      Ex. Coll. 11 & 12.
    Carta Hen. II burgensibus concessa.
      Rawl. B. 356, *fol.* 6^v.
    Carta Johannis burgensibus concessa.
      Rawl. B. 356, *fol.* 6^v.
    Carta Hen. 3 burgensibus concessa.
      Rawl. B. 356, *fol.* 6^v.
    Cartae burgensibus concessae, 1229–1237.
      Rawl. B. 356, *foll.* 5^v, 6^v.
    Writ of Hen. III for observance of the ordinances of the Oxford Parliament of 1256.
      Rawl. C. 358, *fol.* 4.
    Restitutio libertatum villae Oxon. per Edw. III.
      Wood F. 27, art. 32 (*O. C.* 8489).
    Orders of Council to settle differences between the Univ. and City, 1575.
      C. C. C. 367.
    Charta Caroli II burgensibus Oxon. concessa.
      Ex. Coll. 12, *fol.* 61^v.
  Royal visits, 364.
    Ballad on the duke of Monmouth's entertainment there by the City (17th cent.).
      Douce 357, *fol.* 79.
  Coronation service of the Mayor, etc., 365.
    Service of the burgesses at a coronation.
      Ashm. 863, *fol.* 60.

(**City—External Relations.**)

Names of the Mayor etc. who attended the Coronation of James II, 1685.
Tann. 24, *fol.* 109.

To Church and dissent, 366.

Councils (ecclesiastical) at Oxford, 367.

Statuta capituli Lateranensis apud Oxon. A. D. 1220 habiti.
Jes. Coll. 64 ad init.

Constitutiones in concilio Oxoniae factae, 1222.
Rawl. C. 100, *foll.* 105, 114.
Ashm. 1146, *fol.* 43.
Tann. 196, *fol.* 149.

Canones Concilii Oxoniensis (1222 ?)
New Coll. 222, *fol.* 1.

To Parliament, 368.

Petition of citizens to the House of Commons against the Malignants in the latter, A. D. 1647.
Wood F. 27, *art.* 33. (*O. C.* 8489).

Parliaments at Oxford, 369.

Writ of Hen. III for observance of the ordinances of the Oxf. Parliament of 1256.
Rawl. C. 358, *fol.* 4.

Preparations at Oxford for the Parliament, 1625.
C. C. C. 257, *fol.* 131.

Letter from the King's Council to the Univ. requiring rooms for the Parliament to be held at Oxford, 11 July 1625.
Tann. 338, *fol.* 52.

The names of the Lords and Commons assembled in the Parliament at Oxford, A. D. 1643.
Wood F. 32, *fol.* 113 (*O. C.* 8494).

Speech by Charles I to the Parliament at Oxford.
Ashm. 830, *fol.* 279.

Letter from Charles II to the Vice-chancellor about the Parliament to be held at Oxford, 1681.
All S. 253, *fol.* 300.

(City—External Relations.)
Note on Parliaments at Oxford
Wood D. 7(2) (*O. C.* 8519).
To the neighbourhood, 370.
To the University (see *University*, 938).
To other cities, 371.

HISTORY AND ANTIQUITIES IN GENERAL, 380.
(See also *General notes*, 121.)
Notes from the City records.
Ashm. 1115, *fol.* 273.
Tabula calamitatum Oxon. 914–1387.
C. C. C. 267, *fol.* 151^v.
De Oxoniae antiquitatibus libellus, per M. Windesore.
C. C. C. 266, *fol.* 1.
Collectanea ad Oxoniae historiam et antiquitates declarandum, per M. Windesore.
C. C. C. 280.
Papers concerning the history and antiquities of the City.
Wood F. 29^a (*O. C.* 8491).
Ant. à Wood's history and description of the City, a copy with Rawlinson's additions.
Rawl. B. 407^a, 407^b.
Ant. à Wood's notes relating to the history of Oxford and the neighbourhood (transcribed by Hearne).
Rawl. B. 176, *fol.* 15.

To the Conquest, 381.
The foundation of the City.
Wood F. 29^a, *fol.* 2 (*O. C.* 8491).

To 1600, 382.

XVIIth Cent., 383.
Packets of Grants at Oxford in 1643, 1644, 1645.
Dugd. 19 (M. 1) (*O. C.* 6509).
Tumult at Oxford in 1647 (a note).
Wood D. 7 (2) (*O. C.* 8519).

Civil War, 384.
" The Commissioners for victualling Oxford City,"
7 Mar. 164$\frac{3}{4}$.
Ch. Ch. 345, *art.* 7.

(City—History.)

Narrative of affairs at Oxford from 27 Apr. to 30 May 1646, with copy of the treaty between sir T. Fairfax's Commissioners and the Oxford Commissioners, and of a letter from Fairfax to sir Tho. Glemham.
Clar. i. 2240.

Progress of the treaty for the surrender of Oxford, 9 June 1646.
Tann. 59, *fol.* 314.

Proposed articles for the surrender of Oxford, 1646.
Wood F. 27, *art.* 35 (*O. C.* 8489).

Propositions touching the surrender of Oxford (1646?).
Qu. Coll. 284, *fol.* 21.

King's warrant for the surrender of Oxford, 18 May 1646.
Tann. 59, *fol.* 213.

Discontent and disturbances in the garrison, Sept. 1649.
Tann. 56, *foll.* 99, 101.

Suppression of the mutiny by Col. Ingoldsby (Sept. 1649?).
Tann. 56, *fol.* 111.

XVIIIth Cent., 385.

XIXth Cent., 386.

Incidents in chronological order (not otherwise placed: such as accidents, famines, fires, rejoicings, riots, etc.), 387.

Charter of Stephen, dated from Oxford 1136.
Ashm. 860, *fol.* 379.

Bulla Nicholai legati Pontificii contra Burgenses Oxon., A.D. 1214.
Wood D. 18, *fol.* 4 (*O. C.* 8563).

Nota quod primatio super medios motus solis et lunae verificata fuit apud Oxon. anno 1292.
Digb. 149, *fol.* 124.

1354. See *Reln. of Univ. to City* (938).

1361. See *Air* (105).

Anecdote of a mayor, time of Charles I.
Rawl. A. 441, *fol.* 119.

Attestation of the birth of a monstrous child in Cat St., 11 Nov. 1633.
Qu. Coll. 121, *fol.* 301.

(City—History.)

Payment for powder supplied at Oxford, 5 Dec. 1642.
Clar. i. 1639.

Answer of the King to the Parliament's objections to the adjournment of the Law Term (Hilary) to Oxford, [Dec. 1642].
Clar. i. 1641.

"Relation of a lamentable fire [23 Dec. 1644?] in a zealous brother's shop," a poem.
Ashm. 36, *fol.* 160.

Proceedings at a Chapter of the Garter held at Oxford, 17 Jan. 164$\frac{4}{5}$.
Ashm. 1113, *fol.* 180: 1123, *fol.* 51^v.

— 2 Mar. 164$\frac{4}{5}$.
Ibid. 1108, *fol.* 159.

Mischances caused by the wind, 18 Feb. 1661.
Tann. 102, *fol.* 87.

Great storm of hail, May 1664.
Tann. 47, *fol.* 145.

Watch and ward kept in the city after the Great Fire, Sept. 1666.
Tann. 45, *fol.* 103^v.

Account of a riot, 11 Apr. 1683.
Tann. 338, *fol.* 190.

Personal history, in order of names, 388.

Biographical collections, 389.

DOCUMENTS, RECORDS, AND MISCELLANEA, 390.

Almanacs, 391.

Ancient relics (insignia, plate, etc.), 392.

Coins found at Rewley.
Rawl. C. 867, *fol.* 40.

Coin and seal found in St. Giles's parish.
Rawl. C. 867, *foll.* 57^v, 76.

Archives and manuscript collections (charters, etc., as a collection: see also 363), 394.

Charters of the City Hen. II, John, Hen. III, Edw. I, Edw. III, Rich. II.
Wood D. 18 *ad init.* (*O. C.* 8563).

(City—Documents.)

Cartarum formulae, praecipue ad civitatem Oxon. spectantium.

Rawl. A. 357 : *C.* 507, *foll.* 6, 40, 49, 186–200.

Excerpta ex rotulis in archivis Urbis Oxon.

James 26, *p.* 111 (*O. C.* 3863).

Transcripts of Oxford papers, by R. Rawlinson.

Rawl. C. 865–67.

Facetiae (caricatures, etc.), 395.

Literary pieces (see note on 978), 396.

A farewell to Oxford, a poem.

Ashm. 47, *fol.* 126^v.

1644? See *Incidents* (387).

News from Oxford, or the Spy of the Buttery, a poem by John Price, about 1646.

Ashm. 36, *fol.* 83.

Newspapers, Periodicals, etc. 398.

The Moderate Intelligencer.

No. 161 (1648) in Ant. à Wood's hand.

Wood (*printed books*) 514. 43.

(Univ.—General Notes.)

UNIVERSITY.

GENERAL NOTES, 401.

Deeds affecting the University.
Charters Cal. pp. 282, 286, 287, 348.

Notae quaedam Univ. Oxon. spectantes.
Bodl. 816, p. 121? (*O. C.* 2686).

Oxoniensis academiae et collegiorum dilucida descriptio per M. Windesore.
C. C. C. 280, *fol.* 46.

List of papers relating to the University in an iron chest in Magdalen college.
Wood F. 28, *fol.* 154 (*O. C.* 8490).

Name, 402.

Numbers, 403.

List of Fellows, Scholars, and Commoners of every College and Hall, A.D. 1552.
Wood E. 5, *art.* 7 (*O. C.* 8511).

Size and Bounds, 404.

Character and importance, 405.

External appearance, 406.

Buildings (architecture), 407.

Arms, motto, etc., 409.
Arms of the University.
Rawl. C. 867, *fol.* 54.

LOCAL DIVISIONS.

University Institutions and Buildings, 411.

Antony à Wood's History of the Public buildings of the Univ.
Wood   (*O. C.* 8464).

General Notes, 412.

Founders and Benefactors, 413.
Calendarium missarum pro animabus Benefactorum Univ. Oxon.
Wood (*O. C.* 8562). (Lost.)

(**Univ.—Local Divisions.**)

Account of the Savile and other foundations at Oxford: by Hen. Briggs, 1621.
Tann. 73, *fol.* 68.

Verses on Lady Eliz. Pawlet's gift of Needlework to the University, 1636.
Bodl. 22 (*O. C.* 3059): *Malone* 21, fol. 20^v.

Endowments, Estates, revenues, benefices, etc., 414.

Houses and lands of the University lying within the city, Mar. 1636.
Tann. 338, *fol.* 59.

Reasons against the spoliation and secularization of the revenues of the University (17th cent.).
Rawl. C. 739, *fol.* 100.

University Chest, 415 (see also *Finance*, 529).

Ashmolean Museum (Arundel Marbles, Inscriptions, etc.), 416.

Museum Ashmoleanum, carmen academicum.
Ashm. 1136, *fol.* 173.

Statutes of it objected to by dr. Rawlinson.
Rawl. C. 989, *foll.* 112-117.

Ashmole's gifts.
Ashm. 1763, *fol.* 33^v.

Icelandic stones given in 1688.
Rawl. C. 867, *fol.* 79.

Note of removal of the Arundel marbles (1688?).
Ibid., fol. 80^v.

H. Beverland accused of stealing from it, 1690.
Rawl. C. 344, *fol.* 6^v.

Presentation of coins to it by J. Ivie, 1694.
Tann. 25, *fol.* 150: 94, *fol.* 101.

Books sent by Lister to it, Nov. 1699.
Tann. 21, *fol.* 177.

List of books given by dr. Lister to the Ashmolean, 1708.
Wood 276c. 3.

Natural curiosities there said to be ill cared for.
Rawl. C. 989, *fol.* 132.

(Univ.—Local Divisions.)

Bodleian Library, 417.

Ground plot of the Library.
Wood F. 27, *art.* 14 (*O. C.* 8489).

License of Mortmain to sir Thomas Bodley for lands given by him.
Ibid., *art.* 15 (*O. C.* 8489).

Notes by sir Tho. Bodley about the Library.
Ibid., *art.* 16 (*O. C.* 8489).

Heads of statutes for the Library by sir Tho. Bodley, with Hawley's notes on them.
Ibid., *art.* 17 (*O. C.* 8489).

Note on the delivery of the chests containing sir Tho. Bodley's books to the Bodleian.
Qu. Coll. 268, *fol.* 17.

Statuta bibliothecae (17th cent.).
Qu. Coll. 216, *fol.* 145.

Statuta de conservatione bibliothecae.
Tann. 338, *fol.* 37.

Heads of statutes for the government of the Library.
Tann. 338, *fol.* 41.

Statuta bibliothecae.
Rawl. A. 284.

Foreign students admitted to Bodley, 1602–1690.
Wood E. 5, *art.* 3 (*O. C.* 8511).

Catalogus peregrinorum et aliorum admissorum in bibl. 1682–1735.
Rawl. A. 498, *fol.* 51.

Collections for a list of strangers admitted to the Library, 1682–1735: by R. Rawlinson.
Rawl. A. 498, *fol.* 108.

Praefatio Tho. James ad catalogum Bodleianum cum aliis notulis de T. Bodleio: per G. Fulman scripta.
C. C. C. 302, *fol.* 265.

Catalogus librorum bibliothecae Bodleianae, per Tho. James.
Univ. Coll. 155: *Qu. Coll.* 199.

(Univ.—Local Divisions—Bodleian.)

Letter about preparations for a catalogue of the Bodleian by Tho. Lockey (about 1660–65).
Tann. 338, *fol.* 180.

List of prints and portraits sent by R. Rawlinson to the Bodleian, 1750.
Rawl. C. 989, *foll.* 143–4.

(Catalogus librorum MSS. et impressorum in nova loca translatorum, etc.)
Langb. 5–6 (*O. C.* p. 269^a).

Clavis Bibl. Bodleianae [de MSS. translatis in nova loca].
Langb. 4, p. 1 (*O. C.* p. 269^a).

Designatio indiculi librorum [in variis partibus Bibl. Bodleianae].
Langb. 4, p. 151 (*O. C.* p. 269^a).

Clavis MSS. Cantuariensium [i.e. Laudianorum] in Bibl. Bodl.
Langb. 1 (*O. C.* 268^a).

Elenchus MSS. Laudensium prout in classibus suis deponuntur.
Tann. 269, *fol.* 264.

(Comparison of old and new numberings of the Baroccian MSS.)
Langb. 8, p. 265 (*O. C.* p. 270^a).

Greek MSS. at Oxford (short note).
Wood. D. 7 (2) (*O. C.* 8519).

Account of some Bodleian MSS.
Dugd. 48 (*O. C.* 6536).

(Alphabetical catalogue of the Greek MSS., by Edm. Chilmead, A.D. 1636.)
Langb. 7, p. 9 (*O. C.* p. 269^a).

Catalogus bibliothecae Baroccianae, per E. Chilmead.
Tann. 269, *fol.* 10.

Catalogus codd. MSS. Laudensium, per E. Chilmead.
Tann. 269, *fol.* 80.

(**Univ.—Local Divisions**—Bodleian.)
Index cod. Digby 166, by E. Chilmead.
Ibid., fol. 1.
De cod. Digby, 107 (Summa Will. de Conchis) by E. Chilmead.
Ibid., fol. 76.
Recensio quorundam MSS. praecipue Digb., by E. Chilmead.
Ibid., foll. 76, 130, 209.
Catalogus MSS. (Digbeianorum).
Langb. 4, p. 429 (*O. C.* p. 269^a).
Catalogue of 12 unreferenced MSS., A.D. 1654.
Langb. 6, p. 639 (*O. C.*, p. 269^a).
Contents of certain Baroccian and Cromwellian Greek MSS.
Langb. 10 (*O. C.* p. 270^b).
(Accounts of certain Bodleian MSS. by Langbaine.)
Langb. 7, p. 1 etc. (*O. C.* p. 269 ^{b}, *artt.* 10–11).
Langb. 8, p. 293 etc. (*O. C.* p. 270^a).
(Contents of various Bodleian MSS.)
Langb. 8, p. 79 etc. (*O. C.* p. 270^a, *q. v.*).
Ibid. 12, pp. 13, 101, 469: 15: 16: 18, p. 260: 19, pp. 1, 161, etc. (*O. C.* p. 270$^{a, b}$).
Wood (2), 2, p. 33 (*O. C.* 8615): 5, p. 1 (*O. C.* 8618): 7, p. 162 etc. (*O. C.* 8620).
(Comparison of old and new numbers of Digby MSS.)
Langb. 8, p. 287 (*O. C.* p. 270^a).
(Account of various Roe, Baroccian, Laudian and other Greek MSS.)
Langb. 8, p. 293 (*O. C.* p. 270^a).
(Catalogue of Laudian books, printed and MSS.)
Langb. 7, p. 155 (*O. C.* p. 269^a).
Excerpta ex variis libris MSS. et impressis in Bibl. Bodl.
James 30, p. 80 (*O. C.* p. 263^a).
(Catalogus) MSS. quos legavit Tho. Clayton.
Langb. 6, p. 80 (*O. C.* p. 269^a).
Contenta codd. MSS. quos pervolverat Langbainius.
Langb. 4, p. 542 (*O. C.* p. 269^a).

(Univ.—Local Divisions—Bodleian.)

Notes of Dugdale's MSS.
Ashm. 861, *foll.* 410, 502.

Extracts from MSS. about talismans.
Ashm. 434, *fol.* 151–86, cf. 1131, *fol.* 211.

Tabulae contentorum in cod. Gr. Auct. E. 1. 15: et excerpta ex variis codicibus Bodleianis.
Rawl. C. 850, *fol.* 45, etc.

Reference to a MS. given to the Library by Ashmole.
Ashm. 865, *fol.* 372.

Libri Hebræo-Rabbinici in Bibl. Bodleiana recensiti opera H. Jacobii, A. D. 1629.
Casaub. 26, *fol.* 67.
Wood (2) 1, *fol.* 344 (*O. C.* 8614).

Catalogue of printed books in the faculty of Law, by Gerard Langbaine.
Wood (2) 1, *fol.* 1 (*O. C.* 8614).

Oratio quam habuit Tho. James in Bibliotheca Bodleiana ad Regem Jacobum I.
C. C. C. 255, *fol.* 80.

Excerpta ex libro Computorum Bibl. Bodl., 1613–1652.
Wood F. 27, *art.* 38 (*O. C.* 8489).

Letter of archbp. Laud to the Univ. giving 81 MSS. to the Bodleian, 7 Nov. 1640, with the reply of the Univ. 9 Nov.: both in Latin.
Clar. i. 1450–51.

Petition of foreign students in Oxford to the Curators, A. D. 1641.
Wood F. 27, *art.* 18 (*O. C.* 8489).

An order to the Keeper of the University Library for D'Aubigne's Histoire Universelle for the King's use, 30 Dec. 1645.
Clar. i. 2061.

R. Napier studied in it (17th cent.).
Ashm. 1730, *fol.* 168.

(Univ.—Local Divisions—Bodleian.)

Notices by Hearne of various books there, rules for admission, etc.
Rawl. C. 867, *foll.* 36ᵛ, 37, 38, 39ᵛ, 42, 44, 44ᵛ, 45ᵛ-47ᵛ, 49, 50ᵛ, 51ᵛ.

List by Hearne of books publ. in London, not in Bodley.
Rawl. C. 146, *fol.* 31.

Account of the Council of Florence designed to be given to the Library.
Rawl. C. 983, *fol.* 175.

43 letters of Rich. Rawlinson to the Librarian about books, marbles, prints, etc. sent to the Library 1749-53.
Rawl. C. 989, *foll.* 81-142.

Ashmole's benefactions to the Bodleian.
Ashm. 1136, *fol.* 166 : 1731, *fol.* 101ᵛ.

Catalogue of the Bodleian coins, by Ashmole.
Ashm. 808.

— references to the catalogue.
Ibid., 1131, *fol.* 211 : 1136, *fol.* 166.

Crucifix found in St. Frideswide's and preserved in the Library.
Rawl. C. 867, *fol.* 52.

78 letters from B. Willis to H. Owen, Bodley's Librarian, chiefly about coins sent to the Library, 1749-59.
Rawl. C. 989, *foll.* 1-108.

Notes on coins and medals there.
Rawl. B. 399, *fol.* 99ᵛ.

— **Copyright privileges** (including Stationers' Company agreements), 418.

Indenture between the Univ. and the Stationers' Company, Dec. 1610.
Wood F. 27, *art.* 9 (*O. C.* 8489).

Confirmation of the Stationers' gift to the Univ., 28 Jan. 1611.
Ibid., *art.* 10 (*O. C.* 8489.)

(Univ.—Local Divisions—Bodleian.)

— **Picture Gallery**, 419 (but see 441-2).

Lines of Rob. Whitehall to Mrs. Mary More upon her sending sir T. More's picture, by herself, to the Library, 1674.
Rawl. B. 165, *fol.* 51.

Versus E. Waple in effigiem J. J. Scaligeri in bibliotheca.
Rawl. B. 165, *fol.* 18.

— **Radcliffe Building**, 420.

— **Schools quadrangle** (with Proscholium), 421.
(See also *Schools*, old, 498.)

Ground-plan of the "New Schools" (17th cent.).
C. C. C. 280, *fol.* 119^v.

Catalogue of the rarities in the Anatomy School.
Rawl. C. 865, *fol.* 9.

Curiosities and coins in the Anatomy School, 1721.
Rawl. B. 399, *foll.* 89-99, 117-141.

— **Libraries, old**, 422.

Collections relating to the ancient libraries of the Univ., with extracts of statutes etc.
Wood F. 27, *artt.* 11-12 (*O. C.* 8489).

Notes concerning Duke Humphrey's Library in Oxford.
Wood F. 27, *art.* 13 (*O. C.* 8489).

List of books sold in Oxford by Hunt in 1483.
Auct. R. supra 1.

Libri apud Carmelitas Oxonii.
Leland, vol. 3, p. 57 (*O. C.* 5104).

Botanical garden (Physic Garden), 423.

Clarendon Building, 424.

Clarendon Press, 425.

Other University Presses, 426.

Agreement between the Univ. and H. Hills and J. Field, printers, about printing bibles, 7 July 1660.
Tann. 338, *fol.* 91.
Rawl. C. 421, *fol.* 68.

(**Univ.—Local Divisions.**)
Mention of the Oxford printers in 1679.
Tann. 38, *fol.* 114.

Design of publishing all books worthy of note: letter from dr. Fell, 19 June 1681.
Tann. 36, *fol.* 51.

Papers about a dispute as to the right of the Univ. to print Bibles and Prayerbooks, 1688.
Rawl. A. 171, *foll.* 26–36.

Printing in Oxford, generally, 427.
Names of such books as were printed in Oxford about 1627–30.
Qu. Coll., 390, *fol.* 140^v.

State of the affairs of printing in the Univ., 1679.
Tann. 338, *fol.* 183.

External relations (to Stationers' Company, etc.), special rights of printing, 428.

Case between the Univ. and the Stationers' Company (about 1660?), by B. Cooper.
Tann. 338, *fol.* 90.

Dispute about the right of printing Bibles, 1679, in a letter of dr. Fell.
Tann. 33, *fol.* 17: 338, *fol.* 182.

Letter of John Wallis about the right of the Univ. to print Bibles, etc., 15 Apr. 1684.
Tann. 338, *fol.* 200.

Letter of John Wallis on the University's right of printing, 1691.
Qu. Coll. 290, *fol.* 41.

The University and Stationers' Company: letter from Edm. Gibson, 1 Apr. 1697.
Tann. 23, *fol.* 1.

The Stationers' Company and the Oxford Press (letter from A. Charlett), 11 May 1698.
Tann. 22, *fol.* 54; cf. 21, *fol.* 10.

(Univ.—Local Divisions.)

Convocation and Congregation House, with Apodyterium, 429.
   Arms there, 1574.
      Wood. D. 14 (*O. C.* 8548).
   Arms in the Congregation house.
      Wood. F. 33, *fol.* 126^v (*O. C.* 8495).

Old Congregation House in St. Mary's, 430.

Divinity School, 431.
   Arms there, 1574.
      Wood D. 14 (*O. C.* 8548).
   Arms in the Divinity School.
      Wood F. 33, *fol.* 111^v (*O. C.* 8495).
   Plan of one partition of the roof of the Divinity School (17th cent.).
      C. C. C. 280, *fol.* 119^v.

Indian Institute, 432.

Museum and laboratories (Clarendon, etc.), 433.

Radcliffe Library, 434.

Observatory (University), 435.

Park, 436.

St. Mary's (University Church), see *City—local divisions—St. Mary's*, 146; and 430 *above*.

Schools, New Examination, 437.

Sheldonian, 438.
   Carta Theatrum Sheld. universitati confirmans, 25 May 1669.
      Tann. 461, *fol.* 6^v.
   Oratio T. Houghton in inauguratione Theatri Sheldoniani, 1669.
      Tann. 461, *fol.* 177.

Commemoration, Encaenia or Act, 439.
   Oratio Joh. Massey in conclusione Encaeniorum, 7 July 1676.
      Tann. 461, *fol.* 115.
   Letters from the Chancellor to put off the Act, 16 May 1695.
      Tann. 24, *fol.* 35.

(Univ.—Local Divisions.)

Admission to degrees at the Act : see *Degrees* (712).

Sheldonian Press: see under *Clarendon Press* (426).

Taylor Institution, 440.

University Galleries, 441.

  Pictures in general, 442 (see also 419).

    Notes on various portraits in Oxford (17th cent.).
    Tann. 356*, *fol.* 74.

    Notes of an artist's tour through Oxford, 1785.
    Top. Oxf. c. 33.

Collegiate Institutions and Buildings.

  General Notes (colleges and halls), **444.**

    See *Lit. pieces* (Dobbare), 955.

    Excerpta ex tabella Joh. Rouse Collegiorum et Aularum suo tempore in Oxonia.
    Leland Coll. 5 (*O. C.* 5106).

    Arms in the windows of Colleges at Oxford, collected by Dugdale.
    Dugd. 12 (*F.* 1) (*O. C.* 6501).

    Out of Sir W. Dugdale's Collections of Arms in the windows of several Colleges in Oxford before the Civil War.
    Wood D. 19, *fol.* 83 (*O. C.* 8564).

    Monuments, inscriptions, and arms in Colleges, 1659.
    Rawl. B. 397 (in *foll.* 1–217).

    Papers relating to the Colleges and Halls.
    Wood F. 28 (*O. C.* 8490).

    Antony à Wood's History of the Colleges.
    Wood   (*O. C.* 8464).

    Notes of epitaphs etc. in Oxford Colleges: by Ralph Sheldon.
    Wood C. 11 (*O. C.* 8551).

    Collection of monumental inscriptions in Oxford, Bristol, etc.: by R. Rawlinson.
    Rawl. B. 400 [d].

  Founders and benefactors, 445.

(Univ.—Local Divisions.)

Endowments, estates, revenues, benefices, etc., 446.

Old rents of every College according to which they were taxed for Qu. Elizabeth's entertainment.
Tann. 338, *fol.* 27^v.

Of the annual revenue of the Colleges and halls.
Ibid., fol. 203.

Buildings etc., in general, 447.

    Chapels, 448.

    Common Rooms, 449.

    Halls and Offices, 450.

    Libraries, archives, and records, 451.

    Quadrangles and gardens, 452.

    Rooms, 453.

    Plate, 454.

Order of Parliament against carrying away the College plate, 12 July 1642.
Clar. i. 1622.

Abstract of College plate given to Charles I, 20 Jan. 164$\frac{2}{3}$.
Tann. 338, *fol.* 65.

Arms, mottos, etc., 455.

Contributions to Univ.: see *Relation of Univ. to Colleges*, 948.

All Souls', 456.

Statuta Collegii.
C. C. C. 354.

Statuta cum injunctionibus, usque ad 1602.
Tann. 154, *fol.* 1: 340, *fol.* 14.

— ad 1680.
Ibid. 153, *fol.* 1.

Life of the founder, by Rob. Hoveden, 1574.
Wood F. 28, *fol.* 140 (*O. C.* 8490).

Names of the first Warden and Fellows.
Ibid., fol. 144.

Excerpts from the Statutes and Charter of Foundation.
Ibid., fol. 144.

(Univ.—Local Divisions.)

Copy of the foundation charter, 20 May, 1438.
Tann. 153, *fol.* 125 : 340, *fol.* 5.

Carta Henr. VI, 14 Aug. 1442.
Tann. 340, *fol.* 9.

Confirmatio cartae, 1489.
Tann. 340, *fol.* 12.

Visitor's order about disputations, 1519.
Tann. 153, *fol.* 62 : 340, *fol.* 63^v.

Injunctions of the Visitor, 26 Aug. 1541.
Tann. 340, *fol.* 65.

Injunctiones regiae, 1545.
Tann. 340, *fol.* 71.

Short account of the foundation of All Souls', by J. Warner, Warden (about 1550).
Tann. 340, *fol.* 4.

Letter of J. Warner, Warden, about the College Statutes (about 1550).
Tann. 340, *fol.* 72^v.

Fellows, bachelors and undergraduates in 1552.
Rawl. C. 910, *fol.* 23^v.

Some matriculations, 1564–1616.
Rawl. C. 910, *fol.* 22.

Letter of the Visitor about College affairs, 22 Nov. 1570.
Tann. 153, *fol.* 105 : 340, *foll.* 73^v, 200^v.

— 29 June, 1572.
Ibid. 340, *fol.* 75.

Processus super electione R. Hoveden in custodem Collegii, 1571.
Tann. 340, *fol.* 140.

Arms there, 1574.
Wood D. 14 (*O. C.* 8548).

Visitor's injunction about resignations, etc., 1574.
Tann. 340, *fol.* 74.

Orders concerning declamations, 1575.
Tann. 153, *fol.* 83^v : 340, *fol.* 118^v.

(**Univ.—Local Divisions**—All Souls'.)

Visitor's injunction about resignations, 1586.
  Tann. 153, *fol.* 65ᵛ : 340, *fol.* 79ᵛ.

Confirmatio decreti Edm. Grindall de Communiis per J. Whitgift, 1586.
  Tann. 153, *fol.* 63ᵛ : 340, *fol.* 76.

Visitor's interpretation of statute about the dean of Law, 1588.
  Tann. 153, *fol.* 64 : 340, *fol.* 76ᵛ.

Order about lectures, etc., 1588.
  Tann. 153, *fol.* 84 : 340, *fol.* 119.

— about Chapel Services, 1589.
  Ibid. 153, *fol.* 85 : 340, *fol.* 120.

Visitor's injunction about commons, etc., 1593.
  Tann. 153, *fol.* 82 : 340, *fol.* 78.

Visitor's interpretation of statute de dignioribus personis, 1597.
  Tann. 340, *fol.* 79.

Commemoration prayers appointed by Whitgift (16th cent.).
  Tann. 340, *fol.* 91.

Supplement to order of 1589 about College Services, 1604.
  Tann. 340, *fol.* 120ᵛ.

College orders about the kitchen, 26 June, 1606.
  Tann. 153, *fol.* 81 : 340, *fol.* 118.

Visitor's suspension of Whitgift's injunctions concerning Fellows practising the Civil Law, 2 Mar. 160$\frac{9}{10}$.
  Tann. 153, *fol.* 81 : 340, *fol.* 94.

Letter of the Visitor to the Warden about College expenses, 1610.
  Tann. 340, *fol.* 92.

Nomination of officers, 27 June, 1611.
  Tann. 340, *fol.* 142.

Letter on All Souls' affairs, by A. Duck, 16 Dec. 1612.
  Tann. 340, *fol.* 108.

(**Univ.—Local Divisions**—All Souls'.)
Process of the admission of R. Moket as Warden, Apr. 1614.
 Tann. 153, *fol.* 89 : 340, *fol.* 128.

Oratio A. Duck cum archiepiscopo Cantuar. praesentaret duo nominatos ad officium custodis coll. Omnium Animarum, 1614.
 Tann. 340, *fol.* 131^v.

College orders (internal affairs), 1614.
 Tann. 153, *fol.* 86^v : 340, *fol.* 121.

Extracts from sixteen letters of the Visitor about the College, 1614–32.
 Tann. 340, *fol.* 98.

Touching presentation-money in lieu of dinners, 1614–40, by Sir L. Jenkins.
 Tann. 340, *fol.* 122.

Chaplains' petition and Visitor's answer, 1619.
 Tann. 341, *fol.* 94^v.

Reasons why a B.A. at All Souls' cannot be M.A. under 4 years' standing (about 1620).
 Tann. 340, *foll.* 105, 108^v, 431.

Reasons for and against the power of Civilians to take degrees in another faculty (about 1620).
 Tann. 340, *foll.* 99, 105^v, 108^v, 431.

Recommendation of a Fellow by James I.
 Ashm. 64, *fol.* 20^v.

Letters of the Visitor to the Warden about internal affairs of the College, 1624.
 Tann. 340, *foll.* 107, 107^v.

— 1626–9.
 Ibid. 340, *foll.* 109^v sqq.

— 1633.
 Ibid. 340, *fol.* 107^v.

Visitor's injunctions about elections, 1625.
 Tann. 153, *fol.* 105^v : 340, *foll.* 95, 186, 192, 196.

The case of the surplusage money, 1627.
 Tann. 340, *foll.* 110, 112, 439.

(**Univ.—Local Divisions**—All Souls'.)

Mandamus of Charles I to elect to a Fellowship, 2 Nov. 1643.
Tann. 340, *fol.* 148.

Orders about resignations (rejected by the College), 23 Apr. 1657.
Tann. 340, *fol.* 123.

Latin letters from the College to the Visitor (some with the annual accounts, etc.), 1664–88.
Tann. 340, *passim, in foll.* 150–422.

Letter of Miles Smyth, secr. to the Visitor, removing Edw. Pennell unduly elected Fellow, 24 Nov. 1666.
Tann. 340, *fol.* 124.

Two letters of the Visitor about College affairs, 1666–7.
Tann. 340, *fol.* 123^v.

Letters of Tho. Jeames about College affairs, 1673–86.
Tann. 340, *fol.* 124^v, etc.

Letters to the Visitor about candidates for a Fellowship, 1678.
Tann. 340, *foll.* 165, 168, 169.

Visitor's nomination of four Fellows, 1680 (draft).
Tann. 340, *fol.* 440.

Petition of three Fellows for admission to their offices, 1680.
Tann. 340, *fol.* 253.

Papers about the above elections.
Ibid., foll. 254, 255.

Visitor's injunction against resignations, 1680 (draft).
Tann. 340, *foll.* 193, 194.

— Letter of 24 Fellows to the Visitor against the above, 1680.
Ibid., fol. 214.

— legal opinions about the oath in the above, 1680.
Ibid., fol. 216.

— papers by the Sub-warden, North, Prideaux and Digby, about the above, 1680.
Ibid., foll. 218–226, 259.

(**Univ.—Local Divisions**—All Souls'.)

Papers about the Warden's negative voice in the election of officers (1680–81 ?).
    Tann. 340, *foll.* 144, 258–270.

Visitor's interpretation of the statute about Doctors not being Bursar, 1681.
    Tann. 340, *fol.* 345.

Arrangements for the Visitor's visit to the College, 1681.
    Tann. 340, *fol.* 274.

Papers relating to a mandamus of the King's Bench for admitting Ayloffe to a Fellowship, 1681.
    Tann. 340, *foll.* 237, 239, 288, 300, 304, 338, 339, 443.

Latin letter from the College to the Visitor, 1683.
    Tann. 340, *fol.* 370.

College order about allowances, 1683.
    Tann. 340, *fol.* 364.

— approval by the Visitor, 1683.
    Ibid., fol. 364^v.

Letters from the Duke of Ormond to the Visitor about two Fellows, 168$\frac{3}{4}$, 1686.
    Tann. 340, *foll.* 376, 401.

Letter to Sancroft about probationer fellows at All Souls', by Geo. Clarke, 1684.
    Tann. 340, *fol.* 388.

Letter of W. Horton about a remonstrance to the Visitor, 1684.
    Tann. 340, *fol.* 276.

Queries relative to the election of a warden, 168$\frac{4}{5}$.
    Tann. 340, *fol.* 407.

— confirmation of the election of Mr. Finch as Warden (168$\frac{4}{5}$) (draft of a letter by sir Tho. Clarges).
    Ibid., fol. 408.

Letters of the Warden about College affairs, 1687–90.
    Tann. 340, *fol.* 411.

Mandate of James II for presenting Cartwright to the vicarage of Barking, 13 Aug. 1688.
    Tann. 28, *fol.* 160,

(Univ.—Local Divisions—All Souls'.)

Letter of J. Walrond to the Visitor on College affairs, 14 Jan. 16$\frac{98}{99}$.
Tann. 340, *fol.* 425.

Letters and accounts about the expulsion of Jonas Proast from a chaplaincy at All Souls', 1697.
Tann. 23, *fol.* 107, etc. : 340, *fol.* 412 sqq.

Affairs at All Souls', 13 July, 1698; letter from Tho. Rivers.
Tann. 22, *fol.* 199.

The case of the Warden, 19 May–26 June, 1699; three letters from Tho. Rivers.
Tann. 21, *foll.* 59, 74, 130.

Letter of A. Charlett, grievances at All Souls', June, 1699.
Tann. 21, *fol.* 69.

Letter of Tho. Tanner to the Warden for leave to stand for a fellowship at All Souls', in Latin (no date).
Tann. 114, *fol.* 16.

Letters relating to All Souls', about 1715, and in 1719.
Ch. Ch. 248-49.

Addresses of graduates, about 1847.
Top. Oxf. e. 18.

Catalogus MSS^{rum} in bibliotheca Collegii Omnium Animarum.
Wood (2) 3, p. 1 (*O. C.* 8616).

Index to Visitors' injunctions, by Sancroft.
Tann. 340, *fol.* 438.

Memoranda by Sancroft relating to the College.
Tann. 340, *foll.* 441, 442.

Excerpts from the Archives.
Wood D. 2, pp. 137, 147 (*O. C.* 8513).

Monumental inscriptions subsequent to Wood's History, to 1736.
Rawl. B. 400^d, *fol.* 1.

Miscellaneous notices of the College.
Tann. 22, *fol.* 199 : 35, *foll.* 113, 119.

Verses on the Mallard.
Tann. 306, *fol.* 378.

(Univ.—Local Divisions.)

Arms in trick.
Rawl. B. 101, *fol.* 14.

Note on MS. All Souls' 95 (Ptolemy).
Rawl. C. 936, *fol.* 15.

Owned Bodl. MS. *Digby* 44.

Balliol, 457.

Founders and benefactors.
Rawl. C. 867, *fol.* 22.

Charter mentioning " Balliol hall."
Charters Cal. p. 351.

Charter affecting Balliol.
Charters Cal. p. 350.

Names of several fellows of Balliol, 1370–1440.
Ball. Coll. 89. *ad init.*

Catalogue of Fellows, 1502–1682.
Wood F. 28, *fol.* 54 (*O. C.* 8490).

Catalogue of M.A.s, 1607–42.
Ibid., fol. 53.

Case between Balliol and the Halls about the Proctorship, 1668.
Ibid., fol. 44.

Names of Founders and Benefactors.
Ibid., fol. 36.

Abstract of the will of John Snell, founding Scotch scholarships.
Ibid., fol. 47.

List of Fellows, 1520–1680.
Tann. 356, *fol.* 79.

Arms in the College, 1574.
Wood F. 14 (*O. C.* 8548).

Catalogus magistrorum aliaque ad Coll. Balliolense spectantia, per M. Windesore.
C. C. C. 280, *fol.* 28.

Balliofergus, a history of the College, by Henry Savage.
Rawl. B. 406.

(Univ.—Local Divisions.)

List of eminent members of Balliol and Oriel, written in the 17th cent.
Qu. Coll. 280, *fol.* 81.

Letter of J. Robinson, bp. of Bristol, to the College on becoming Visitor (about 1714?).
Rawl. B. 376, *fol.* 153.

Papers relating to W. Cruwys's appeal to the Visitor against the Master and Fellows, 1719.
Rawl. B. 376, *foll.* 49, 156–159.

Papers relating to Dr. Warner's scholarships.
Tann. 338, *foll.* 227, seqq.

Excerpts from the Archives.
Wood D. 2, pp. 107, 274 (*O. C.* 8513).

Arms in the College.
Wood F. 33, *fol.* 107 (*O. C.* 8495).

Index MSS^{rum} in bibliotheca coll. Balliolensis, cum conjecturis Langbainii.
Wood (2) 4 (*O. C.* 8617).

Libri in bibliotheca collegii Balliolensis.
Leland Coll. 3, p. 58 (*O. C.* 5104).

Note of a MS. there.
Rawl. C. 850, *fol.* 135^v.

(See also *New Inn Hall*, 478.)

Brasenose, 458.

List of Founders and benefactors.
Wood 28, *fol.* 162 (*O. C.* 8492): *Rawl. C.* 865, *fol.* 1^v.

Names of Fellows in 1538.
Wood 28, *fol.* 162 (*O. C.* 8492).

Admission, resignation, etc., of some Fellows, 1543–55.
Ibid., *fol.* 165.

Arms there, 1574.
Wood D. 14 (*O. C.* 8548).

Letter concerning the choice of a Principal by Fellows of B. N. C., 10 Oct. 1608.
Ashm. 1729, *fol.* 181^v.

(**Univ.—Local Divisions.**)

Ceremony of the Consecration of the Chapel.
Wood F. 28, *fol.* 158 (*O. C.* 8490).

License to accept lands, etc., from Sir J. Grimston, 22 May, 1696.
Rawl. A. 241, *fol.* 187^v.

Excerpts from the Archives.
Wood D. 2, p. 290 (*O. C.* 8513).

Pension out of the Thenford tithes given to the College.
Ashm. 1162, *fol.* 31.

Christ Church (Cardinal College), 459.

Charters affecting Ch. Ch.
Charters Cal. pp. 46, 49, 283–86, 312, 588, 611, 661.

Statuta Collegii Cardinalis, 1525.
Ch. Ch. 339.

Excerpta ex codice Statutorum Coll. Cardinalis Oxon.
James 7, p. 88 (*O. C.* 3844).

Sundry orders of the Dean and Chapter (Charles I's time?).
Ch. Ch. 345, *art.* 4.

Statutes and decrees of the Dean and Chapter of Ch. Ch. (Watkins collection).
Wood C. 7 (1) (*O. C.* 8541).

Letters, bonds, etc., relating to Ch. Ch., Oseney, etc., 1519–1631.
Top Oxf. c. 22.

Fundatores et nomina Monasteriorum suppressorum ad fundandum Collegium Thomae Wolsey card. Ebor. in Acad. Oxon.
Dodsw. 26, *fol.* 23 (*O. C.* 4168).

Grant from card. Campeggio to card. Wolsey of timber for the building of Cardinal college, 22 Sept. 1529.
Ch. Ch. 344, *fol.* 55.

Cartularium dotationis Decano et Capitulo ecclesiae Cathedralis Christi, 15 Sept. 1542.
Ch. Ch. 344, *fol.* 1.

(Univ.—Local Divisions—Ch. Ch.)

The lands assigned by the King to the Cathedral Church in Oxford, 1 Oct. 1546.
   Ch. Ch. 344, *fol.* 16 : *Wood F.* 28, *fol.* 176 (*O. C.* 8490).

Yearly value of the suppressed monasteries belonging to Cardinal College.
   Tann. 343, *fol.* 57.

Parsonages to be appropriated to Cardinal College.
   Tann. 343, *fol.* 58^v.

Charter of foundation of the episcopal see and of the Dean and Chapter of the Cathedral Church of Christ, 4 Nov. 1546.
   Ch. Ch. 344, *fol.* 48.

Charter of actual dotation (Ch. Ch.), 11 Dec. 1546.
   Ch. Ch. 344, *fol.* 26.

Extract from the journal book of the expenses of building the College.
   Tann. 338, *fol.* 313.

List, with notes, of the Bishops of Oxford, and Deans and Canons of Ch. Ch. from its foundation (Watkins collection).
   Wood C. 7 (2) (*O. C.* 8541).

List of admissions to Ch. Ch., 1547–1581.
   Wood F. 28, *fol.* 172 (*O. C.* 8490).

Various Catalogues of the Canons, students, etc., of Ch. Ch., 1547–1619 (Watkins collection).
   Wood C. 8 (*O. C.* 8542).

Qu. Mary's remission of tithes to Ch. Ch., 2 July, 1555.
   Ch. Ch. 344, *fol.* 44.

Letter from Queen Elizabeth to the College relative to the Westminster studentship, 6 June, 1561, in Latin.
   Tann. 338, *fol.* 316.

Elections from Westminster to Ch. Ch., and to Trin. Coll. Cambridge, 1561–1689.
   Wood F. 28, *fol.* 170 (*O. C.* 8490).

Expenses of the College on the Queen's visit, 1566.
   Rawl. C. 878, *fol.* 1 : *Gough Oxf.* 68.

(Univ.—Local Divisions—Ch. Ch.)

Arms there, 1574.
   Wood D. 14 (*O. C.* 8548).

Epistola praebendariorum studentium ecclesiae Cathedralis Christi Oxon. Elizabethae Reginae (July, 1575).
   Auct. F. 5. 13, p. 301.

Receipt for annuity allowed by the Dean and Chapter to J. Sancterentianus, 17 Dec. 1583.
   Tann. 79, *fol.* 206.

Arguments about the precedency of the Canons of Ch. Ch. by Tho. Thornton (16th cent.).
   Rawl. B. 404, *fol.* 8.

Dr. Thornton's reason about the succession of Prebendaries.
   Wood F. 28, *fol.* 169 (*O. C.* 8490).

Petition from Students in behalf of dr. King to King James I, 1604.
   Wood F. 28, *fol.* 171 (*O. C.* 8490).

Letters patent of James I for annexing a Canonry to the Regius Professorship of Divinity, 1606.
   Ch. Ch. 345, *art.* 1.

Lines on Technogamia (the Marriage of the Arts) played there, 1621.
   Ashm. 38, *fol.* 31.

Lines on the play acted by the students of Ch. Ch. before the King at Woodstock, 1621.
   Malone 19, pp. 98, 99 : *Ashm.* 36, *fol.* 283.

Reply of Charles I to the Students' complaints, 30 Jan. 1629.
   Ch. Ch. 345, *art.* 5.

Lord Coventry's decision as to Canons' lodgings, 24 Sept. 1632.
   Ch. Ch. 345, *art.* 6.

Letters patent annexing a Prebend of Ch. Ch. to the Public Oratorship, 21 Dec. 1635, in Latin.
   Clar. i. 600.

— reply of the Univ. 20 March 163$\frac{5}{6}$, in Latin.
   Ibid., i. 679.

(**Univ.—Local Divisions—Ch. Ch.**)

Letters patent of Charles I for annexing a prebendal stall at Ch. Ch. to the Public Oratorship, 1636.
Ch. Ch. 345, *art.* 3.

Steps for exempting Ch. Ch. from the ordinance for abolishing Deans and Chapters, Oct. 1648.
Tann. 456, *foll.* 3, 5.

Lines on the Ch. Ch. men expelled in the Parliament time.
Ashm. 36, *fol.* 144^v.

Letter from the Dean and Chapter to Sheldon, giving an account of money expended on the fabric, etc., from 1661–1670.
Tann. 147, *fol.* 71.

Permission to Ch. Ch. to print a private form of prayers, 8 Oct. 1669.
Ch. Ch. 345, *art.* 12.

Letter from the Prince of Orange about the deprivation of Will. Ellis from his Studentship, because he went in the Prince's suite to Cambridge, dated 11 Jan. 167$\frac{1}{2}$.
Ch. Ch. 345, *art.* 9.

Case of the Vicechancellor, etc., as to the Canons preaching in the Cathedral (167$\frac{2}{3}$).
Ch. Ch. 345, *art.* 10.

— Reply of the Dean and Chapter, 6 Mar. 167$\frac{2}{3}$.
Ibid., *art.* 11.

Answer of the Vicechancellor, etc., to the dean and canons on their refusal to preach in their turns at St. Mary's, 1673.
Qu. Coll. 278, *fol.* 276.

The Case between the Univ. and Ch. Ch. about University sermons at the Cathedral and St. Mary's.
Wood F. 27, *art.* 37 (*O. C.* 8489).

Case between the Univ. and Ch. Ch. about the Dean and Canons preaching only at Ch. Ch.
Rawl. B. 404, *fol.* 1.

The Lord Chancellor's judgement, as Visitor, on an

(Univ.—Local Divisions—Ch. Ch.)
appeal by Will. Shipley, undergraduate of Ch. Ch., 20 June, 1678.
Ch. Ch. 345, *art.* 13.

Verses on Tom of Christ Church newly cast, 1680.
Tann. 366, *fol.* 67^v.

Affairs of the College, 1683.
Tann. 305, *fol.* 141.

Proceedings of the Chapter in the case of Smith and Beane, master-students, convicted of riotous conduct, 1694–1705.
Tann. 314, *fol.* 205.

Monumental Inscriptions subsequent to Wood's History, to 1750.
Rawl. B. 400^d, *fol.* 4.

Address of dean Aldrich to Qu. Anne, etc., at Ch. Ch., 1702.
Worc. Coll. 58, *fol.* 277.

Inscriptions on the foundation stones of the New Buildings, 1705; Library notes, etc.
Rawl. C. 867, *foll.* 35, 39^v, 40^v, 60^v.

Inscriptions on the foundation stone of Peckwater quad, 1706.
Tann. 338, *fol.* 315.

Atrium Peckwateriense, poëma auctore J. Prescot (18th cent.).
Magd. Coll. 234, *fol.* 93^v.

Conciones iv brevissimae apud Aedem Christi Oxon. annis 1720–25 habitae.
Rawl. C. 17.

Notes by Brown Willis of the observance of St. Frideswide's Day at Ch. Ch.
Rawl. C. 989, *foll.* 43^v, 53, 66, 67.

Addresses of graduates, about 1847.
Top. Oxf. e. 18.

Christ Church—accounts, etc. 1555–1632.
Top. Oxf. c. 23.

F

(Univ.—Local Divisions.)

Themata octo a quodam Aedis Christi alumno.
Rawl. C. 556.

Lines on Ch. Ch. window and Magd. wall.
Ashm. 38, *fol.* 46; 47, *fol.* 94^v.

Arms, in trick.
Rawl. B. 101, *fol.* 14.

See also *Canterbury College*, 486: *Cathedral*, 154: *St. Frideswide's*, 262.

Corpus Christi, 460.

Statuta collegii (the original MS.).
Laud Misc. 621: *cf.* C.C.C. 412–15.

Excerpta ex statutis coll. Corporis Christi.
James 17, p. 168 (*O. C.* 3854).

Alumnorum C.C.C. carmina in adventum Elizabethae, 1566 (?).
C.C.C. 280, *fol.* 171.

Arms there, 1574.
Wood D. 14 (*O. C.* 8548).

Proceedings of the commissioners in the case of Fulman and others ejected from their fellowships in 1648.
C.C.C. 301, *fol.* 165.

Monumental inscriptions subsequent to Wood's History, to 1750.
Rawl. B. 400^d, *foll.* 3, 106.

Addresses of graduates, about 1847.
Top. Oxf. e. 18.

Collegii origo.
C.C.C. 280, *fol.* 169.

History of C.C.C., collated from Ant. à Wood.
Rawl. C. 867, *fol.* 2.

Varia ad historiam C.C.C. spectantia.
C.C.C. 280, *fol.* 211; 303–305; 408; 421–23; 432; 435–7: (library) 416–20.

Excerpts from the Archives.
Wood D. 2, p. 609 (*O. C.* 8513).

(**Univ.—Local Divisions.**)
Papers by Vaughan Thomas about the Presidents, Writers, etc. of C.C.C.
Top. Oxf. c. 2.

Note of Arms in C.C.C.
Wood B. 14 (*O.C.* 8585): *F.* 33, *fol.* 119^v (*O.C.* 8495).

Arms, in trick.
Rawl. B. 101, *fol.* 14.

Exeter, 461.
Charters affecting Stapledon hall.
Charters Cal., pp. 288, 290.

Nota de somnio cujusdam in coll. Exon. anno 1547.
Digb. 103, *fol.* 40^v.

Arms there, 1574.
Wood D. 14 (*O. C.* 8548).

Rental of manors and farms in the XVIth cent.
Tann. 338, *fol.* 415.

Letter of thanks from the college to Napier for helping to rebuild the kitchen, 1624.
Ashm. 1730, *fol.* 148.

Lord chief justice Holt's argument in the case between the Visitor and D^r. Bury the Rector, 16 June 1694.
Tann. 280, *fol.* 153.

Excerpts from the Archives.
Wood D. 2, pp. 71, 95, 306, 314, 318, 356 (*O.C.* 8513).

Inscription over Chapel door.
Rawl. B. 479, *fol.* 119.

Bodl. MS. Digb. 176 datum est "in usum coll. Merton et Exon."

Hertford (new foundation), **462.**

Jesus, 463.
Extracts from the statutes.
All S. 222, *fol.* 136.

Endowments, statutes, etc.
Rawl. C. 867, *foll.* 69^v–75.

(Univ.—Local Divisions.)
Papers relating to Jesus college.
   All S. 240, *fol.* 510.
Copies of Charters to Jesus college.
   All S. 216, *fol.* 81 : *Charters Cal.*, pp. 284-85.
Report of a case respecting sir L. Jenkins' will.
   All S. 264, *fol.* 132.
Letter from chancellor Ellesmere about the headship, 1613.
   Rawl. C. 867, *fol.* 68.
Proposal for establishing lectures for Welsh students in law.
   Tann. 338, *fol.* 404.
Common-room account book, 1703-22.
   Add. A. 205.
Chancery decree about W. Lewis's charities, 1737.
   Rawl. C. 451, *fol.* 1.

Keble, 464.

Lincoln, 465.
Catalogue of Fellows, 1436-1572.
   Wood F. fol. 126 (*O. C.* 8490).
— 1577-1681.
   Ibid., fol. 133.
Concerning Trape's scholars.
   Ibid., fol. 137.
List of Rectors, by Ant. à Wood (17th cent.).
   Tann. 338, *fol.* 224^v.
Charter affecting Lincoln.
   Charters Cal., p. 284.
Arms there, 1574.
   Wood D. 14 (*O. C.* 8548).
Addresses of graduates, about 1847.
   Top. Oxf. e. 18.
Catalogus MSS^{rum} in bibliotheca coll. Lincoln.
   Wood (2) 3, p. 61 (*O. C.* 8616).
Disticha de Angliae regibus ex fenestris in aula coll. Lincoln.
   C.C.C. 258, *fol.* 65^v.

(Univ.—Local Divisions.)

Sermons preached at Linc. coll. and elsewhere.
Magd. Coll. 245.

Excerpts from the Archives.
Wood D. 2, pp. 51, 65 (*O. C.* 8513).

Arms in Lincoln college.
Wood F. 33, *fol.* 109^v (*O. C.* 8495).

Magdalen, 466.

Statuta.
Rawl. C. 945, *fol.* 225.

Magdalen college lists, by — Burn.
Gough Oxf. 80.

Charters affecting Magdalen.
Charters Cal., pp. 306, 424.

Chronological memoirs of Magd. coll. 1458–1776, by the Rev. R. Bryne, 5 vols.
Gough Oxf. 32–36.

Case of dr. Coveney president, 1558, cited by dr. Hen. Fairfax in 1687.
Tann. 29, *fol.* 85.

Arms there, 1574.
Wood D. 14 (*O. C.* 8548).

Bp. Cooper's Injunctions to the College, 17 Oct. 1585.
Gough Oxf. 8.

Rental of college manors and farms in the 16th cent.
Tann. 338, *fol.* 263.

Agreement in a dispute between the College and W. Sidner, 1613.
Tann. 338, *fol.* 241.

Proceedings for the recovery of the mitre taken out of the college by M. Baker in 1646.
Tann. 338, *fol.* 243.

Royal mandate for election to a demyship, 20 July 1660.
Tann. 338, *fol.* 246.

Rent-roll, 1661.
Wood F. 28, *fol.* 148 (*O. C.* 8490).

Signatures of the President and Fellows, 1678.
Tann. 41, *fol.* 96.

(**Univ.—Local Divisions**—Magdalen.)

State of the case between some Fellows and the Visitor about the divinity reader (about 1680?).
Tann. 338, *fol.* 250.

Letter of the Visitor to the archbp. of Canterbury (Sancroft) about his proceedings against Magdalen college, Aug. 1684.
Tann. 32, *fol.* 121.

Accounts of the Visitation in 1687.
Rawl. B. 398, *foll.* 1, 47.

Heads of the proceedings in the order in which they occurred, 1687.
Tann. 29, *fol.* 84.

Proceedings against D^r. Hough and the Fellows, 1687.
Tann. 456*, *fol.* 21.

Account of proceedings against Magdalen college, 1687-88, in letters from W. Sherwin to dr. Tho. Turner.
C.C.C. 345.

Letters, petitions, etc. on the same subject.
Ibid. 355.

Account of the proceedings of bp. Cartwright in the same matter.
Ibid. 301, *fol.* 225.

Account of what took place before the Commissioners, 13 June, 1687.
Tann. 29, *fol.* 90.

D^r. Tho. Smith's account of his own conduct before the Commission, 1687.
Ibid., fol. 91.

Copy of the journal of the Visitors, 1687.
Ibid., fol. 88.

Account of the Visitation.
Ibid., fol. 93.

Account of what passed between the King and the Fellows at Ch. Ch. 4 Sept. 1687.
Tann. 29, *fol.* 86 : *Rawl. A.* 189^a, *fol.* 21.

Letter from J. Proast to bp. Cartwright one of the Commissioners, 24 Oct. 1687.
Tann. 29, *fol.* 105.

(Univ.—Local Divisions—Magdalen.)

Letter from R. W., giving an account of the Commissioners' proceedings on 16 Nov. 1687.
Ibid., fol. 112.

Letters and queries in the college case addressed to dr. Tho. Bayley, with his answer, 1687.
Rawl. C. 983, *fol.* 117.

Matters in Johnston's Account, but not in the Oxford Narrative, 1687.
Tann. 29, *fol.* 84ᵛ.

Elections of demies and fellows, 1698.
Tann. 22, *fol.* 191.

Trial respecting the nomination to the headship of Magdalen Hall, 1694.
Rawl. C. 867, *fol.* 26.

Monumental inscriptions subsequent to Wood's History, to 1750.
Rawl. B. 400ᵈ, *fol.* 11.

Addresses of graduates, about 1847.
Top. Oxf. e. 18.

Catalogus MSSʳᵘᵐ in bibliotheca coll. Magdalenensis ab H. Clay confectus, A.D. 1637.
Langb. 7, p. 299 (*O. C.* p. 269 a): *Tann.* 269, *fol.* 155.

MS. of Eusebii Chronicon in the Library.
Rawl. C. 850, *fol.* 134ᵛ.

Excerpts from the Archives.
Wood D. 2, pp. 151, 161 (*O. C.* 8513).

Epitaphia Magdalenensium.
Gough Oxf. 37.

Gratiarum actio in coll. Magdalenensi.
Rawl. C. 945, *fol.* 501.

Lines on Ch. Ch. window and Magd. wall.
Ashm. 38, *fol.* 46; 47, *fol.* 94ᵛ.

Arms.
Ashm. 802, *fol.* 187.

Arms, in trick.
Rawl. B. 101, *fol.* 14.

(Univ.—Local Divisions.)

Merton, 467.

Statuta coll. Mertonensis, 1274.
Tann. 339, *fol.* 3.

Excerpta ex statutis collegii de Merton.
James 8, p. 154 (*O. C.* 3845).

Abstract of the Statutes, etc., by Sancroft.
Tann. 339, *foll.* 50, 52.

Notes on the foundation of the College, etc.
Rawl. C. 867, *fol.* 61.

Catalogus sociorum Collegii de Merton, ad ann. 1676 et Custodum collegii, ad ann. 1661.
Gough Oxf. 11.

Excerpta ex catalogo libelli de nominibus Sociorum coll. de Merton.
Leland Coll. 3, p. 54 (*O. C.* 5104).

Charters affecting Merton.
Charters Cal., pp. 283, 287.

Ordinances of the Visitor (Peckham), 1284.
Tann. 339, *foll.* 27, 40, 47.

Ordinances of the Visitor (Chicheley), 1425.
Tann. 339, *foll.* 32, 44, 48^v.

Ordinance of the Visitor (Parker), 1567.
Tann. 339, *fol.* 36.

Letter to the Visitor from Warden Bichley about the latter's power at College elections, 1574.
Tann. 339, *fol.* 428.

Arms there, 1574.
Wood D. 14 (*O. C.* 8548).

Extract from the College Register about the election of officers, 1593.
Tann. 339, *fol.* 430.

Expulsion of Colmar and suspension of Fisher, Bentham and Brisenden from their fellowships, 21 Oct. 1598.
Tann. 339, *fol.* 55.

(**Univ.—Local Divisions**—Merton.)
— restitution of Fisher, 1599.
   Ibid., fol. 55ᵛ.

Case between Merton and Wadham about the rights of the Austin friars.
   Wood F. 28, *fol.* 223 (*O. C.* 8490).

Petition of the college to the King for confirmation of their possessions, with the King's answer, Dec. 1632.
   Tann. 339, *foll.* 59, 60.

Letter from Laud to the college, about Earles's petition to hold his fellowship with a rectory, 31 July 1634.
   Tann. 339, *fol.* 61.

Extract from college Register about Knightley's donation for a lecture, 1635.
   Tann. 339, *fol.* 62.

Laud's articles of visitation, 30 Mar. 1638.
   Tann. 339, *fol.* 63.

Ordinances of the Visitor (Laud), 1640.
   Tann. 339, *fol.* 17.

List of postmasters, with notices, by Ant. à Wood, 1642–53.
   Tann. 456, *fol.* 90.

Papers about the deprivation of Rich Hine, fellow, 1675.
   Tann. 339, *foll.* 73–101.

Papers relating to disputes between the Warden and the fellows, 1675.
   Tann. 339, *foll.* 92–105, 176 sqq., 347 sqq.

Papers about the deprivation of H. Freeman, under-butler, 1675.
   Tann. 339, *foll.* 66–71.

Papers about the right of the senior fellow to the lease of the Burmington tithes, 1675–76.
   Tann. 339, *foll.* 110–117, 418–19.

Papers about nominations to postmasterships, 1676–77.
   Tann. 339, *foll.* 118–127, 129–168.

Mr. Lane's case about the power of choosing Fellows at Merton, 1679.
   Ex. Coll. 12, *fol.* 74.

(**Univ.—Local Divisions**—Merton.)

D^r. Bernard's case about punishing and expelling a Fellow of Merton, 1679.
Ibid., fol. 81.

Papers about elections to a fellowship and a Commission of enquiry, 1679–80, and 1681.
Tann. 182–384, 386–394.

Papers about the rights of the senior fellow over the Burmington tithes, 1685–86.
Tann. 339, *foll.* 395–431.

Papers relating to a dispute between the Warden and M^r. Bernard, fellow, 1685–87.
Tann. 339, *foll.* 411–422.

Petition of the college to the Visitor about a royal mandate to elect to a fellowship (1686?).
Tann. 339, *fol.* 421.

Monumental inscriptions subsequent to Wood's History, to 1736.
Rawl. B. 400^d, *fol.* 19.

Letters relating to Merton, about 1715, and about 1719.
Ch. Ch. 248–49.

Election of fellows, 1731.
Rawl. A. 275, *fol.* 122.

Case between Merton and S. Good about the impropriation of Malden.
Tann. 104, *fol.* 123.

Catalogus MSS^{rum} in bibliotheca coll. de Merton.
Wood (2), 3, p. 21 (*O. C.* 8616).

Libri in bibliotheca coll. de Merton.
Leland Coll. 3, p. 59 (*O. C.* 5104).

MSS. of Roger Bacon there.
Ashm. 335, *fol.* 150.

Collations from a Merton MS. of Eschenden.
Ashm. 576.

Note of a MS. there.
Rawl. C. 850, *fol.* 135^v.

(Univ.—Local Divisions.)

Bodl. MS. Digb. 176 datum est " in usum coll. Merton et Exon."

Inscription on the brass of Walter Clerke.
Rawl. C. 867, *fol.* 36ᵛ.

Oaths taken by fellows and others.
Tann. 339, *fol.* 1.

Arms in Merton college.
Wood F. 33, *fol.* 117 (*O. C.* 8495).

Arms, in trick.
Rawl. B. 101, *fol.* 14.

See also *St. Alban Hall*, 479.

New, 468.

Charters affecting New college.
Charters Cal., pp. 283, 351.

Controversy between Fynes and Wickham about kinship to William of Wykeham.
Wood F. 28, *fol.* 102 (*O. C.* 8490).

Extracts from the Register from 1522.
Ibid., fol. 110.

Archbishops, Bishops, Archdeacons, Chancellors, Canons, Prebendaries, Regius Professors, Heads of Houses and Teachers of Scholars, from New College.
Ibid., fol. 113.

Benefactors.
Ibid., fol. 119.

Notes on Vestments of the College, the Cemetery, the site of the College.
Ibid., fol. 121.

Fellows, bachelors and undergraduates in 1552.
Rawl. C. 910, *fol.* 20ᵛ.

Some matriculations, 1564–1642.
Rawl. C. 910, *fol.* 19.

Arms there, 1574.
Wood D. 14 (*O. C.* 8548).

(**Univ.—Local Divisions.**)

Catalogus MSS^{rum} in bibliotheca coll. Novi, A. D. 1624.
Langb. 7, p. 331 (*O. C.* p. 269 *a*).

List of fellows 1632–40, with their birthplaces, etc.
Tann. 338, *fol.* 407.

Verses of New College men on lady Eliz. Powlet's gift to the University, A. D. 1636.
Bodl. 22 (*O. C.* 3059).

Letter of the Warden (Beeston) on his election, to the Visitor, 15 July 1679.
Tann. 338, *fol.* 225.

Monumental inscriptions subsequent to Wood's History to 1750.
Rawl. B. 400^d, *foll.* 25, 107.

Letter of the Warden of Winchester college to the Warden of New college, about admitting T. Prince to the latter college, 12 Aug. 1711: in Latin.
Tann. 20, *fol.* 1.

Excerpts from the Archives.
Wood D. 2, pp. 244, 278 (*O. C.* 8513).

Tituli librorum in studiis scholarium Wintoniae Oxon. repertorum, anno 1489.
Digb. 31 *ad fin.*

Catalogue of MSS. in New college library, 1624.
Tann. 269, *fol.* 172.

Account of some MSS. in the college library.
Tann. 269, *fol.* 205.

Note about MSS. 41, 281 (Ptolemy) in the Library.
Rawl. C. 851, *fol.* 41^v: 936, *fol.* 15.

Epitaphs etc. in New College cloister.
Wood D. 11, part 2 (*O. C.* 8518).

Inscription over the Chapel door.
Rawl. B. 479, *fol.* 119.

Arms in New college.
Wood F. 33, *fol.* 116 (*O. C.* 8495).

(Univ.—Local Divisions.)

Oriel, 469.

Catalogue of MSS. in the college library (17th cent.).
Tann. 269, fol. 219.

Statuta collegii, manu T. Hearne.
Rawl. B. 180, fol. 133.

Notes of the foundation etc. of Oriel college.
C. C. C. 302, fol. 205.

Extracts from the muniments.
Wood C. 1, p. 1 (O. C. 8515).

Collectanea ex archivis.
Wood F. 28, fol. 57 (O. C. 8490).

Catalogus Praepositorum et Sociorum usque ad ann. 1665.
Ibid., fol. 63.

Extract relating to Thomas de Kirketon's resignation of the Provostship (1414).
Tann. 338, fol. 249.

Custom of the Crown to recommend provosts, discountenanced by archbp. Parker (about 1570?).
Tann. 155, fol. 176^v.

Arms there, 1574.
Wood D. 14 (O. C. 8548).

List of eminent members of Balliol and Oriel, written in the 17th cent.
Qu. Coll. 280, fol. 81.

Catalogus MSS^{rum} in bibliotheca coll. Orielensis.
Langb. 7, p. 423 (O. C. p. 269 b).

On a MS. codex canonum in the college library, by bp. Barlow.
Qu. Coll. 266, fol. 102.

Figures in windows, name, etc.
Rawl. C. 867, foll. 49^v–50, 55, 58^v.

Arms, in trick.
Rawl. B. 101, fol. 14.

"Domus beataê Mariae" (Oriel?) owned MS. Digb. 191.
See also *St. Mary Hall*, 481.

(Univ.—Local Divisions.)

Pembroke, 470.

Statuta Collegii, 1624.
   Wood F. 28, *fol.* 246 (*O. C.* 8490).

Acceptance by the college of a fellowship founded by Charles I for natives of Jersey and Guernsey, 29 Apr. 1636.
   Tann. 338, *fol.* 177.

List of Pembroke men who were officers in Charles I's army.
   Wood F. 28, *fol.* 241 (*O. C.* 8490).

Papers about the deprivation of H. Wyatt from his fellowship, 1661.
   Tann. 338, *foll.* 406-9.

Extracts from the Matriculation register of the College (?), 1668–1672.
   Wood D. 5 (*O. C.* 8524).

Defence of the procedure of the Fellows with their petition to the Visitor (about 1685 ?).
   Wood F. 28, *fol.* 242.

Exceptions of the Fellows to the Commissioners' account sent to them (about 1685 ?).
   Ibid., fol. 244.

Oratio habita in aula per C. T. (18th cent.).
   Magd. Coll. 234, *fol.* 69.

Leases from the University, of London houses for maintenance of Channel Island scholars.
   Rawl. C. 421, *fol.* 62.

Excerpts from the Archives.
   Wood D. 2, p. 621 (*O. C.* 8513).

Queen's, 471.

Charters affecting Queen's College.
   Charters Cal., pp. 283, 284, 309.

Survey of Queen's college, in H. VIII's time.
   Gough Oxf. 77.

Arms there, 1574.
   Wood D. 14 (*O. C.* 8548).

(Univ.—Local Divisions.)
Livings and schools in the College gift, with valuations and holders, A. D. 1639.
Wood F. 28, *fol.* 75 (*O. C.* 8490).
Reasons for augmentation of the Taberdars' places, by dr. Langbaine, etc.
Ibid., fol. 78.
Collections out of the Statutes and Registers.
Ibid., fol. 93.
List of Fellows for 40 years after the foundation, etc.
Ibid., fol. 96.
Benefactors of the College.
Ibid., fol. 98.
Oratio Henr. Washington taberdarii occasione jubilaei Collegii, 15 Aug. 1740.
Rawl. C. 318.
Collections relating to Queen's college, by Edw. Rowe Mores, 9 vols.
Gough Oxf. 12–17, 38–40.
Excerpta ex libro obituali.
Ashm. 826, *fol.* 131; 833, *fol.* 481.
Notae ex archives coll. Reginensis de eodem collegio.
Langb. 8, p. 171 (*O. C.* p. 270 *a*).
Excerpts from the Archives.
Wood D. 2, p. 125 (*O. C.* 8513).
Controversy about ordination in the chapel.
Qu. Coll. 194, *fol.* 86.
Dissertationes per scholares Reginenses habitae.
Qu. Coll. 220, 232.
Catalogus codicum MSS. in bibliotheca collegii.
Qu. Coll. 204, *fol.* 66: *Langb.* 7, p. 411 (*O. C.*, p. 269 *b*): *Tann.* 269, *fol.* 213.
See also *St. Edmund Hall*, 480.

St. John's, 472.
Catalogue of the Fellows 1555–1617, by Griffin Higgs.
Wood F. 28, *fol.* 204 (*O. C.* 8490).
License of Mortmain to St. John's college.
Ibid., fol. 213.

(**Univ.—Local Divisions**—St. John's.)

List of College lands in the county of Oxford.
Ibid., fol. 214.

Short history of the College, with lists of benefactors, writers, etc., by Joseph Taylor.
Ibid., fol. 215.

Charter affecting St. John's.
Charters Cal., p. 284.

Sir Thomas White's last letter to St. John's College, 1566, printed by dr. Will. Holmes in 1728.
Rawl. B. 250, *fol.* 80.

Names of undergraduate Fellows at the elections of President in 1572 and 1577.
Tann. 338, *foll.* 342, 344.

Account of the dramatic entertainments and revels at St. John's, 1607–8.
St. J. 52, *fol.* 26.

Papers about the election of a president, 1611.
Tann. 338, *foll.* 321, 328–364.

Petition from four Fellows to the Chancellor of the University about their graces refused, Apr. 1611.
Ibid. 338, *fol.* 323.

— Other papers about the same affair, Apr. 1611.
Ibid., foll. 324–27, 365–72.

Letter from the Visitor to the King about the visitor's power in College disputes, 5 Aug. 1611.
Ibid. 338, *fol.* 345.

Estate of the College, 1611 and 1621.
Ibid. fol. 373.

Account of money laid out on building, 1616–17.
Tann. 338, *fol.* 381.

Petition of sir W. Paddie, etc., to the King about founding a choir in the College, 1622.
Ibid. 338, *fol.* 389.

Recantation by Rich. Spinke, Fellow of St. John's, read in the college chapel and in congregation, Feb. 163$\frac{4}{5}$.
Tann. 303, *fol.* 108.

(Univ.—Local Divisions—St. John's.)

In aream novam Johannensem ode encomiastica, per Gul. Creede collegii socium (circa A. D. 1635).
Tann. 306, *fol.* 87.

Verses spoken in St. John's at the King and Queen's entertainment there, 1636.
Malone 21, *fol.* 52ᵛ.

Money received and paid in connexion with the Canterbury rooms, 1636-47.
Tann. 338, *fol.* 398.

Petition of the college to Laud about sir W. Paddie's legacy, 23 Jan. 163⅞.
Ibid. 338, *fol.* 391.

— Laud's order in the matter, 25 May 1638.
Ibid., fol. 393.

Acquittance for Geo. Benson's donation, 24 June 1639.
Tann. 338, *fol.* 397.

Archbp. Laud's legacy to the College, in his will, Jan. 164¾.
Clar. i. 1816.

Offer of Fellows to supply places of ejected clergy, 1662.
Tann. 48, *fol.* 26.

Address to Charles II and his consort in the Library of St. John's, Sept. 1663.
Tann. 306, *fol.* 365; 314, *fol.* 101.

— to the Duchess of York on the same occasion.
Ibid., 306, *fol.* 366; 314, *fol.* 102.

Donation of Tobias Rustat for exhibitions, etc., 1665.
Tann. 157, *fol.* 31.

St. John's College brewhouse accounts, 1681-84.
Top. Oxf. e. 14.

Transcript of the Chapel register of St. John's college, 1690-1752: by R. Rawlinson.
Rawl. B. 402ᵇ.

Monumental inscriptions subsequent to Wood's History, to 1750.
Rawl. B. 400ᵈ, *fol.* 10.

(Univ.—Local Divisions.)

Batells, and other accounts, 1733.
Top. Oxf. b. 2.

Satirical epitaph on a Fellow, 1733.
Rawl. C. 936, *fol.* 93.

Papers between the bp. of Oxford and St. John's college concerning Gloucester college.
Wood F. 28, *fol.* 310 (*O. C.* 8490).

Carmina Tho. Paynter de casu qui faciem sibi deformaverat, collegii D. Joh. Bapt. praesidi dicata.
Tann. 306, *fol.* 118.

Excerpts from the archives.
Wood D. 2, pp. 625, 637 (*O. C.* 8513).

Liber precum matutinarum vespertinarumque in usum Collegii, Graeco-Latine (17th cent.).
Greek Misc. 52.

Verses on the picture of Charles I in the library.
Tann. 306, *fol.* 363.

Arms, in trick.
Rawl. B. 101, *fol.* 14.

See also *St. Bernard's College*, 493.

Trinity, 473.

Admissions of Scholars, with details about them, 1556–1600.
Wood F. 28, *fol.* 172 (*O. C.* 8490).

Benefactors to the Library, etc.
Ibid., fol. 183.

Account of sir Thomas Pope, founder.
Ibid., fol. 189.

List of some Fellows from 1556, with notes of arms, pictures, etc., in the College.
Ibid., fol. 194.

Arms there, 1574.
Wood D. 14 (*O. C.* 8548).

Letter from Edw. Saunder bequeathing his library to Trinity college, 1640.
Qu. coll. 121, p. 34.

(Univ.—Local Divisions.)

Recommendation of Tho. Cracroft for the headship, by dr. Goodwin, 1658.
Rawl. A. 62, *fol.* 503.

Letters from Mr. John Foyle to the President about the expulsion of Henry Knollys, esq. (17th cent.).
Wood 276e, 32.

Letter of bp. Geo. Morley to the college on their refusing to elect — Turner to a scholarship (17th cent.).
Tann. 338, *fol.* 318.

Signatures of the President and Fellows, 1679.
Tann. 46, *fol.* 117.

Complaint before the college Visitor against Mr. Barker, 1698.
Tann. 22, *fol.* 121.

Letter of A. Charlett about the sentence against Hen. Barker, fellow, 19 Aug. 1698.
Tann. 22, *fol.* 121.

Addresses of graduates, about 1847.
Top. Oxf. e. 18.

Excerpts from the Archives.
Wood D. 2, p. 618 (*O. C.* 8513).

See also *Durham College*, 487.

University, 474.

Statuta, 1292.
Rawl. C. 863, *fol.* 3.

Charters affecting Univ. coll.
Charters Cal., pp. 290, 308.

Nomina magistrorum sociorum et alumnorum, 1381-1654.
Wood F. 28, *fol.* 1 (*O. C.* 8490).

Houses bought with William of Durham's money.
Ibid., fol. 11.

Names of Benefactors, with form of prayers for them.
Ibid., fol. 12.

Concerning Sir Simon Bennet's foundation.
Ibid., fol. 14.

Collections concerning the election of Thomas Thornton as Master, 1654: made by G. Langbaine.
Ibid., fol. 17.

(Univ.—Local Divisions.)

Langbaine's Collections out of the Statutes.
Wood F. 28, *fol.* 21.

Ordinations mag. Walteri Skirlaw.
Ibid., fol. 27.

Ordinationes comitis Northumbriæ.
Ibid., fol. 29.

Statuta, 1475–78.
Ibid., fol. 30ᵃ.

Arms there, 1574.
Wood D. 14 (*O. C.* 8548).

Account of the consecration of the Chapel of Univ. College, 20 Mar. 166$\frac{5}{8}$, by dr. Blandford.
Qu. Coll. 285, *fol.* 15.

Form for consecration of the Chapel, 166$\frac{5}{8}$.
Rawl. B. 224, *fol.* 18.

Drawing of part of Univ. Coll. quadrangle, 1668, by Ant. à Wood.
Wood 276ᵇ, *fol.* 116.

Signatures of the Master and Fellows, 1679.
Tann. 46, *fol.* 14.

Letter of A. Charlett about disputes at Univ. coll. about a fellowship, 25 June, 1698.
Tann. 21, *fol.* 94.

— Dº. 18 June, 1699.
Ibid. 21, *fol.* 116.

Papers about the election of Will. Denison as fellow, 1699.
Tann. 21, *fol.* 94, 104 : 22, *foll.* 127, 136, 141, 143, 150, 158, 175.

Notices of the College, 1699.
Tann. 21, *foll.* 164, 175, 181.

Letter from the earl of Leicester to the College, nominating to a scholarship, July, 1701.
Tann. 20, *fol.* 48.

Letter by R. B. respecting the case of mr. Cockman and the right of visiting University College, 26 Mar. 1728.
Top. Oxf. d. 5.

Commission for visiting the college, March, 1729.
Tann. 338, *fol.* 219.

(Univ.—Local Divisions.)

Legacies left to the College by J. Freeston.
Ibid. fol. 217.

Petition to the Visitor by E. Watkins as near of kin to R. Gunsley (about a fellowship?).
Tann. 338, *fol.* 221.

Sir S. Bennett's benefaction.
Rawl. C. 867, *fol.* 28.

De Magna Aula Universitatis Oxon.
Wood D. 18, *fol.* 14 (*O. C.* 8563).

Excerpts from the Archives.
Wood D. 2, p. 1 (*O. C.* 8513).

Catalogus MSS^{rum} in bibliotheca coll. Universitatis.
Wood (2) 3, p. 65 (*O. C.* 8616).

Pictures, statues of Anne and James II, etc.
Rawl. C. 867, *foll.* 36, 45, 48^v, 49, 51.

Arms, in trick.
Rawl. B. 101, *fol.* 14.

Arms in Univ. coll.
Wood F. 33, *fol.* 105 (*O. C.* 8495).

Wadham, 475.

Indenture between the City and Dorothy Wadham conveying the site of Wadham college.
Wood F. 28, *fol.* 224 (*O. C.* 8490).

Names of Fellow-Commoners and Commoners, 1615–1670, by Nich. Lloyd.
Ibid., fol. 225.

Some collections from the College archives.
Ibid., foll. 198, 227.

List of Wardens and Fellows to 1681.
Ibid., fol. 232.

Admission of Wardens, Fellows, Scholars, and some Chaplains, 1613–94.
Ibid., fol. 241.

Extracts from the Chapel register: Bur. 1583–1676.
Wood D. 5 (*O. C.* 8524).

Case between Merton and Wadham about the rights of the Austin friars.
Wood F. 28, *fol.* 223 (*O. C.* 8490).

(**Univ.—Local Divisions.**)
Legacy to the college by J. Knightbridge, 1677.
Tann. 158, *fol.* 105.
Testimonium Collegii de vita R. Napier.
Ashm. 1730, *fol.* 238.
See also *Austin Friars*, 669.

Worcester, 476.
Charter of foundation, 22 Oct., 1698.
Rawl. A. 241, *fol.* 261.
— Ratification of it, 18 Nov., 1698.
Ibid., fol. 263.
Extract from sir Tho. Cooke's Will.
Rawl. C. 867, *fol.* 64ᵛ.
See also *Gloucester College*, 488.

Halls (sometimes included under *Colleges*, see 444), 477.
Excerpta ex tabella Joh. Rouse Collegiorum et Aularum suo tempore in Oxon.
Leland Coll. 5. (*O. C.* 5106).
Case between Balliol and the Halls about the Proctorship, 1668.
Wood F. 28, *fol.* 44 (*O. C.* 8490).

New Inn (now part of Balliol College), 478.
Principals found in New college accounts.
Wood F. 28, *fol.* 124ᵛ (*O. C.* 8490).
Names of members who refused to subscribe to the act of Uniformity, Sept. 1662.
Tann. 338, *fol.* 411.

St. Alban (now part of Merton College), 479.
Dispute with St. Peter's in the East about right of entrance to the Hall to mark the parish bounds (17th cent.): by Ant. à Wood.
Rawl. 402ᵃ (at beginning).

St. Edmund, 480.
Names of the scholars, 1573–1693.
Wood F. 28, *fol.* 267 (*O. C.* 8490).
Inscriptions on the plate of the hall, when sold in 1679.
Ibid., fol. 299.

(Univ.—Local Divisions.)
List of benefactors to the hall.
Wood F. 28, *fol.* 306.

Benefactors.
Rawl. C. 865, *fol.* 7.

Claim to a MS. of the Univ. statutes.
Rawl. C. 421, *fol.* 58.

Owned MS. *Rawl. C.* 900.

Catalogus bibliothecae per T. Hearne.
Rawl. C. 851, *fol.* 87.

St. Mary, 481.

Customs and dues paid at St. Mary hall.
Tann. 338, *fol.* 412.

Private Halls, 482.

Old Institutions which have ceased to exist, 483.

Chests and pledges, 484.

Notae de libris variis in cautionem in cistis Universitatis depositis, etc.
Digb. 160. *fol.* 223 : 216, *fol.* 61^v : 225 *ad fin.*

— in cista Dunken.
Ibid., 160, *fol.* 223.

Custodes cistarum Universitatis Oxon. 1510–1519.
Wood E. 5, *art.* 4 (*O. C.* 8511).

Colleges, etc., 485.

Canterbury college (Bened.), 486.
Of Canterbury College.
Wood F. 29^a, *fol.* 260 (*O. C.* 8491).
See also *Christ Church*, 459.

Cardinal college: see *Christ Church*, 459.

Durham college (Bened.), 487.
Charta fundationis coll. Dunelmensis apud Oxon. per Tho. de Hatfeld.
Jes. Coll. 78, *fol.* 169.

Donation of the site of Durham College to the Dean and Chapter of Durham by King Hen. VIII.
Wood F. 28, *fol.* 188 (*O. C.* 8490).

(Univ.—Local Divisions.)
Collectanea de T. Hatfield et Rich. Aungerville of Bury.
Ibid., fol. 190.
Extract from grant of Hen. VIII to Dean and Chapter of Durham, etc.
Rawl. C. 865, *fol.* 28.
Of Durham college.
Wood F. 29ᵃ, *fol.* 260 (*O. C.* 8491).
See also *Trinity College*, 473.

Gloucester college (Bened.), 488.
Carta fundationis Aulae Glocestrensis.
Dodsw. 10, *fol.* 300 (*O. C.* 4152).
Carta John Giffard pro fundatione prioratus S. Benedicti postea Aulae Gloucestrensis nuncupati, 1283.
Rawl. B. 252, *fol.* 11.
Carta Joh. abbatis Glouc. de monachis in dictum prioratum migrantibus.
Ibid., fol. 11ᵛ.
Papers in the case of Gloucester college between the bp. of Oxford and St. John's college, in the time of Elizabeth and James I.
Wood F. 28, *fol.* 310 (*O. C.* 8490).
Liber donationum ad sacellum aedificandum, etc. (17th cent.).
Worc. Coll. 59.
Of Gloucester college.
Wood F. 29ᵃ, *fol.* 260 (*O. C.* 8491).
Arms in Gloucester college.
Wood F. 33, *fol.* 103 (*O. C.* 8495).
See also *Worcester College*, 476.

Hart hall, 489.
Charters affecting it.
Charters Cal., pp. 287, 288.
Arms there, 1574.
Wood D. 14 (*O. C.* 8548).
Rules and statutes of Hart hall, 1740.
Top. Oxf. c. 24.

(Univ.—Local Divisions.)

Customs and dues paid at Hart hall.
Tann. 338, *fol.* 413.

Case of Glastonbury exhibitions at Hart hall, 1664.
Wood F. 28, *fol.* 256 (*O. C.* 4890).

· Collectanea Ger. Langbainii de Hart hall ex archivis coll. Oxon.
Ibid., fol. 260.

Hertford college (old foundation), 491.
Names of benefactors to Hertford college, etc.
Top. Oxf. c. 25.

Magdalen hall, 492.
Arguments at Westminster in the suit between the Chancellor and Magdalen college about presenting a Principal to Magdalen hall, A.D. 1694.
Wood D. 18, *fol.* 47 (*O. C.* 8563).

Trial between Magd. college and Magd. hall about the headship of the latter, 1694.
Rawl. C. 867, *fol.* 26.

Concerning the expulsion of Mr. Ford of Magdalen Hall, 1631.
Wood F. 27, *art.* 25 (*O. C.* 8489).

St. Bernard's college (Cisterc.), 493.
Chartae Hen. Chicheley archiep. Cant. de collegio S. Bernardi, 1437.
Univ. Coll. 167, *fol. circa* 55–60.

Charter affecting St. Bernard's College.
Charters Cal., p. 283.

Of St. Bernard's college.
Wood F. 29ª, *fol.* 258 (*O. C.* 8491).

St. George's college in the Castle (Sec. Canons), 494.
Charters affecting St. George's college and parish.
Charters Cal., pp. 332, 337, 351.

The college or church of St. George.
Wood F. 29ª, *fol.* 206 (*O. C.* 8491).

Of St. George's.
Wood F. 29ª, *fol.* 306 (*O. C.* 8491).

(Univ.—Local Divisions.)

St. Mary's college (Aust. Canons), 495.

Memorandum ad orandum pro . . . animabus Thome Holden et Eliz. uxoris sue fundatorum collegii beate Marie de Oxon., qui obiit 19 Edw. IV (1479–80).
Tann. 196, *fol.* 248.

Charter affecting St. Mary's college.
Charters Cal., p. 116.

Proposal to purchase the site of St. Mary's college (16th cent.).
Rawl. B. 450, *fol.* 252.

Of St. Maries college.
Wood F. 29ª, *fol.* 247 (*O. C.* 8491).

Halls (pre-Laudian), 496.

Litterae patentes de modo retaxandi domos a scholaribus inhabitatas 40 Hen. III, etc.
C. C. C. 280, *fol.* 9.

Enquiry into the primary and original state and nature of halls.
Top. Oxf. c. 26.

Aularum catalogus per M. Windesore.
C. C. C. 280, *foll.* 49, 54.

Names of several principals of the old halls in Oxford.
Wood D. 7 (1) (*O. C.* 8529).

Concerning the Halls of an unknown situation.
Wood F. 29ª, *fol.* 130 (8491).

Names of some old Halls.
Wood 4, *fol.* 199 (*O. C.* 8562).
(Lost.)

Dr. Wallis's dissertation on the case of the (Old) Halls, 1693.
Ex. Coll. 12, *fol.* 79.

Statuta poenalia Aulae cujusdam in Univ. Oxon.
Bodl. 487, *fol.* 105 (*O. C.* 2067).

Arthur Hall.
Charters affecting it.
Charters Cal., pp. 287, 288.

(Univ.—Local Divisions.)

Beam Hall.
  Charter affecting Beam hall.
    Charters Cal., p. 252.

Black hall.
  Charters affecting Black hall.
    Charters Cal., pp. 287, 355.

Bodyns.
  See *Halls*—Hampton hall.

Broadgates hall.
  Principals found in New College accounts.
    Wood F. 28, *fol.* 124ᵛ (*O. C.* 8490).

Chequer hall.
  Charter affecting it.
    Charters Cal., p. 292.

Durham hall.
  Charter affecting it.
    Charters Cal., p. 308.

Elm hall.
  Charter affecting it.
    Charters Cal., p. 355.

Grove hall.
  Charter affecting it.
    Charters Cal., p. 350.

Hart hall.
  See *Hart hall* (489).

Hampton hall.
  Charter affecting "Hampton hall or Bodyns."
    Charters Cal., p. 308.

Ludlow hall.
  Charter affecting it.
    Charters Cal., p. 308.

Perilous hall.
  Charter affecting it.
    Charters Cal., p. 282.

Plummer hall.
  Charter affecting it.
    Charters Cal., p. 307.

(Univ.—Local Divisions.)

St. John's hall.
  Charter affecting it.
    Charters Cal., p. 352.

St. Stephen's hall.
  Charters affecting it.
    Charters Cal., pp. 288, 290.

Staple hall.
  Charter affecting it.
    Charters Cal., p. 354.
  Book which belonged to the hall.
    Ashm. 748.

Stapledon hall.
  See *Exeter college* (461).

Vine hall.
  Charter affecting it.
    Charters Cal., p. 351.
  Principals found in New College accounts.
    Wood F. 28, *fol.* 124 (*O. C.* 8490).

Schools, old, 498.
  Charter affecting the Civil Law School.
    Charters Cal., p. 350.
  Letter about the house, etc. occupying the site of the old Logic School, 12 Nov. 1661.
    Tann. 338, *fol.* 100.

GOVERNMENT (Incorporation and Constitution), 500.
  Apology for the government of the University of Oxford against Henry VIII, by Roger Jones.
    Wood D., 18 (*O. C.* 8559).
  Copy of Act 13 Eliz. cap. 29 for the Incorporation and liberties of the Universities of Oxford and Cambridge.
    Tann. 121, *fol.* 52 : 338, *fol.* 3.

Hebdomadal Board (afterwards Council), 501.

Convocation, 502.
  Extracts from the registers of Congregation and Convocation, 1448–63, 1505–1604.
    Wood D. 3, p. 1 (*O. C.* 8514).

(Univ.—Government.)
Excerpts from the Register of Convocation, 1640-90.
   Wood   (*O. C.* 8562).
      (Lost.)
Index libri Convocationis, 1647-1741.
   Top. Oxf. e. 17.
Proceedings of Convocation, 12 Apr. 1648.
   Tann. 338, *fol.* 85.
List of members of Convocation, 1785.
   Add. C. 182.
— 1794.
   Top. Oxf., e. 4.
Printed list of Convocation, 1884-85, with MS. addresses.
   Top. Oxf. d. 1.

Congregation, 503.
Extracts from the registers of Congregation and Convocation, 1448-63, 1505-1604.
   Wood D. 3, p. 1 (*O. C.* 8514).

Delegacies, Commissions, and Boards in general, 504.
Commissioners for a present to the King, 1636-37.
   Rawl. C. 421, *fol.* 96.
Proceedings of the delegates of Convocation, 16 July—1 Aug. 1662.
   Tann. 338, *fol.* 143.

Statutes and decrees in general, 505.
Statuta univ. Oxon ("D").
   Bodl. 337 (*O. C.* 2874).
Statuta quaedam Univ. Oxon.
   Bodl. 487, *fol.* 95 (*O. C.* 2067).
Statuta Univ. Oxon. transcripta ex libris Vice-Canc. et Procuratorum.
   Arch E. —, pp. 1, 117 (*O. C.* 2944).
Excerpta ex libro statutorum Academiae.
   C. C. C. 261, *fol.* 88.
Extracts from the old books of Statutes.
   Wood (*O. C.* 8562).
      (Lost.)

(Univ.—Government.)

Statuta Univ. Oxon. edita per Commissionarios regis Edvardi VI.
Arch E. —, p. 78 (*O. C.* 2944).

Statuta Univ. Oxon. edita per card. Reg. Pole, A.D. 1556.
Arch. E. —, p. 83 (*O. C.* 2944).

Some papers touching the reformation of the Statutes (early xviith cent.?).
Wood F. 27, *art.* 23 (*O. C.* 8489).

Bryan Twyne's preface to the Laudian Statutes (different from the printed copy).
Wood —, *fol.* 211 (*O. C.* 8562).
(Lost.)

Ordinationes et statuta Universitatis, 1629.
All S. 125, *fol.* 18.

Remonstrance to Parliament of some in the University against archbishop Laud and his Statutes (about 1650).
Wood (*O. C.* 8562).
(Lost.)

Papers on the statutes and privileges of the University (about 1670?).
All S. 239, *fol.* 538.

Proclamations, petitions, letters, condemnations, etc., 506.

Liber epistolarum Regum et Magnatum ad Univ. Oxon. una cum Responsis (Reg. FF).
Bodl. 282 (*O. C.* 2949).

Literae Universitatis ad diversos.
C. C. C. 301, and 316, *fol.* 55.

Salutationes secundum usum Oxoniae seu Epistolarum formulae.
Auct. F. 3. 9, p. 414 (*O. C.* 3581).

Litterae missae ad Joh. Halton, Episc. Carliolensem per Cancell. et Univ. Oxon., circa A. D. 1296.
Wood F. 27, *art.* 31 (*O. C.* 8489).

Articuli reprobati tanquam errores a magistris Theologiae Oxoniae A. D. 1314.
Mert. Coll. 84 *ad fin.*

(Univ.—Government.)

Epistola Universitatis ad Ric. II de abolendo schismate, 1395.
Magd. Coll. 53, *fol.* 317.

Epistola Univ. ad regem Ric. II, responsoria ad Epistolam Acad. Paris. de dissidio inter Papas, 1398.
Digb. 188, *fol.* 47.

Condemnatio Joh. Wyclif Oxoniae facta (14th cent.).
James 12 (*O. C.* 3849).

Determinatio Acad. Oxon. de Papae potestate in regno Angliae (14th cent.).
James 12 (*O. C.* 3849).

Literae testimoniales Universitatis de Johanne Wyclif, 1406.
C. C. C. 301, *fol.* 11.

Literae Academiae ad Hen. V de reformatione ecclesiae, 1414.
C. C. C. 301, *fol.* 12 : 183, *fol.* 16^v.

Epistola Universitatis ad Synodum Londinensem, 1420.
Univ. Coll. 76, *fol.* 619.

Academiae epistola ad Martinum V papam, 1427.
C. C. C. 318, *fol.* 197.

Academiae epistolae IV ad Ric. Fox episc. Winton., 1487–1511.
C. C. C. 280, *foll.* 194, 199, 200.

Epistola Academiae ad Henr. VIII commendans opus Edw. Pouelli contra Lutheranos.
C. C. C. 318, *fol.* 1.

The judgement of the Univ. of Oxford concerning Tho. Cartwright, on Church Discipline (A.D. 1573 ?).
Seld. supr. 44, p. 22 (*O. C.* 3432).

Academiæ epistola ad Jacobum I Regem, de operibus ejus, 29 May 1620.
Tann. 290, *fol.* 61 : *Rawl. C.* 739, *fol.* 105^v.

Reply of the Univ. to the Letters patent annexing a Ch. Ch. Prebend to the Public Oratorship, 20 Mar. 163$\frac{5}{8}$.
Clar. i. 679.

(Univ.—Government.)

Letter of the Univ. to archbp. Laud, thanking him for a gift of MSS., 9 Nov. 1640.
Clar. i. 1451.

Petition of the Univ. to Parliament, 24 Apr. 1641.
Wood F. 27, *art.* 2 (*O. C.* 8489).

Letter of thanks from the Univ. to Lenthall, 1 Nov. 1648.
Tann. 57, *fol.* 397.

Letter of thanks from the Univ. to the Mayor of London for the petition to Parliament for continuance of Tithes, 1653.
Wood F. 27, *art.* 44 (*O. C.* 8489).

Proclamation of the Vice-chancellor against wearing wigs and reading sermons, 1674.
Tann. 338, *fol.* 185.

Epistola eccl. et acad. Genevensis ad Univ. Oxon. cum responso, 1706.
Tann. 338, *fol.* 209.

Address of the Univ. on the foundation of a Professorship of Modern History, about 1718.
Ch. Ch. 249.

Epistolae Cancellarii et Magistrorum Oxon. ad Bonifacium papam.
Seld. supr. 65, p. 74 (*O. C.* 3453).

Academiae epistola ad Rob. de Winchecumbe (n. d.).
C. C. C. 149, *fol.* 220.

Epistola Academiae de Johanne de Chelmelegh testimoniales (n. d.).
C. C. C. 149, *fol.* 220.

Law Courts, trial of all kinds, 507.

Extracts from the Register of the Chancellor's Court, 1434–69.
Wood (*O. C.* 8562).
(Lost.)

Extracts from the registers of the Chancellor's Court, 1434–69, 1498—17th cent.
Wood D. 3, p. 63 (*O. C.* 8514).

(Univ.—Government.)

Citations in the Chancellor's Court (selected), from the Restoration to 1706.
Top. Oxf. c. 27.

Notes in behalf of a University Court-leet (about 1700?).
Tann. 338, *fol.* 23.

Privileges, 508 (see also *Relations to the City*, 938).
Registrum privilegiorum Universitatis Oxoniensis, per Rob. Hare.
Bodl. 906.

Collectanea ex chartis Academiae de libertatibus.
Wood —, *fol.* 202 (*O. C.* 8562). (Lost.)

Papers on the statutes and privileges of the University, (about 1670?).
All S. 239, *fol.* 538.

Some privileges of the Univ. extracted out of the Public Records.
Wood F. 27, *art.* 42 (*O. C.* 8489).

Collections concerning the Privileges of the University, out of the Archives, made by Chr. Potter.
Wood — (*O. C.* 8589). (Lost.)

Nota de confirmatione libertatum univ. per Papas varios et regem Ric. II.
Rawl. B. 202, *fol.* 263^v.

Confirmatio omnium chartarum et privilegiorum Univ. Oxon. (temp. Caroli I).
Gough Oxf. 6.

Case of dr. Joseph Crowther, principal of St. Mary Hall, claiming exemption from the Court of Chancery, 1683.
Tann. 338, *foll.* 191, 192, 197.

The Univ.'s plea for their claim of Privilege in the King's Courts.
Wood —, (*O. C.* 8484). (Lost.)

Wills, administrations, and inventories, 509.
Some collections out of the Will-office in Oxford.
Wood —, *fol.* 223 (*O. C.* 8562). (Lost.)

H

(Univ.—Government.)

University Police, 511.
  Notes from a diary on the care of the 'Night-walk' (17th cent. ?).
    All. S. 214, *fol.* 126ᵛ.

Procedure, public, 512.
  Aliquot directiones procedendi in rebus academicis.
    Bodl. 918 (*O. C.* 2910).

Officers and Offices, 513.
  De supremis Acad. Oxon. magistratibus, Cancellariis scil., Commissariis, Procancellariis, et Procuratoribus commentarius, auctore Briano Twyno, 883–1556 (imperfect).
    Wood F. 27, *art.* 52 (*O. C.* 8489).
  List of officers supposed liable to taxation, 1661.
    Tann. 338, *fol.* 106.

Chancellor, 514.
  Charter affecting the Chancellor.
    Charters Cal., p. 319.
  Catalogus Cancellariorum, 1268–1604.
    Arch. E. —, p. 132 (*O. C.* 2944).
  List of chancellors, 1483–1648.
    Tann. 338, *fol.* 6.
  Cancellarii (catalogus), per M. Windesore.
    C. C. C. 280, *foll.* 52, 77.
  Collections of Miles Windsore towards a catalogue of Chancellors.
    Wood F. 27, *art.* 50 (*O. C.* 8489).
  List of Chancellors, 1505–1641.
    Univ. Coll. 128, *fol.* 5.
  List of Chancellors, 1505–1643.
    Rawl. C. 788, *fol.* 2ᵛ : 876, *fol.* 2ᵛ.
  Letter from the Chancellor (the earl of Pembroke) to the Univ. for the afflicted French (17th cent.).
    Wood F. 21, p. 93 (*O. C.* 8485).
  Appeal of some members of the Univ. against the election of archbp. Laud as Chancellor, in Latin, 23 Apr. 1630, with two petitions, 25 and 27 Apr. 1630.
    Tann. 82, *fol.* 301.

(**Univ.—Government.**)
De Cancellario nato Universitatis Oxon.
Wood F. 27, *art.* 49 (*O. C.* 8489).
Ceremony of signifying to the Chancellor his election.
Tann. 338, *fol.* 213.
Chancellor's Court, see *Law Courts* (Univ.), 507.

High Steward, 515.

Vice-chancellor (or Commissary), 516.
List of Vice-chancellors, 1483-1648.
Tann. 338, *fol.* 6.
Collections of Miles Windsore towards a catalogue of Vice-chancellors.
Wood F. 27, *art.* 50 (*O. C.* 8489).
List of Vice-chancellors, 1533-1640.
Univ. Coll. 128, *fol.* 6.
List of V. C.s 1550-1640.
Rawl. C. 788, *fol.* 6ᵛ: 876, *fol.* 5.
Excerpts from the Computus of the Vice-chancellor, 1550-54.
Wood D. 2, p. 338 (*O. C.* 8513).
The Vice-chancellor's accounts, 9 Aug. 1661-18 Sept. 1662.
Tann. 338, *foll.* 92, 165.
Inventory of goods and papers delivered by the Vice-chancellor to his successor, 17 Oct. 1662.
Tann. 338, *fol.* 163.
Memorandum book of Dr. Hodson, vice-chancellor, 1818-22, chiefly of matters brought before him in Mich. T. 1818.
Top Oxf. c. 31.

Pro-vicechancellor, 517.

Proctors, 518.
Catalogus Procuratorum, 1315-1604.
Arch. E. —, p. 132 (*O. C.* 2944).
List of Proctors, 1435-1525.
Tann. 2, *fol.* 141.
A catalogue of proctors, 1550-1676.
Wood F. 27, *art.* 36 (*O. C.* 8489).

(Univ.—Government.)

Cyclus Procuratorius ad latitudinem Oxoniae [*sic*], per M. Windesore.
>C. C. C. 280, *fol.* 117.

Cyclus Procuratorum : accedunt Statuta Carolina de eodem.
>*Tann.* 338, *fol.* 50.

List of Proctors, 1563–1628.
>*Univ. Coll.* 128, *fol.* 21.

Of the standing necessary for a Proctor.
>*Wood F.* 27, *art.* 36 (*O. C.* 8489).

Dispute about Proctors between Magd. & Merton and Ch. Ch. & Brasenose, 1662.
>*Tann.* 338, *foll.* 123, 125.

Legal opinion about Mr. Dod's succession to the Proctorship (Ch. Ch.), 1659.
>*Tann.* 338, *fol.* 89.
>*Wood F.* 27, *art.* 27 (*O. C.* 8489)^v.
>>(Lost.)

Case between Balliol and the Halls about the Proctorship, 1668.
>*Wood F.* 28, *fol.* 44 (*O. C.* 8490).

Pro-proctors, 519.

Oratio Joh. Massey, proprocuratoris munere functi, 7 July 1677.
>*Tann.* 461, *fol.* 119.

Burgesses, 521.

A demurre about the Burgesses of both Universities, drawn up by sir Edw. Coke.
>*Wood F.* 27, *art.* 51 (*O. C.* 8489).

Elections (poll-books, etc.), 522.

Petition against the returning sir Tho. Edmonds Burgess, 1625–6: with the Vice-Chancellor's answer.
>*Wood* (*O. C.* 8562). (Lost.)

Notices of the election of burgesses, 1698.
>*Tann.* 22, *foll.* 197, 199, 202, 203.

Three letters of A. Charlett about University members' elections, etc. July–Aug. 1698.
>*Tann.* 22, *foll.* 16, 119, 202.

(Univ.—Government.)
Letter of Tho. Rivers about the same, 13 July 1698.
Ibid. 22, *fol.* 199.
Letter of Tho. Tanner, about the same, 2 Aug. 1698.
Ibid., 22, *fol.* 197.
Poll for Members of Parliament for the Univ., 23 Mar. 1768.
Gough Oxf. 4.
Poll book, Heber v. Nicholl, 1821.
Top Oxf. d. 7, *c.* 32.
Poll book, Inglis v. Peel, 1829.
Top. Oxf. c. 38.

Public Orator, 523.
Letters patent annexing a Prebendal stall at Ch. Ch. to the public Oratorship, 21 Dec. 1635: in Latin.
Clar. i. 600 : *Ch. Ch.* 345, *art.* 3.
— reply of the Univ. 20 Mar. 163$\frac{5}{6}$, in Latin.
Ibid., i. 679.

Keeper of the Archives, 524.

Registrar, 525.
Registrars of the University, 1508–1659.
Wood E. 5, *art.* 6 (*O. C.* 8511): *Rawl. C.* 867, *fol.* 28.

Bedells, Architypographus, and inferior officers, 526.
Bedelli Acad. Oxon. 1508–1634.
Wood E. 5, *art.* 5 (*O. C.* 8511).
Ballad concerning the Bedells (esp. John Bell) by J. E. (about 1700 ?).
Tann. 306, *fol.* 302.
Ballad on the election of a bedell in place of D. Edwards, by J. E. (about 1700 ?)
Tann. 306, *fol.* 302^v : 466, *fol.* 65^v.
Notice of Hearne's election as architypographus, Jan. 171$\frac{4}{5}$: by R. Rawlinson.
Rawl. B. 250, *fol.* 72^v.
University Yeomen Bedels' books, 18th cent.
Add. B. 63.

Other (Chaplain, etc.), 527.

(Univ.—Government.)

Elections to Offices, 528.
    Proposita in Convocatione de suffragiis in Electionibus Academicis, 1628.
        Wood F. 27, *art.* 24 (*O. C.* 8489).

Finance (Fees, rates, taxes, etc.—see also *Univ. Chest*, 415), 529.
    Order of the Vice-chancellor for levying tolls on the Thames, 15 June 1638.
        Bodl. 338, *fol.* 63.
    Proviso for excepting the Univ. from the acts of assessments, 1661.
        Tann. 338, *fol.* 101.
    Fees for the degrees of B.D. and D.D.
        Rawl. C. 421, *fol.* 63.

CLASSES OF MEMBERS, 530.
    Graduates, 531.
        Professors, Readers, Lecturers, (see 708), Teachers (usually including the higher study of the subjects, but see *Ancient subjects of study*, 755, and *Course of Studies*, 701), 532.
        Antony à Wood's History of the Lectures etc. of the Univ.
            Wood   (*O. C.* 8464).
        Regius Professors, 533.
        Abstract of James I's Patents for the endowment of the Regius Professors of Divinity, Physic and Law.
            Wood F. 27, *art.* 19 (*O. C.* 8489).
        Deputy Professors, 534.
        Theology, 535.
            Divinity (Regius), 536.
            Letters patent of James I for annexing a Canonry at Ch. Ch. to the Regius Professorship of Divinity, 1606.
                Ch. Ch. 345, *art.* 1.
        Divinity (Margaret), 537.
        Hebrew, 538.
        Pastoral Theology, 539.

(Univ.—Classes—Professors.)
Ecclesiastical History, 541.
Exegesis, 542.
Interpretation, 543.
Septuagint (Grinfield Lecturer), 544.
Rabbinical Studies (Reader), 545.
Select Preachers (see also *University Sermons*), 546.
Bampton Lecturers, 547.

Law, 548.
Civil Law (Regius), 549.
Roman Law (Reader), 551.
English Law (Vinerian), 552.
International Law, 553.
Jurisprudence, 554.
Indian Law (Reader), 555.

Medicine and Natural Science (including Mathematics), 556.
Medicine (Regius), 557.
 ,, (Lichfield Lecturers), 558.
Geometry (Savilian), and the Savilian foundation, 559.
Fundatio duarum lecturarum in disciplinis Mathematicis per cl. Savilium.
Wood B. 14, *foll.* 94, 97 (*O. C.* 8587).
Statuta Saviliana, 1619.
Tann. 338, *fol.* 43.
Estates assigned for the Savilian mathematical endowment, 1636–37.
Rawl. C. 421, *foll.* 3, 5.
Account of the Mathematical chest, 1660.
Rawl. C. 421, *fol.* 7.
Astronomy (Savilian), 561.
Mathematics (study of), 562.
Natural Philosophy, 563.
Experimental Philosophy, 564.
Physics (Lee's Reader), 565.
Chemistry, 566.
Chemistry (Aldrichian Demonstrator), 567.
 ,, (Lee's Reader), 568.
Mineralogy, 569.

(Univ.—Classes—Professors.)

Geography (Reader), 570.

Geology, 571.

Anatomy, 572.

   Copy of Tomlins's will, about his Anatomy Lecture founded at Oxford, 1623.

      Wood F. 27, *art.* 45 (*O. C.* 8489).

Anatomy (Lee's Reader), 573.

Physiology, 574.

Zoology, 575.

Anthropology (Reader), 576.

Botany, 577.

Rural Economy, 578.

Arts, 579.

   Classics, higher study of (see 611), 580.

Greek, 581.

   „ (Reader), 582.

   Greek, higher study of, 583.

Latin, 584.

   „ (Reader), 585.

   Latin, higher study of, 586.

Sanskrit, 587.

Arabic (Laudian), 588.

   Statuta lecturae Arabicae Laudianae.

      C. C. C. 301, *fol.* 131.

   Notice of Matth. Pasor's Arabic lecture at Oxford, by Henry Briggs, 1627.

      Tann. 72, *fol.* 211.

Arabic (Lord Almoner's), 589.

Oriental Studies, higher, 590.

Chinese, 591.

Hindustani (Teacher), 592.

Persian   „   593.

Telugu   „   594.

Celtic, 595.

Anglo-Saxon, 596.

English language and literature, 597.

German (Teacher), 598.

French   „   599.

Italian   „   600.

(Univ.—Classes.)

Spanish (Teacher), 601.
Comparative Philology, 602.
Moral Philosophy (Whyte), 603.
　Account of the Langdon Hills endowment of the Prof. of Moral Philosophy, 1661-2.
　　Rawl. C. 421, *foll.* 56-7.
　Abstract of title of lands given by dr. Whyte to the University.
　　Tann. 338, *fol.* 61.
Moral Philosophy (Waynflete), 604.
Logic, 605.
Ancient History (Camden), 606.
　Notice of the election of the Camden professor of history, 1688.
　　Tann. 28, *fol.* 15.
Ancient History (Reader), 607.
Modern History (Regius), 608.
　Establishment of the professorship of Modern History, 1724.
　　Rawl. C. 151, *fol.* 184.
　Address of the Univ. on the foundation of a Professorship of Modern History (about 1724?).
　　Ch. Ch. 249.
Modern History (Chichele), 609.
Indian History (Reader), 610.
Classical Archæology, 611.
Political Economy, 612.
Music (Professor, Choragus, and Coryphæus), 613.
Poetry, 614.
Fine Art, 615.
Drawing (Master), 616.
Doctors and Masters, 617.
　Supplicatio Episcopi Linc. Papae Bonifacio VIII ut Doctores et Magistri Univ. Oxon. licentiam habere possint legendi in aliis Univv. (c. A.D. 1300).
　　Wood F. 27, *artt.* 6 and 31 (*O. C.* 8489).
　Nomina inceptorum in quavis facultate, 1502-1680, per Ant. à Wood.
　　Wood F. 13 (*O. C.* 8475).

(Univ.—Classes.)
Catalogue of all Doctors and Masters in Oxford, 1565–1616.
Seld. supr. 98 (*O. C.* 3486).
Names of the Doctors and Masters of Arts in every College, A. D. 1616.
Wood B. 14 (*O. C.* 8587).
· List of doctors proceeding in the years 1660–61.
Tann. 338, *fol.* 105.
Regent masters: see *Regency*, 722.

Bachelors, 618.
Nomina baccalaureorum determinantium 1519–1680, per Ant. à Wood.
Wood F. 14 (*O. C.* 8476).

Private tutors, 619.

Undergraduate members (students, scholars, clerks: see also 640), 620.
Placitum coram rege de pensione cuidam pauperi scholari assignata (1405–6).
Rawl. C. 426, *fol.* 136.
Number of scholars and students in 1612.
Tann. 338, *fol.* 28.
List of books bequeathed by dr. Raynolds of C. C. C. to various students at Oxford.
Wood D. 10 (*O. C.* 8546).
That *Clericus* is used for any scholar in the University.
Wood F. 27, *art.* 40 (*O. C.* 8489).

Unattached students (=Non-collegiate), 622.

Senior men, 623.

Junior men (freshmen), 624.

Noblemen, 625.

Terrae filius, 626.
Two speeches by the Terræ Filius, 1703.
Bodl. 338, *foll.* 205, 207.
Speech of Rob. Roberts as Terrae filius, 1703.
Tann. 338, *fol.* 205.
Vice-chancellor's form of proposing the public burning of the intended Terrae filius speech 13 July 1713.
Tann. 338, *fol.* 208.

(Univ.—Classes.)

Members of Colleges and Halls, 630.

 List of Fellows, Scholars, and Commoners of every College and Hall, A.D. 1552.
  Wood E. 5, *art.* 7 (*O. C.* 8511).

 Reasons why questions of expelling a scholar or fellow do not belong to the Common Law.
  Tann. 338, *fol.* 49.

College Officers and government, 631.

 Visitors, 632.
  Letters on Visitatorial power, about 1715.
   Ch. Ch. 248.

 Heads of Houses, 633.
  Heads of different colleges and halls from their foundation, by E. R. Mores.
   Gough Oxf. 49.
  List of heads of Colleges and Halls.
   Tann. 338, *fol.* 13.
  Draught of an act to invest in the Crown all Headships, &c., for a time (about 1715).
   Ch. Ch. 248.

 Fellows, 634.
 Bursars, 635.
 Tutors, 636.
 Lecturers, see *College exercises*, 637.
 Chaplains, 638.
 Choir, 639.

Undergraduates (see also 620), 640.

 Fellow-Commoners, 641.
 Scholars, 642.
  Regula proposita in quodam Collegio anno 1513 de electione scholarium per sortes.
   Digb. 167, *fol.* 32^v.

 Exhibitioners, 643.
 Commoners, 644.
 Batellers, 645.
 Servitors, 646.

Servants, 647.

(Univ.—Classes.)

College expenses, 648.
 Batels and Commons, 649.

College exercises (collections, lectures, prizes, etc.), 650.
 [For the actual exercises, see *Literary pieces* (978).]

College morals and discipline, 651.

College penalties, 652.

Nations, 653.

Privileged persons, 654.
 List of matriculated citizens, 1662.
  Rawl. C. 421, *fol.* 113^v.

Religious Orders, 660.
 Roman Catholics, 661.
  Ordines religiosi Oxonienses, per M. Windesore.
   C. C. C. 280, *fol.* 77.
  Twelve petitions against Roman Catholics, University and City.
   Gough Oxf. 54.

 Monks, 662.
  Austin Canons, 663.
   Capitulum generale canonicorum regularium ord. S. Augustini apud Fredeswidam celebratum, 6 Maii 1234.
    Tann. 196, *fol.* 118.
   — A. D. 1337.
    Ibid., fol. 148^v.
   (See *Oseney Abbey*, 255: *St. Frideswide's*, 262: *St. Mary's College*, 495.)

  Benedictines (Black monks), 664.[1]
   Of the order of St. Benedict in Oxford.
    Wood F. 29^a, *fol.* 260 (*O. C.* 8491).
   Literae Prioris et Conventus Norwicensis ad Priorem Nigrorum Monachorum Oxon.
    Bodl. 692, *fol.* 116 (*O. C.* 2508).
   Literae ad studentes ordinis Benedictini Oxoniae degentes.
    Bodl. 692, *foll.* 30, 60, 100^v, 110^v, 116 (*O. C.* 2508).

(**Univ.—Classes.**)
(See *Canterbury College*, 486.)
(„ *Durham College*, 487.)
(„ *Gloucester College*, 488.)
(„ *Godstow Nunnery*, 247.)

Carthusians, 665.

Cistercians, 666.
(See *Rewley Abbey*, 256.)
(„ *St. Bernard's College*, 493.)

Cluniacs, 667.

Friars, 668.

Austin Friars and house, 669.
Of the Austin friars.
Wood F. 29ᵃ, *fol.* 192 (*O. C.* 8491).
Breve ad quod damnum pro tenemento fratribus Ord. August. in Oxon. concedendo, 1294–5.
Wood F. 27, *art.* 41 (*O. C.* 8489).
Conveyance to the city of the site of the Austin Friars, 31 Eliz. (1588–89).
Rawl. C. 936, *fol.* 85.
Case between Merton and Wadham about the rights of the Austin friars.
Wood F. 28, *fol.* 223 (*O. C.* 8490).
(See also *Wadham College*.)

Carmelites (White) and house, 671.
Of the Carmelites.
Wood F. 29ᵃ, *fol.* 180 (*O. C.* 8491).
Charter affecting the prior of the Carmelites.
Charters Cal., p. 283.
Libri apud Carmelitas Oxonii.
Leland, vol. 3, p. 57 (*O. C.* 5104).

Crossed or Crutched Friars, and house, 672.
Of the Crouched friars.
Wood F. 29ᵃ, *fol.* 204 (*O. C.* 8491).

Dominicans (Black, Preaching) and house, 673.
Of the house of Dominican friars.
Wood F. 29ᵃ, *fol.* 170 (*O. C.* 8491).

(Univ.—Classes.)
Processus in Curia Romana inter fratres Praedicatores et Acad. Oxon. anno 1312.
Digb. Rot. 1.

Acta fratrum praedicatorum et Magistrorum Univ. Oxon. in Curia Romana de gradibus Religiosorum Oxon.
Wood D. 18, *fol.* 1 (*O. C.* 8563).

Libri apud Praedicatores Oxon.
Leland Coll. 3, p. 59 (*O. C.* 5104).

Franciscans (Grey, Minorites) and house, 674.
Of the Franciscan friars.
Wood F. 29ᵃ, *fol.* 174 (*O. C.* 8491).

Nomina eorum qui theologiam in scholis Franciscanorum Oxoniae legerunt.
Leland Coll. 4, p. 236 (*O. C.* 5105).

Description of the state of their library in Leland's time.
Leland Coll. 3, p. 60 (*O. C.* 5104).

Owned MS. *Digb.* 90.

Mathurines (Trinitarians) and Trinity house, 675.
Of the house of the Holy Trinity.
Wood F. 29ᵃ, *fol.* 201 (*O. C.* 8491).

Sack or Penance, friars of, and house, 676.
The Pœnitentiarian friars.
Wood F. 29ᵃ, *fol.* 205 (*O. C.* 8491).

Secular Canons, 677.
(See *St. Frideswide's*, 262: *St. George's College*, 494.)

Secular Clergy, 678.

Nuns, 679.
(See *Godstow*, 247: *St. Frideswide's*, 262.)

Jesuits, 681.

Protestant, 682.

Church of England, 683.
Index of ordinations of Oxford writers, time of Ch. II–1738, by R. Rawlinson.
Rawl. C. 801, *fol.* 29.

Dissenters (see *Mansfield College*, 177), 684.

(Univ.—Classes.)

Greek Church, 686.

Jews, 687.
> (See *Conversorum domus*, 244).

Other (Lollards, Military Orders, etc.), 688.
> Charter affecting the Templars' land in Oxford.
> *Charters Cal.*, p. 305.

> De banniendo et expellendo a villa Oxon. omnes fautores certorum haereticorum: de debatis in Univ. Oxon. sedandis, 1385: de Lollardibus et aliis haeresim praedicantibus extra Univ. Oxon. amovendo, 1395, etc.
> *Wood F.* 32, *foll.* 3 et seqq. (*O. C.* 8494).

Other Classes (Socialists, etc.), 689.

COURSE OF STUDIES (General conditions), 701.
> Epistolae duae Joh. Rainoldi ad Tho. Kingsmillum de disciplina scholastica apud Oxoniam (early 17th cent.).
> *Qu. Coll.* 354, *fol.* 65.

Preliminaries to residence, 702.

Matriculation, 703.
> Quaedam ex registro matriculae.
> *Wood D.* 3 (at end?) (*O. C.* 8514).

> Collections out of the Matriculation books, 1564–1647.
> *Wood E.* 5, *art.* 7 (*O. C.* 8511).

> Similar collections, 1540–1690, arranged alphabetically.
> *Wood D.* 1 (*O. C.* 8512).

> Matriculations Jan.–Apr. 1715.
> *Rawl. B.* 399, *fol.* 1.

Residence, 704.

Terms and Vacations, 705.

Declarations and Oaths (see 717), 706.
> Forms of Oaths and Graces: in Latin.
> *Arch. E.* —, p. 142 (*O. C.* 2944).

Subscription to the xxxix. Articles, etc. (Religious Tests), 707.

(Univ.—Studies.)

Lectures, Collections, Declamations, Disputations
(Answering under Bachelor, Austins, In Parviso or Generals, Juraments, Quadragesimals or Lent disputations, Quodlibeticae, etc.), **Opponency, etc.,** 708.

[For the actual lectures, disputations, etc., see *Lit. pieces* (978).]

Days for the Collectors in Lent, 1662.
Rawl. C. 421, *fol.* 66.

Examinations in general, 711.

Degrees in general, 712.

Acta fratrum praedicatorum et Magistrorum Univ. Oxon. in Curia Romana de gradibus Religiosorum Oxon.
Wood D. 18, *fol.* 1 (*O. C.* 8563).

Statuta de gradibus academicis, 1251, etc. (in Processu fratrum Praedicatorum in Curia Romana anno 1312).
Digb. Rot. 1.

Admissions to degrees at the Act, 1563-1638.
Rawl. C. 788, *fol.* 36.

— 1563-1645.
Ibid. 876, *fol.* 27.

Degrees conferred at a visit of Charles I, 31 Aug. 1636.
Rawl. C. 876, *fol.* 97.

Orders of delegates of Convocation about procedure in taking degrees, etc., 1655.
Wood F. 27, *art.* 26 (*O. C.* 8489).

Degrees conferred, 9 and 12 Sept. 1661.
Tann. 338, *foll.* 99, 103.

Honorary degrees, 713.

Catalogus virorum gradu D.C.L. insignitorum, 1677.
Qu. Coll. 280, *fol.* 80.

Terms connected with the taking of a degree, 714.

Dispensation, 715.

Notes of dispensations from degrees, 1681-96.
Gough Oxf. 95.
(See *Responsions*, 728.)

Determining, 716.
(See also *Lectures*, 708.)

Graces (see 706), 717.

(Univ.—Studies.)
Presentation, 718.
Vesperies, 719.
Inception, 721.
  Expensae factae circa inceptionem doctt. Joh. Langdon in Theologia, et Ric. Godmersham in Jure Canonico, A.D. 1400.
    Tann. 165, *fol.* 146 (cf. *fol.* 148): 342, *fol.* 104.
  Notae de Inceptione, per Joh. Laverne.
    Bodl. 692, *foll.* 18ᵛ, 27ᵛ, 28, 34, 34ᵛ, 37ᵛ (*O.C.* 2508).
  Regency, Regent Masters, 722.
Special Studies, 726.
  Arts (and Artists), 727.
  Responsions (Little Go, Smalls), 728.
    Dispensation relative to Responsions, 1 Nov. 1646.
      Tann. 338, *fol.* 72.
    Examination in lieu of Responsions, 729.
    Questionists, 731.
  Moderations, 732.
    Honours, 733.
      Classical, 734.
      Mathematical, 735.
    Pass, 736.
    Sophists, 737.
  Final Schools (Great Go), 738.
    Honours, 739.
      Literae humaniores, 740.
      Mathematics, 741.
      Law, 742.
      Modern History, 743.
      Modern Languages and Literature, 744.
      Natural Science, 745.
      Oriental Studies, 746.
      Theology, 747.
    Pass, 748.
      Group A, 749.
        ,,   B, 750.
        ,,   C, 751.
        ,,   D, 752.

(Univ.—Studies.)

B.A. degree, 753.
   Admissiones baccalaureorum in Artibus, 1505–1580.
      Gough Oxf. 1*.
   Admissiones omnium Bacc. in Artibus, 1505–1690.
      Wood E. 6 (*O. C.* 8506).
   Nomina baccalaureorum determinantium, 1518–81 [from MS. Wood F. 14].
      Gough Oxf. 7.
   Notes of "determinantes," 1737–69.
      Top. Oxf. d. 9.

M.A. degree, 754.
   Varia de capiendo gradu Magistri in Artibus.
      Magd. 38, *fol.* 32.
   Nomina incipientium in Artibus, 1502–13.
      Gough Oxf. 7.
   Admissiones omnium Magistrorum in Artibus, 1505–1691.
      Wood E. 29 (*O. C.* 8507).
   List of M.A.s, 1563–1628.
      Univ. Coll. 128, *fol.* 21.
   Notes of "Incipientes," 1737–69.
      Top. Oxf. d. 9.

Ancient subjects of study (Arts), 755.
   Opera Joh. Laverne monachi ex aula Gloucestrensi, continentia notas miscellaneas de Lecturis, Disputationibus, Inceptione, etc., Oxoniae habitis.
      Bodl. 692 (*O. C.* 2508).

(Trivium), 756.
   Notulae de trivio.
      Langb. 12, p. 93 (*O. C.* p. 270 *a*).

Grammar, 757.
   Errores in grammatica, logica et philosophia naturali ab archiep. Cantuariensi anno 1284 condemnati.
      Digb. 168, *fol.* 157^v.
   Admissiones ad informandum in grammatica, 1508–1567.
      Wood E. 5, *art.* 2 (*O. C.* 8511).

(Univ.—Studies.)

Logic, 758.
    Errores in ... logica ab archiep. Cant. anno 1284 condemnati.
        Digb. 168, *fol.* 157ᵛ.

Rhetoric, 759.
    Admissiones ad informandum in Rhetorica, 1508–1567.
        Wood E. 5, *art.* 2 (*O. C.* 8511).

(Quadrivium), 760.
    Notulae de quadrivio.
        Langb. 12, p. 93 (*O. C.* p. 270 *a*).

Music, see *Music*, 792.

Arithmetic, 762.

Geometry, 763.

Astronomy, 764.

(Tongues), 765.

Greek, 766.

Hebrew, 767.

Philosophy, 768.

Moral, 769.

Metaphysical, 771.

Natural, 772.
    Errores in ... philosophia naturali ab archiep. Cant. anno 1284 condemnati.
        Digb. 168, *fol.* 157ᵛ.

History, 773.

Oriental studies, 774.
    Collectanea de antiquo statu linguarum Orientalium in academia Oxon.
        Langb. 12, pp. 65, 95, 150 (*O. C.* p. 270 *a*).

Law, 778.
    Declaratio magistrorum regentium contra facultatem Juris canonici et civilis, &c. (15th cent.).
        Tann. 196, *fol.* 1.
    Sermon of Roger Bitson against the Canon and Civil Law, 4 Dec. 1435.
        Ibid., fol. 1ᵛ.

(Univ.—Studies.)
Prophetia de dissensione inter magistros et facultatem juris (Carmen).
Tann. 196, *fol.* 2ᵛ.

Canon, 779.
Admissiones omnium Bacc. et Doctorum in Jure Canonico, 1505-1690.
Wood E. 7 (*O. C.* 8508).

Civil, 781.
S.C.L. degree, 782.
B.C.L. degree, 783.
Admissiones omnium Bacc. in Jure Civili, 1505-1690.
Wood E. 7 (*O. C.* 8508).
D.C.L. degree, 784.
Admissiones omnium Doctorum in Jure Civili, 1505-1690.
Wood E. 7 (*O. C.* 8508).
List of D.C.L.s, 1563-1628.
Univ. Coll. 128, *fol.* 21.
(See *Honorary degrees*, 713.)

Medicine and Surgery, 785.
Epistola Henr. VIII de gradibus in Medicina, " 2 Mar. 1535."
Tann. 338, *fol.* 25.
B.M. degree, 786.
Admissiones omnium Bacc. in Medicina, 1505-1689.
Wood E. 8 (*O. C.* 8509).
List of Bachelors of Medicine at Oxford, 1691-1734: by R. Rawlinson.
Rawl. B. 250, *fol.* 68.
D.M. degree, 787.
Admissiones omnium Doctorum in Medicina, 1505-1689.
Wood E. 8 (*O. C.* 8509).
List of D.M.s, 1563-1628.
Univ. Coll. 128, *fol.* 21.

(Univ.—Studies.)

Theology, 788.
[For disputations, etc., see under *Lit. pieces* (978).]
Nomina eorum qui Theologiam in scholis Franciscanorum Oxoniae legerunt.
Leland Coll. 4, p. 236 (*O. C.* 5105).
Admissiones Opponentium in Theologia, 1505-1539.
Wood E. 9 (*O. C.* 8510).

B.D. degree, 789.
Admissiones Bacc. in Theologia, 1505-1690.
Wood E. 9 (*O. C.* 8510).
List of B.D.s, 1563-1628.
Univ. Coll. 128, *fol.* 8.
List of B.D.s, 1565-1641.
Rawl. C. 788, *fol.* 8.
— 1565-1647.
Ibid. 876, *fol.* 9.
List of B.D.s in Oxford, 1644 and 1647.
Rawl. C. 876, *end.*

D.D. degree, 791.
Nomina incipientium in Theologia, 1502-13.
Gough Oxf. 7.
Admissiones Doctorum in Theologia, 1505-1690.
Wood E. 9 (*O. C.* 8510).
List of D.D.s, 1563-1628.
Univ. Coll. 128, *fol.* 21.
List of D.D.s in Oxford, 1644 and 1647.
Rawl. C. 876, *end.*
(See *Honorary degrees*, 317.)

Music, 792.

Mus. Bac. degree, 793.
Admissiones Bacc. in Musica, 1504-1670.
Wood E. 5, *art.* 1 (*O. C.* 8511).

Mus. Doc. degree, 794.
Admissiones Doctorum in Musica, 1504-1670.
Wood E. 5, *art.* 1 (*O. C.* 8511).

(Univ.—Studies.)
Letter of John Wallis, about proceeding to the Mus. Doc. degree; 15 June 1703.
Tann. 338, *fol.* 201.

University Scholarships, 795.
  Craven (with Craven Fellowships), 796.
  Radcliffe travelling, 797.
  Vinerian Law, 798.
  Ireland, 799.
  Eldon Law, 800.
  Boden Sanskrit, 801.
  Mathematical, 802.
  Kennicott Hebrew, 803.
  Pusey and Ellerton Hebrew, 804.
  Denyer and Johnson Theological, 805.
  Hertford, 806.
  Taylor, 807.
  Burdett-Coutts Geological, 808.
  Abbott, 809.
  Derby, 810.
  Davis Chinese, 811.

University Exhibitions, 812.

University Prizes, 813.
  Chancellor's Latin Verse, 814.
        ,,   English Essay, 815.
        ,,   Latin Essay, 816.
  Newdigate English Verse, 817.
  Ellerton Theological Essay, 818.
  English Sacred Poem, 819.
  Arnold Historical Essay, 820.
  Stanhope Historical Essay, 821.
  Gaisford Greek Verse, 822.
        ,,   Greek Prose, 823.
  Johnson Essay, 824.
  Hall and Hall-Houghton, 825.

(Univ.—Studies.)
Lothian Historical Essay, 826.
Conington, 827.
Cobden, 828.
Rolleston, 829.
Green Moral Philosophy, 830.

LIFE AND MANNERS.
General Notes, 831.
Expenses, 832 (see 907).
Fragment of R. Rawlinson's private accounts when at St. John's College, about 1710.
Rawl. C. 865, *fol.* 31.
Morals and Discipline, 833.
Orders from the Chancellor concerning the good government of the University, 1589.
Wood F. 27, *art.* 22 (*O. C.* 8489).
Penalties, 834.
Religious, 835.
University Services, Sermons, and Preaching (bidding prayer, etc.: see also *Select Preachers*, 546, and *Bampton Lecturers*, 547), 836.
Proclamation of the Vice-chancellor against reading (Univ.) sermons, 1674.
Tann. 338, *fol.* 185.
Proceedings against F. Nicholson of Univ. college for a questionable sermon at St. Mary's, 1680.
Tann. 37, *foll.* 59, 71.
Preacher summoned before the vice-chancellor (letter from dr. Fell, 29 June 1680).
Tann. 37, *fol.* 59.
The order of preaching the University sermons at St. Mary's and elsewhere (17th cent.).
Univ. Coll. 128, *fol.* 1.
Order of Univ. preachers.
Rawl. C. 788, *fol.* 1 : 876, *fol.* 1.
Bidding prayer before sermons.
Ibid., 945, *foll.* 5, 180, 527.

(**Univ.—Life and Manners.**)
Latin sermon, before the University? (14th or 15th cent. ?).
Ball. Coll. 75, *fol.* 106.
Courses for preaching the Tuesday lectures at St. Mary's, about 1656.
Wood (*O. C.* 8562).
(Lost.)
List of Lent preachers, 1662.
Tann. 338, *foll.* 112, 114.
Case between the Univ. and Ch. Ch. respecting the Dean and Canons preaching only at Ch. Ch., 1673.
Wood F. 27, *art.* 37 (*O. C.* 8489).
Rawl. B. 404, *fol.* 1.
Answer of the Vice-chancellor etc. to the dean and canons of Ch. Ch. on their refusal to preach in their turns at St. Mary's.
Qu. Coll. 286, *fol.* 276.
Case of the Vice-chancellor etc. as to the Canons of Ch. Ch. preaching in the Cathedral (167$\frac{3}{4}$).
Ch. Ch. 345, *art.* 10.
— Reply of the Dean and Chapter, 6 Mar. 167$\frac{3}{4}$.
Ibid., art. 11.

University Services, etc., pre-Reformation (Masses, etc.), 837.
Calendarium missarum pro animabus Benefactorum Univ. Oxon.
Wood (*O. C.* 8562).
(Lost.)
Old University Masses for particular persons and occasions, especially on St. Scholastica's day.
Bodl. 918 (*O. C.* 2910).

Missions, 838.

Clubs and Societies, 839.

Intellectual and Literary (State of Learning, etc.), 840.
State of learning in Oxford, temp. Hen. VIII.
Wood D. 7 (2) (*O. C.* 8519).

Reading in general, 841.

(Univ.—Life and Manners.)

Books, 842.
    Tituli librorum in studiis scholarium Wintoniae Oxon. repertorum, anno 1489.
      Digb. 31, *ad fin.*
  Clubs and Societies, 843.

Political, 844.
    Letters concerning a reform of the Universities in point of Jacobitism, 1715.
      Ch. Ch. 248.

North and South (old disputes), **845.**
    Quaedam de dissensionibus inter scholares Boreales et Australes: ex archivis domus Congreg. Oxon.
      Wood F. 27, *art.* 7 (*O. C.* 8489).
  Clubs and Societies, 846.

Scientific, 847.
  Clubs and Societies, 848.
    Royal Society, as the " Philosophical Society of Oxford." Proceedings and correspondence 1681–90, with Rules of 1651.
      Ashm. 1810–13.

Artistic, 849.
  Music, 850.
    Clubs and Societies, 851.

  Dramatic, 852.
    Account of the dramatic entertainments and revels at St. John's college, 1607–08.
      St. John's 52, *fol.* 26.
    Lines on the comœdians of Oxford and Cambridge (about 1620?).
      Malone 19, p. 125.
    Lines on the Ch. Ch. play acted at Woodstock, 1621.
      Ashm. 36, *fol.* 283.
    Lines on Technogamia played at Ch. Ch. (James I's reign).
      Ashm. 38, *fol.* 31.
    Clubs and Societies, 853.

Other Clubs and Societies, 854.

(Univ.—Life and Manners.)

Social, 855.
 Etiquette, 856.
 Amusements, 857.
  Archery, 858.
  Athletics, 859.
  Bell ringing, 860.
  Bicycling, etc., 861.
  Billiards, 862.
  Boating, 863.
   „ see also *Sailing*.
  Boxing and wrestling, 864.
  Cards, 865.
   Whist, 866.
  Chess, 867.
  Coursing, 868.
  Cricket, 869.
  Croquet, 870.
  Cycling, see *Bicycling*.
  Dancing (Balls, etc.), 871.
  Feasting (dinners, teas, wines, etc.), 872.
   Charges of the earl of Leicester's dinner at Oxford, 6 Sept. 1570.
    Wood F. 27, *art.* 3 (*O. C.* 8489).
  Fencing, 873.
  Fishing, 874.
  Fives, 875.
  Football, 876.
  Gambling, 877.
  Games, indoor, other than cards or chess, 878.
  Gymnastics, 879.
  Hockey, 880.
  Horse-racing, 881.
  Hunting, 882.
  Lawn Tennis, 883.
  Polo, 884.
  Racquets, 885.
  Ratting, 886.

(Univ.—Life and Manners.)
Riding and driving, 887.
Notice of the design of Henry Hyde 4th earl of Clarendon to found a riding school at Oxford, 1753.
Rawl. C. 989, *fol.* 198.
Rowing, see *Boating*.
Sailing, 888.
Shooting, 889.
Pigeon-shooting, 890.
Skating, 891.
Swimming, 892.
Tennis, 893.
Volunteers, 894.
Walking, 895.

Clubs and Societies, 896.
Freemasons, 897.
Union Society, 898.

Personal, 900.
Dress (Hair, etc.), 901.
Proclamation by the Vice-chancellor against wearing wigs, 1674.
Tann. 338, *fol.* 185.
Academical costume, 902.

Diet, 903.
Drinking, 904.
Drunken habits of the University, in Charles II's time.
Rawl. C. 406, *fol.* 100.
Language—University slang, 905.
Smoking, 906.
Debts, 907 (see 832).

EXTERNAL RELATIONS, 911.

To foreign lands and the Colonies, 912.
Rate levied on the Colleges for relief of the Protestants of Piedmont (about 1660).
Rawl. C. 421, *fol.* 72.

(Univ.—External Relations.)

To the Pope, 914.

Processus inter fratres Praedicatores et Academiam Oxon. in Curia Romana, anno 1312.
Digb. Rot. 1.

Acta fratrum praedicatorum et Magistrorum Univ. Oxon. in Curia Romana de gradibus Religiosorum.
Wood D. 18, *fol.* 1 (*O. C.* 8563).

Bulla Johannis XXII papae ad Acad. Oxon. de constitutionibus Clementis V, A. D. 1318.
Digb. 218, *fol.* 206.

Determinatio Acad. Oxon. de potestate Papae in regno Angliae (14th cent.).
James 12 (*O. C.* 3849).

Academiae epistola ad Martinum V papam, 1427.
C.C.C. 318, *fol.* 197.

Sententia Univ. de jurisdictione episc. Romani, 27 Jun. 1534.
Tann. 90, *fol.* 65.

Indulgences, 915.

Indulgentiae concessae omnibus qui concionibus Theologorum in ecclesiis Oxon. intererunt A. D. 1313.
Wood F. 27, *art.* 5 (*O. C.* 8489).

Foreigners in Oxford, 917.

Foreign students admitted to the Bodleian Library, 1602–1690.
Wood E. 5, *art.* 3 (*O. C.* 8511).

Petition of foreign students in Oxford to the Curators of the Bodleian Library, A. D. 1641.
Wood F. 27, *art.* 18 (*O. C.* 8489).

To the country at large, 918.

Letters patent of Charles I granting lands chiefly for Jersey and Guernsey fellowships.
Tann. 338, *fol.* 54.

Notice of the Jersey and Guernsey Fellowships.
Ibid., fol. 188.

Acceptance by Pembroke college of a fellowship for natives of Jersey and Guernsey, 1636.
Tann. 338, *fol.* 177.

(Univ.—External Relations.)

Local Examinations, 919.

Migration, 922.

To the Crown, 925.

 Acta Oxonii circa divortium Henr. VIII, 1530.
  Tann. 90, *fol.* 59.

 Letter of the Privy Council to the University concerning schismatical books, 1573.
  C. C. C. 301, *fol.* 88.

 Oratio in domo Convocationis cum Jacobus I rex opera sua Academiae daret, 29 Maii, 1620.
  Ashm. 1153, *fol.* 68.

 Acceptance by Pembroke college of a fellowship founded by Charles I, 29 Apr. 1636.
  Tann. 338, *fol.* 177.

 Commissioners of the Univ. for a present to the King, 1636–37.
  Rawl. C. 421, *fol.* 96.

 Draught of an act to invest in the Crown all Headships of Colleges, etc. for a time (about 1715).
  Ch. Ch. 248.

Visitations, 927.

 Declaratio regis Ric. II, quod jus visitandi universitatem pertinet ad archiep. Cantuariensem, 1 Jun. 1397.
  Rawl. B. 202, *fol.* 263 : *C.* 737, *fol.* 24.

 Resolution and proceedings concerning the visitation of the Univ., agreed upon by the King and Parliament, 1411.
  Tann. 127, *fol.* 187^v.

 Caroli II delegatio ad universitatem visitandam, 1660.
  C. C. C. 301, *fol.* 161.

 Letters of Charles II appointing Commissioners to visit the University, 1660.
  e Mus. 246 (*O. C.* 3735).
  C. C. C. 319, *fol.* 222.

 Of Royal Visitations : written about 1718.
  Ch. Ch. 249.

(Univ.—External Relations.)
Royal Charters (see also 973), 928.
  University Charters.
    Ex. Coll. 11 and 12.
  Charta Henrici VIII Universitati concessa.
    Ex. Coll. 155, *fol.* 33.
  Orders of the Council to settle differences between the Univ. and City, 1575.
    C. C. C. 367.
  Caroli I confirmatio chartarum regiarum Universitati concessarum, 1635-6.
    Qu. Coll. 378, *fol.* 1.
    Ex. Coll. 11, *fol.* 1 : 12, *fol.* 4.
  Analysis and abstract of the Charter of Charles I to the Univ. 1636.
    Wood F. 27, *art.* 28, 29 (*O. C.* 8489).

Royal Letters, Mandamuses, etc., 929.
  Letter from Hen. VII to the University.
    Wood F. 31, *fol.* 29 (*O. C.* 8493).
      (Lost.)
  Letters of Hen. VIII to the University.
    C. C. C. 316, *fol.* 57.
  Qu. Mary's remission of tithes to Ch. Ch., 2 July 1555.
    Ch. Ch. 344, *fol.* 44.
  Custom of the Crown to recommend provosts of Oriel, discountenanced by archbp. Parker (about 1570 ?).
    Tann. 155, *fol.* 176ᵛ.
  Letters patent of James I for annexing a Canonry at Ch. Ch. to the Regius Professorship of Divinity, 1606.
    Ch. Ch. 345, *art.* 1.
  The King's directions to the Universities, about 1617.
    Ch. Ch. 290, p. 551.
  Reply of Charles I to complaints of the students of Ch. Ch., 30 Jan. 1629.
    Ch. Ch. 345, *art.* 5.
  K. Charles I's answer to the petition of Merton college, with the petition, Dec. 1632.
    Tann. 339, *foll.* 60, 59.

(**Univ.—External Relations.**)

Letters patent of Charles I for annexing a prebendal stall at Ch. Ch. to the Public Oratorship, 1636.
Ch. Ch. 345, *art.* 3.

Mandamus of Charles I to All Souls to elect a Fellow, 2 Nov. 1643.
Tann. 340, *fol.* 148.

Royal mandamus to Magdalen college to elect to a demyship, 20 July 1660.
Tann. 338, *fol.* 246.

Letter of Charles II to the Vice-Chancellor about a Parliament at Oxford, 1681.
All S. 253, fol. 300.

Petition of Merton college to its Visitor about a royal mandate to elect to a fellowship (1686?).
Tann. 339, *fol.* 421.

Mandamus of James II to All Souls to present to the vicarage of Barking, 13 Aug. 1688.
Tann. 28, *fol.* 160.

Royal Visits, 930.

Notae ex variis orationibus etc. A.D. 1566, cum regina Elizabetha academiam visitaret.
Rawl. C. 753, *foll.* 47–61^v.

Notae ex oratione Tho. Thornton apud Oxon. anno 1566 habita, cum Regina adesset.
Rawl. C. 753, *fol.* 61^v.

Rents of Colleges according to which they were taxed for Qu. Elizabeth's entertainment.
Tann. 338, *fol.* 27^v.

Carmina alumnorum C. C. C. in adventum Elizabethae, 1566 (?).
C. C. C. 280, *fol.* 171.

Expenses of Ch. Ch. when the Queen visited it, 21 July 1566.
Top. Oxf. e. 9.
Rawl. C. 878, *fol.* 1.

Notices to Colleges about the entertainment of the King, Queen and prince, 1605.
C. C. C. 301, *fol.* 93.

(Univ.—External Relations.)
Song on Charles I coming to Oxford.
Ashm. 36, *foll.* 259, 316.
Order for the King's entertainment, 1636.
C. C. C. 301, *fol.* 127.
Degrees conferred at a visit of Charles I, 31 Aug. 1636.
Rawl. C. 876, *fol.* 97.
Verses spoken in St. John's library at the entertainment of the King and Queen, 1636.
Malone 21, *fol.* 52ᵛ.
(For papers relating to Charles I's personal and public affairs during his stay at Oxford during the Civil War, see the printed Indexes to the Clarendon State Papers in the Bodleian.)
Account of the reception of Kings, Princes, Chancellors, etc., 1661-87.
Wood D. 19 (*O. C.* 8566).
Address to Charles II in the Library of St. John's, Sept. 1663.
Tann. 306, *fol.* 365 : 314, *fol.* 101.
Account of Charles II's entry into Oxford, 16 Mar. 168⁹⁄₇.
All S. 242, *foll.* 37, 258.
Account of what passed between the King and the Fellows of Magdalen at Ch. Ch., 4 Sept. 1687.
Tann. 29, *fol.* 86.
Proceedings in the University on the visit of the King, 1695.
Tann. 456*, *fol.* 43.
Address to Qu. Anne etc. by dean Aldrich at Ch. Ch.
Worc. Coll. 58, *fol.* 277.
Account of the visit of the Prince Regent etc. in 1814.
Top. Oxf. c. 1.
Account of the visit of the Allied Sovereigns in 1814.
Bodl. Arch. F.

To the Church and Dissent, 932.
Epistola a Roberto archiep. Cantuariensi de erroribus apud Oxoniam condemnatis (13th or 14th cent. ?).
Merl. Coll. 267, *fol.* 109.

(Univ.—External Relations.)

Articuli reprobati tanquam errores a magistris Theologiae Oxoniae A. D. 1314.
Mert. Coll. 84 *ad fin.*

Compositio inter archidiac. Oxon. et Univ., 1345.
Tann. 300, *fol.* 118ᵛ.

Epistola Universitatis ad Ric. II de abolendo schismate, 1395.
Magd. Coll. 53, *fol.* 317.

Letters patent of Rich. II affirming the visitatorial jurisdiction of the archbp. of Canterbury, 1 June 1397.
Tann. 127, *fol.* 187.

Literae testimoniales Universitatis de Johanne Wyclif, 1406.
C. C. C. 301, *fol.* 11.

Petitiones quoad reformationem ecclesiae militantis editae Oxon. a mag. Ric. Ullerston, A. D. 1408.
Langb. 12, p. 29 (*O. C.* p. 270 *a*).

Epistola Universitatis ad Henr. V de reformatione ecclesiae universalis (about 1415 ?).
C.C.C. 183, *fol.* 16ᵛ.

Epistola Universitatis ad Synodum Londinensem, 1420.
Univ. Coll. 76, *fol.* 619.

Act of Parliament 27 Hen. VIII exempting the Universities from Firstfruits and Tenths.
Barlow   (*O. C.* 6457).

Judgement of the University on Tho. Cartwright, concerning Church Discipline (A. D. 1573?).
Seld. supr. 44, p. 22 (*O. C.* 3432).

The archbp. of Canterbury's right to visit the Universities determined in Council, 21 June 1636.
Tann. 158, *fol.* 97: 299, *fol.* 135.

Literae regiae de visitatione univ. Oxon. et Cantab. per archiep. Cantuar., 30 Jan. 163⅚.
Tann. 158, *fol.* 99.

K

(**Univ.—External Relations.**)

Two letters of Rich. Zouche on exempting the Univ. from the ordinance for abolishing Deans and Chapters, Oct. 1648.
Tann. 356, *foll.* 3, 5.

To Parliament, 933.

Order of Parliament about College Plate, 12 July 1642.
Clar. i. 1622.

Petition of the Univ. to Parliament, 24 Apr. 1641.
Wood F. 27, *art.* 2 (*O. C.* 8489).

Vote of thanks to the University (by Parliament?) for not subscribing the Solemn League and Covenant, 1665.
All S. 204, p. 25.

To Visitations and Commissions, 934.

Diaries, letters, orders, instructions, etc. relating to the Visitation of the University, A. D. 1647–48.
Wood F. 35 (*O. C.* 8497).

Papers connected with the Parliamentary visitation of Oxford, 1647–165–.
E Mus. 77 (*O. C.* 3736).

Commission for visiting the Universities, 27 Sept. 1647.
Tann. 338, *fol.* 83.

Names of Visitors, and their powers.
Ibid., fol. 77.

Reasons against the Commission.
Ibid., foll. 78, 81.

Charles I's proposals relative to this Visitation.
Ibid., fol. 80.

Opening of the Visitation, treatment of the Visitors by the University, 5 June 1647.
Ibid., fol. 74.

Order of the Visitors to remove the Pres^t of St. John's, 17 Mar. 174$\frac{7}{8}$.
Ibid., fol. 76.

Letter of G. Langbaine condemning the Visitors' Regulations, 8 Nov. 1653.
Tann. 52, *fol.* 60.

(**Univ.—External Relations.**)
Letter about the reception of the Parliamentary Commission at Oxford, Oct. 1647.
   Clar. i. 2636.
Appeal of the University against the Visitation, Oct. 1647.
   Clar. i. 2735.
Account of the proceedings of the Committee of Lords and Commons for the reformation of the University, 28 Dec. 1647.
   Clar. i. 2735.
Draft of a commission for visiting the Univ. (Charles II).
   Tann. 338, *fol.* 95.

Acts of Parliament concerning the University, 936.
Act of Parliament 27 Hen. VIII exempting the Universities from Firstfruits and Tenths.
   Barlow   (*O. C.* 6457).

Parliaments at Oxford: see *City* part (369).

To the neighbourhood, 937.

To the city (Town and Gown), 938.
De magna discordia inter academicos et oppidanos, 1264, (copy by Thomas Hearne).
   Rawl. B. 201, *fol.* 192ᵛ.
Differences between the scholars and townsmen, A.D. 1297–8.
   Wood F. 27, *art.* 46 (*O. C.* 8489).
Planctus Univ. Oxon. contra laicos, poëma (A. D. 1353).
   Wood (2) 7, p. 191 (*O. C.* 8620). *Bodl.* 859, *fol.* 292ᵛ (*O.C.* 2722). *Rawl. B.* 176, *fol.* 60 (manu Tho. Hearne).
Brevia et caetera munimenta conflictum inter Univ. et civitatem in die S. Scholasticae tangentia, 1355.
   Rawl. C. 356.
Notae de conflictu inter scholares et cives anno 1354.
   Digb. 57, *fol.* 28ᵛ.
Relation of the conflict between Scholars and Townsmen, 10 Feb. 135⅔.
   Wood F. 27, *art.* 47 (*O. C.* 8489).
Notes of the townsmen who presented themselves before the University on St. Scholastica's Day, 1737–74.
   Top. Oxf. d. 9.

(Univ.—External Relations.)

St. Scholastica's day: see also *University Services*—Pre-Reformation (837).

Orders of Council to settle differences between the University and City, 21 June 1575.
C. C. C. 367.

Papers relating to orders of the Chancellor to butchers etc. not to kill meat in Lent, 1578–1630.
Rawl C. 421, *foll.* 78–112.

The summe and effect of greivances susteined by the citty at the hands of the universitie: also greivances done to the universitie by the cittie (time of James I).
Top. Oxf. d. 6.

Placita quaedam inter Acad. et Civitatem Oxon. de Ricardo Paynter noctivagatore, 1609–10.
Wood F. 27, *art.* 21 (*O. C.* 8489).

Order of the Lords of the Council concerning the controversy between the Univ. and Town, 1612, June 22.
Wood   (*O. C.* 8562).
(Lost.)

Grievances exhibited by the Univ. against the City, 17 June, 1634.
Tann. 338, *fol.* 30.

Letters relating to the differences between the Univ. and City, 1635.
Tann. 338, *foll.* 56, 58.

Four grievances of the City against the Univ., 1635.
Tann. 338, *fol.* 30.

Doubts of the Univ. concerning the City Charter (1635 ?).
Tann. 338, *fol.* 35.

Matters in controversy between the Univ. & City discussed at Lambeth, 28 Apr. 1636.
All S. 216, *fol.* 96.

Complaint of the City, Answer of the University, and Replication of the City.
Wood F. 27, *art.* 1 (*O. C.* 8489).

Points in controversy between the Univ. and City, 1640.
Wood F. 27, *art.* 39 (*O. C.* 8489).

(Univ.—External Relations.)
Complaints made by the City against the University before the House of Lords, 1640.
Wood F. 27, *art.* 36 (*O.C.* 8489).
(Lost.)
The case between the Proctor Allibond and Alderman Nixon, A. D. 1640.
Wood D. 18, *fol.* 44 (*O. C.* 8563).
Orders agreed on between the University and City about the rights of the former (1643?).
Queen's Coll. 278, *fol.* 18ᵛ.
Heads of answer to objections of the City in their Petition, 1648.
Wood F. 27, *art.* 30 (*O. C.* 8489).
Proviso exempting the Univ. from the acts of Assessment, 1661.
Tann. 338, *fol.* 101.

To other universities, 939.
Supplicatio Oliveri Episc. Linc. Papae Bonifacio VIII ut Doctores et Magistri Univ. Oxon. licentiam habere possint legendi in aliis Universitatibus (*c.* A. D. 1300).
Wood F. 27, *art.* 6 (*O.C.* 8489).

English, Welsh, Scotch, or Irish, 941.

Cambridge, 942.
See *Incorporation* (944).

Foreign, 943.
Subscription for the Heidelberg professors (letters to Hen. Briggs, 1627-8).
Tann. 72, *foll.* 211, 228, 308.
Epistola ecclesiae et academiae Genevensis ad univ. Oxon. cum responso, 1706.
Tann. 338, *fol.* 209.

Incorporation, 944.
Case of Fleetwood, Fellow of All Souls, D.C.L. Padua, seeking to be incorporated ad eundem at Oxford (about 1630?).
Tann. 340, *fol.* 117.
List of Cambridge men admitted at Oxford, to about 1750.
Rawl. C. 947.

(Univ.—External Relations.)

Affiliation, 945.

To Schools, 946.

Education of Women, 947.

To Colleges, etc., within itself, 948.
> Decimae et primitiae Collegiorum, ab Henr. VIII condonatae, A.D. 1536.
> *Tann.* 338, *fol.* 50.

HISTORY AND ANTIQUITIES IN GENERAL, 950.
> Bellesitensis academia e tenebris eruta et in lucem vindicata, per M. Windesore.
> *C. C. C.* 280, *fol.* 15.
>
> Collectanea ad Oxoniae historiam et antiquitates declarandum per M. Windesore.
> *C. C. C.* 280.
>
> Registrum FF, epistolae ad Universitatem Oxoniensem, cum responsis.
> *Bodl.* 282 (*O. C.* 2949).
>
> Collectanea ad Universitatem spectantia.
> *C. C. C.* 301 and 302.
>
> Collectanea Langbainii de Acad. Oxon. ex Historicis desumpta.
> *Wood F.* 27, *art.* 48 (*O. C.* 8489).
>
> Antony à Wood's History of the University to A.D. 1660.
> *Wood* (*O. C.* 8463).
>
> Notes on Wood's Historia Univ. Oxoniensis, by Will. Fulman.
> *Wood D.* 9 (*O. C.* 8540). (See 962, *Wood*: 973.)
>
> Index to A. Wood's Historia et Antiquitates Universitatis Oxoniensis : by Wood.
> *Wood F.* 22 (*O. C.* 8499).
>
> John Pointer's Antiquities and Curiosities of the University of Oxford (publ. in 1749).
> *Rawl. B.* 405.

Mythical and legendary, 951.
> Excerpta ex libris Joh. Rouse de antiquitate Oxon. Academiae.
> *Leland Coll.* 5, *art.* 16 (*O. C.* 5106).

(Univ.—History.)
De antiquitate academiae.
   Qu. Coll. 258, *fol.* 79.
De academiae primordiis.
   Tann. 338, *fol.* 1.

Relative antiquity of Oxford and Cambridge, 952.
Collections of Brian Twyne in answer to sir Simon D'Ewes' speech in the House of Commons for the antiquity of Cambridge, 9 Mar. 164½.
   Wood F. 27, *art.* 53 (*O. C.* 8489).

To 1600, 954.
Planctus Univ. Oxon. contra laicos (A. D. 1353), poëma.
   Wood (2) 7, p. 191 (*O. C.* 8620).
   Bodl. 859, *fol.* 292ᵛ (*O. C.* 2722).
   Rawl. B. 176, *fol.* 60 (manu Tho. Hearne).
De tempore instituendi publicas lectiones in Acad. Oxoniensi.
   C. C. C. 263, *fol.* 228.
Litterae concessae Universitati Oxon. a Joh. Halton, episc. Carliol., circa A. D. 1296.
   Wood F. 27, *art.* 31 (*O. C.* 8489).
Petitiones quoad reformationem ecclesiae militantis editae Oxon. a mag. Ric. Ullerston, A. D. 1408.
   Langb. 12, p. 29 (*O. C.*, p. 270 *a*).
Apology for the Government of the University against Hen. VIII.
   Wood D. 18 (*O. C.* 8559).
Letters from the earl of Dorset, chancellor (1591–1608), about University business.
   Wood F. 31, *fol.* 49 (*O. C.* 8493).
         (Lost.)

xviith cent., 955.
Diary of Tho. Crossfield at Oxford, 1626–1640, 1653.
   Queen's Coll. 390, *fol.* 4.
Account of the University and its leading men, 1642–60, by Antony à Wood.
   Wood F. 31 (*not O. C.* 8493).
Papers connected with the Parliamentary Visitation, 1647.
   E Mus. 77 (*O. C.* 3736).

(Univ.—History.)

Oratio in proscriptione Oxoniensi, 1647, per T. Carles.
C. C. C. 301, *fol.* 135.

Versus de statu Oxoniae, A. D. 1648, auctore J. B.
C. C. C. 317, *fol.* 297^v.

Rustica academiae nuper reformatae descriptio 1648, per mag. Petrum Allibond: poëma.
Ball. Coll. 336, *fol.* 12.
C. C. C. 317, *fol.* 298.

Letter from A. W(oodhead) at Oxford to mr. Denman about affairs in Oxford, 10 Oct. 1648.
Clar. i. 2895.

Account of the reception of Kings, Princes, Chancellors, &c., with other solemnities in the University, 1661–87.
Wood D. 19 (*O. C.* 8566).

Oxford news, letter of A. Charlett, 13 May, 1698.
Tann. 22, *fol.* 53.

— 17 Mar. 1699.
Ibid. 21, *fol.* 17.

— 27 Apr. 1699.
Ibid. 22, *fol.* 132.

— 1 May, 1699.
Ibid. 21, *fol.* 10.

— 16 May, 1699.
Ibid. 21, *fol.* 70.

— May, 1699.
Ibid. 21, *foll.* 45, 67, 68, 71, 80.

Letter from Tho. Rivers: university news, 17 May, 1698.
Tann. 22, *fol.* 48.

— 2 June, 1698.
Ibid., fol. 20.

— 29 June, 1698.
Ibid., fol. 24.

— 29 July, 1698.
Ibid., fol. 191.

Four letters from W. A. (William Adams?) of Ch. Ch. to Tho. Tanner about University news, 1699.
Tann. 21, *foll.* 39, 63, 90, 132.

(Univ.—History.)
Dialogue in verse between a serving man and a clown on the state of Oxford: *beg.* " Howe nowe, John a dogg " (17th cent.).
All S. Coll. 155, *fol.* 242ᵛ.

Civil War, 956.

Musterings etc. of the University, 1642–4.
Wood (*O. C.* 8558).
(Lost.)

— transcript by Hearne.
Rawl. B. 225, *fol.* 51.

Order of Parliament to apprehend certain Heads of Colleges for helping the King, 12 July, 1642.
Wood F. 27, *art.* 34 (*O. C.* 8489).

Preparations to be made at Oxford for the King's service, 164⅔.
Clar. i. 1810.

xviiith cent., 957.

xixth cent., 958.

Incidents, (not otherwise placed) in chronological order (see note on 387), 961.

St. Scholastica's Day, A. D. 1355.
(See *Relation to City*, 938).

Account of a riot, 11 Apr. 1683.
Rawl. C. 739, *fol.* 21.

Humphrey Wanley at the Three Tuns, Oxford, 28 Mar. 1699.
Tann. 21, *fol.* 22.

Personal history, in order of names, 962.
Cheynell.
Objectiones contra magistrum Cheynell in domo Congregationis Oxon. 17 Dec. 1641, ne ad gradum B.D. promoveretur, cum responsionibus ejus.
Wood B. 14, *fol.* 94 (*O. C.* 8587).

(**Univ.—History.**)

Midsummer Moon, being a character of mr. Cheynell the Arch Visitor of Oxford and Mongrel-President of St. John's.
   Wood D. 19, *fol.* 49 (*O. C.* 8565).

Dod, —, of Ch. Ch.
   Opinions about his election as Proctor, 1659.
   Wood 27, *art.* 27 (*O. C.* 8489).
             (Lost.)

Dodwell.
   M^r. Barbour the Proproctor's case about Dodwell, 1677.
   Wood   (*O. C.* 8562).
             (Lost.)

Ford, —
   Concerning the expulsion of mr. Ford of Magdalen Hall, 1631.
   Wood F. 27, *art.* 25 (*O. C.* 8489).

Gloucester, Humphrey, duke of.
   Missa pro H. duce Gloucestriæ qui obiit 1441.
   Bodl. 918 (*O. C.* 2910).

Knight.
   The case of mr. Knight of Broadgate hall.
   Wood D. 18, *fol.* 45 (*O. C.* 8563).

Laverne, John.
   His common-place book, letters, etc., while Benedictine student at Gloucester College, Oxford: in Latin.
   Bodl. 692 (*O. C.* 2508).

Parkinson, James.
   Articles against James Parkinson, Fellow of Lincoln College.
   Wood F. 18, *fol.* 51 (*O. C.* 8563).

Pococke, dr. Edward.
   Petition of Heads of Houses, M.A.s, etc., to the Committee for regulating the University, in behalf of dr. Pocock (1649 or 1650).
   Wood F. 27, *art.* 43 (*O. C.* 8489).

Wood, Anthony.
   Animadversions on the Popish bias of Wood's History of the University, by A. Charlett, 1691.
   Tann. 114, *fol.* 54.

(Univ.—Documents.)
Biographical Collections, 963.
> Athenae and Fasti Oxonienses, printed, with MS. notes by their author, A. à Wood (2 vols.).
> > *Wood* (*O. C.* 8500–1).
>
> Gutch's Continuation of Wood's account of Oxford writers, 1668–1811 (short notices).
> > *Top. Oxf. c.* 34–7.
>
> Diocesan and University Register of Oxford, 1713–1866 (selected lists and biographical notices).
> > *Top. Oxf. c.* 28.

DOCUMENTS, RECORDS, AND MISCELLANEA, 970.
> Transcripts of Oxford papers, by R. Rawlinson.
> > *Rawl. C.* 865–67.

Almanacs, 971.
> Letter of John Wallis about St. Matthias' day, misplaced in the Oxford Almanac for 1684.
> > *Tann.* 107, *fol.* 50.

Ancient relics (insignia, plate, etc.), 972.
> Arms in the windows of Colleges, collected by Dugdale.
> > *Dugdale* 12 (F. 1), (*O. C.* 6501).

Archives, manuscript collections, charters, etc., as a collection, 973.
> "Out of the archbishop's Registers about the University."
> > *Wood* (*O. C.* 8562).
> > (Lost.)
>
> Out of some papers in the School Tower, entitled Viæ, Vici, Nocumenta, &c.
> > *Wood* (*O. C.* 8562).
> > (Lost.)
>
> Notice of the subscription book to the Articles, 1615–39, being in dr. Hutton's possession (169$\frac{8}{9}$).
> > *Tann.* 22, *fol.* 177.
>
> Receipt by the Keeper of the Archives for certain books and papers belonging to the Univ., 5 Feb. 166$\frac{2}{3}$.
> > *Tann.* 338, *fol.* 169.

(Univ.—Documents.)
Contents of some of the Collectanea volumes of Brian Twyne, in the University archives: by Ant. à Wood.
Wood D. 18 (*O. C.* 8537).

Extracts from and Indexes to the Books of the Vice-chancellor and Proctors.
Arch. E., —, pp. 113, 135, etc. (*O. C.* 2944).

Catalogue of MSS. quoted in Wood's Historia et Antiqqu. Universitatis Oxoniensis, 1674.
Wood E. 4 (*O. C.* 8561).

Calendar, 974.

Facetiae (caricatures, etc.), 975.

Honours' Register (Ten-Year Book), 976.

Gazette, 977.

Literary pieces (with cross-reff., from here, if special), such as comedies, disputations, essays, novels, plays, poems, songs, speeches, tales, tragedies (see also 272, 506, 931), 978.

    See *Cathedral* (223).
    „ *Royal Visits* (364 and 930).
    „ *Ashmolean* (416).
    „ *Bodleian Library* (417).
    „ *Botanical Garden* (423).
    „ *Sheldonian Theatre* (438).
    „ *All Souls* (456).
    „ *Christ Church* (459).
    „ *Pembroke College* (470).
    „ *St. John's* (472).
    „ *Proclamations,* etc., of the Univ. (506).
    „ *Bedells* (526).
    „ *Terrae filius* (626).
    „ *Dramatic life* (852).
    „ *History of Univ.* (954).
    „ *History of Univ.,* 17th cent. (955).
    „ *Civil War* (Univ.), 956.

Grievances of the University presented to dr. Palmer, M.P., to be read in Parliament, 1658: in verse.
Tann. 366, *fol.* 62.

(Univ.—Documents.)

Verses upon some public characters in the University, 1664.
    Tann. 306, *fol.* 371.

Verses on the University, by Tho. Palmer (17th cent.).
    Ashm. 36, *fol.* 210.

Carmina in obitus variorum Oxoniensium, etc. (17th cent.).
    C. C. C. 325.

Poemata in Comitiis recitata, 1733.
    Rawl. C. 155, *fol.* 367.

"Dobbare de Collegiis," 18 Latin verses (13th or 14th cent.).
    C. C. C. 233, *fol.* 81.

Quaestiones theologicae Oxoniae disputatae.
    Digb. 216.

Quaestiones in vii artibus scholis (Oxon. ?) disputatae.
    Digb. 92, *foll.* 80–95.

Determinationes Gul. Widford in Univ. Oxon. contra Wyclevistas.
    Digb. 170.

De laude Universitatis Oxoniensis poëma : auctore Tryvytlam (a copy by Tho. Hearne).
    Rawl. B. 182, *fol.* 155^v.

Questiones in Physica Aristotelis prout in scholis Oxon. disputantur, auctore Joh. Sharpe.
    Digb. 49.

Variae disputationes Inceptorum quorundam Oxoniensium, sec. XV.
    C. C. C. 116.

Libel on Oxford, 1564, a poem by Thomas Buckley.
    Tann. 465, *fol.* 105.

Epistle on the state of the University, in Qu. Elizabeth's time, Latin and English, imperfect.
    Ashm. 1537, *fol.* 111.

Oratio panegyrica quum quidam baccalaureus pro gradu magistri in artibus praesentaretur.
    Digb. 55, *fol.* 203.

(**Univ.—Documents.**)

Lists of authors of Oxford verses, printed in various collections, 1603-41.
Top. Oxf. e. 10.

Mercurius Rusticus, comœdia, cujus scena est Hinxey.
Wood D. 18 (*O. C.* 8557).

On the scholars flocking to Woodstock to the King, 1621 (verse).
Tann. 366, *fol.* 67.

Lines on the scholars of Oxford who resorted to Woodstock when the King was there, 1622.
Malone 19, p. about 100.

Oratio habita a Griffino Higgs coram Acad. Oxon. A.D. 1623.
Wood D. 19, *fol.* 45 (*O. C.* 8565).

Speech by Rich. West in the Music School at the Act, 1640.
Tann. 88, *fol.* 9.

Poems, English and Latin, chiefly on Oxford subjects (17th cent., first half).
Douce 409.

Newspapers and Periodicals, 979.

OXFORD.

PART II.

INDEX, IN ALPHABETICAL ORDER

(*The numbers refer to the sections in part* 1.)

Abbott Scholarship, 809.
Accidents (City), 387.
   ,,   (Univ.), 961.
Act, 439.
Acting, see *Dramatic Life*.
Acts of Parliament relating to City, 368.
   ,,   ,,   University, 936.
Administration of Effects, 509.
Affiliation to the University, 945.
Air (Meteorology), 105.
Aldermen, 286.
Alehouses, 174.
All Saints (parish and church), 133.
All Souls' College, 456.
Almanacs (City), 391.
   ,,   (Univ), 971.
Almshouses, 173.
Amusements (City), 353.
   ,,   (Univ.), 857.
Anatomy, Lee's Reader in, 573.
   ,,   Professor of, 572.
Ancient Buildings (City), 24.
   ,,   (Univ.), 483.
Ancient History, Camden Professor of, 606.
   ,,   Reader in, 607.
Ancient Relics; insignia, plate, etc. (City), 392.
   ,,   ,,   (Univ.), 972.
Ancient Subjects of Study, 755.
Anglo-Saxon, Professor of, 596.
Animals, 112.
Answering under Bachelor, 708.

Anthropology, Reader in (Univ.), 576.
Antiquities (City), 38, 392.
   „   (Univ.), 95, 972.
Apodyterium, 429.
Appearance, general, of Oxford, 115.
Arabic, Laudian Professor of, 588.
   „   Lord Almoner's Professor of, 589.
Archæology, Professor of Classical, 611.
Archery (Univ.), 858.
Architecture (City), 116.
   „   (Univ.), 407.
Architypographus, 526.
Archives (City), 394.
   „   (College), 451.
   „   (Univ.), 973.
   „   „   see also *Keeper of the Archives*, 524.
Arithmetic, old study of, 762.
Arms, (City), 129.
   „ (Colleges), 455.
   „ (Univ.), 409.
Arnold Historical Essay (prize), 820.
Art, see *Fine Art*.
Artistic life (City), 347.
   „   (Univ.), 849.
Arts, Professors in (Univ.), 579.
   „ study of (Univ.), and artists, 727.
   „   „ , ancient, 755.
Arundel Marbles, 416.
Ashmolean Museum, 416.
Assay of weights and measures, 179.
Assize of bread and ale, 180.
Assizes, criminal, 273.
Astronomy, old study of, 764, cf. 105.
   „   Professor of, 561.
Asylums, 176.
Athletics (Univ.), 859.
Austin Canons, 663.
   „ friars, and house, 669.
Austins, 708.
B.A. degree, 753.

B.C.L. Degree, 783.
B.D.   „   789.
B.M.   „   786.
B. Mus. „   793.
Bachelors (Univ.), 618.
Bacon's study, 241.
Bailiffs, 285.
Balliol College, 457.
Balls, 871.
Bampton Lecturers, 547.
Banks, 164.
Baptists, 321.
Batels (college), 649.
Batellers, 645.
Beaumont (palace, etc.), 242.
Bedells and inferior officers (Univ.), 526.
Bell-ringing, (Univ.), 860.
Benedictines, 664.
Benefactors, see *Founders*, etc.
Benefices (College and Univ.), see *Endowments*.
Bicycling, etc. (Univ.), 861.
Bidding prayer, 836.
Billiards (Univ.), 862.
Binsey, 156.
Biographical collections (City), 389.
       „   „   (Univ.), 963.
Black friars, 673.
Black monks, 664.
Blue Coat Schools, 198.
Boards (Univ.), 504.
Boating (Univ.), 863.
Bocardo, 246.
Boden Sanskrit Scholarship, 801.
Bodleian Library, 417.
Books and reading (see *Libraries*), 842.
Botanical Garden, 423.
Botany, 111.
       „   Professor of (Univ.), 577.
Botley, 157.
Bounds (City), 123.

Bounds (Univ.), 404.
Boxing (Univ.), 864.
Brasenose College, 458.
Bridges, 218.
Broad Street, 221.
Buildings (Oxford in general), 116.
   ,,   public (City), 163.
   ,,   old City, 24.
   ,,   college, 447.
   ,,   public (Univ.), 407.
   ,,   old Univ., 483.
Burdett-Coutts Geological Scholarship, 808.
Burgesses (City), 281.
   ,,   (Univ.), 521.
Burials, 169.
Bursars (College), 635.
Cabs, 209.
Calendar (Univ.), 974.
Cambridge University, relative antiquity of, 952.
   ,,   ,,   relations of Oxford University to, 942.
Camden's Professor, 606.
Canals, 166.
Canditch, 266.
Canon Law, 779.
Canterbury College, 486.
Cardinal College, 459.
Cards (Univ.), 1865.
Carfax (parish and church), 143
   ,,   (quarter and conduit), 222.
Caricatures (City), 395.
   ,,   (Univ.), 975.
Carmelites (white friars) and house, 671.
Carriers, 209.
Carthusians, 665.
Castle (Oxford), 167.
   ,,   see also *St. George's College*, 494.
Cathedral, 154.
   ,,   see also *Christ Church*, 459.
   ,,   see also *St. Frideswide's*, 262.
   ,,   School, 199.

Catholics, see *Roman Catholics*.
Cells, 248.
Celtic, Professor of, 595.
Cemeteries, 168.
Census, 122.
Ceremonies, see *Public Ceremonies*.
Chancellor (Univ.), 514.
Chancellor's Court, 507.
    ,,   English Essay (prize), 815.
    ,,   Latin Essay (prize), 816.
    ,,   Latin Verse (prize), 814.
Chapels (College), 448.
    ,,   dissenting, 171.
Chaplain of the University, 327.
Chaplains (College), 638.
Character and Importance of Oxford (City), 124.
    ,,   ,,   (Univ.), 405.
Charters (as a MS. collection), (City), 394.
    ,,   ,,   (Univ.), 973.
    ,,   Royal (single) (City), 363.
    ,,   ,,   (Univ.), 928.
Chemistry, Professor of (Univ.), 566.
    ,,   Demonstrator in (Univ.), 567.
    ,,   Lee's Reader in (Univ.), 568.
Cherwell (river), 223.
Chess (Univ.), 867.
Chests (Univ.), 484.
Chichele Professor of Modern History, 609.
Chinese, Professor of, 591.
    ,,   Scholarships, 811.
Choirs (College), 639.
Cholera, 113.
Choragus, 613.
Christ Church, 459.
Church of England (City), 319.
    ,,   ,,   (Univ.), 683.
Church and Dissent (relations of City to), 366.
    ,,   ,,   (relations of Univ. to), 932.
Churches (City), 132.
Cistercians, 666.

Cities (relations of Oxford to other), 371.
Citizens, lists of, 122.
City, 121–399.
„ (relations of Univ. to the), 938.
Civil Law, Professor of, 549.
„ study of, 781.
Civil War (City), 384.
„ (Univ.), 956.
Clarendon Building, 424.
„ Laboratory, 433.
„ Press, 425.
Classes of the Community (City), 300.
„ Members (Univ.), 530.
Classical Archæology, Professor of, 611.
„ Honours (Moderations), 734.
Classics, higher study of, 580.
Clergy, secular, 678.
Clerks (clerici), 620.
„ of the Market, 181.
Clubs and Societies, Artistic (City), 351.
„ „ „ (Univ.), 854.
„ „ Commercial (City), 342.
„ „ Intellectual and Literary (City), 338.
„ „ „ „ (Univ.), 843.
„ „ Political (City), 344.
„ „ „ (Univ.), 846.
„ „ Religious (City), 336.
„ „ „ (Univ.), 839.
„ „ Scientific (City), 345.
„ „ „ (Univ.), 848.
„ „ Social (City), 355.
„ „ „ (Univ.), 896.
Cluniacs, 667.
Coaching, 211.
Cobden Prize, 828.
Coffee-houses, 243.
Coins, see *Ashmolean* (416), *Bodleian* (417), *Mint* (187), *Ancient relics*, 392 and 972, etc.
Collections (College), 650.
„ (Univ.), 708.

College exercises, 650.
,, expenses, 648.
,, morals and discipline, 651.
,, officers and government, 631.
,, penalties, 652.
,, servants, 647.
Colleges, etc., relations of Univ. to, 948.
,, and Halls, members of, 630.
,, ,, old, 485.
Collegiate Institutions and Buildings, 441.
Colonies, relations of the Univ. to, 912.
Comedies, see *Literary pieces*.
Commemoration or Act (Univ.), 439.
Commercial Character (City), 126.
,, Life (City), 339.
Commissary, 516.
Commissions appointed by the University, 504.
,, , relations of Univ. to Parliamentary, 934.
Common People (City), 308.
,, Rooms (College), 449.
Commoners, 644.
Commons (College), 649.
Comparative Philology, Professor of, 602.
Condemnations, 506.
Congregation (Univ.), 503.
,, house of, 429.
,, old house of, 430.
Congregationalists, 322.
Conington Prize, 827.
Conversorum Domus, 244.
Convocation (Univ.), 502.
,, house of, 429.
Copyright privileges of the Bodleian, 418.
Corn Exchange, 207.
Cornmarket Street, 224.
Coronation Service of the Mayor, 365.
Coroners' Inquests, 273.
Corpus Christi College, 460.
Coryphæus, 613.
Costume, academical, 902.

Council (Hebdomadal), 591.
   ,,   (Town), 271.
Councils (Ecclesiastical) at Oxford, 367.
Country at large, relations of City to, 361.
   ,,   ,,   relations of Univ. to, 918.
Course of studies (Univ.), general conditions, 701.
Coursing, 868.
Cowley St. John's, 158.
Craven Scholarships and Fellowships, 796.
Cricket (Univ.), 869.
Criminals (City), 276.
Croquet, 870.
Crossed or Crutched Friars, and House, 672.
Crown, relations of City to the, 362.
   ,,   relations of Univ. to the, 925.
D.C.L. Degree, 784.
   ,,   Hon. Degree, 713.
D.D.   ,,   791.
   ,,   Hon. Degree, 713.
D.M.   ,,   787.
D. Mus.   ,,   , 724.
Dancing, 871.
Dantesburne Church, 245.
Davis Chinese Scholarship, 811.
Debts (members of Univ.), 907.
Declamations, 708.
Declarations and Oaths (Univ.), 706.
Decrees (Univ.), 505.
Degrees in general (Univ.), 712.
   ,,   terms connected with the taking of, 714.
Delegacies and Boards in general (Univ.), 504.
Denyer and Johnson Theological Scholarship, 805.
Deputy Professors, 534.
Derby Scholarship, 810.
Descriptions, general, of Oxford (guides), 115.
Determining, 716.
Diet (members of Univ.), 903.
Dinners, 872.
Discipline (City), 332.
   ,,   (College), 651.

Discipline (Univ.), 833.
Diseases, etc., 113.
Dispensation, 715.
Disputations, 708.
Dissent, relations of city to, 366.
„ (Univ.), 932.
Dissenters (City), 320.
„ (Univ.), 684.
Dissenting Chapels, 171.
Divinity, Margaret Professor of, 537.
„ Regius Professor of, 536.
„ School, 431.
Doctors and Masters (Graduates), 617.
Documents, Records, and Miscellanea (City), 390.
„ „ „ (Univ.), 970.
Domesday Survey and Hundred Rolls, 128.
Dominicans (Black, Preaching Friars), and house, 673.
Drainage, 114.
Dramatic Life, etc. (City), 349.
„ (Univ.), 852-3.
Drawing Master, (Univ.), 616.
Drawings of Oxford, 115.
Dress (City), 358.
„ (Univ.), 901.
„ „ (academical costume), 902.
Drinking (Univ.), 904.
Driving, 887.
Durham College, 487.
Earth (geology), 106.
East Bridge, 228.
Ecclesiastical History, Professor of, 541.
Eldon Law Scholarship, 800.
Elections (City), poll-books, etc., 282.
„ (Univ.), „ 522.
„ „ to offices, 528.
Ellerton Theological Essay (prize), 818.
Encaenia, 439.
Endowments and Estates (City), 164.
„ „ (Collegiate), 440.
„ „ (Univ.), 414.

English Essay (prize), 815.
,, language and literature, Professor of, 597.
,, Law, Professor of (Vinerian), 552.
,, Sacred Poem (prize), 819.
English, Scotch, or Irish Universities, relations of Univ. to, 941.
Essays, see *Literary pieces*, 978.
Estates (City), 164.
,, (College), 440.
,, (Univ.), 414.
Etiquette (Univ.), 856.
Examination in lieu of Responsions, 729.
Examinations in general (Univ.), 711.
Exegesis, Theological Professor of, 542.
Exeter College, 461.
Exhibitioners (College), 643.
Exhibitions (Univ.), 812.
Expenses (College), 648.
,, (Univ.), 832.
Experimental Philosophy, Professor of, 564.
External Appearance (City), 115.
,, ,, (Univ.), 406.
,, Relations (City), 360.
,, ,, (Univ.), 910.
Facetiae (City), caricatures, etc., 395.
,, (Univ.), ,, 975.
Fairs, 341.
Famines (City), 387.
,, (Univ.), 961.
Feasting, 872.
Fees (Univ.), 333.
Fellow-Commoners, 641.
Fellows of Colleges, 634.
Fencing (Univ.), 873.
Final Schools (Univ.), 738.
Finance (City), 232.
,, (Univ.), 333.
Fine Art, Professor of, 615.
Fires (City), 387.
,, (Univ.) 961.
Fireworks, see *Rejoicings*, public.

Fishing (Univ.), 874.
Fives (Univ.), 875.
Floods, 108.
Flys, 209.
Folly Bridge, 225.
   ,,   see also *Bacon's Study*, 241.
Football (Univ.), 876.
Foreign Lands, relations of Univ. to, 912.
   ,,   Universities, relations of Univ. to, 943.
Foreigners in Oxford, 917.
Forestallers, 182.
Founders and Benefactors (City), 164.
   ,,   ,,   (Colleges), 445.
   ,,   ,,   (Univ.), 413.
   ,,   ,,   see also *University Services*.
Franciscans (Grey Friars, Minorites), and house, 674.
Freemasons (City), 356.
   ,,   (Univ.), 897.
Freemen (City), 307.
French Teacher (Univ.), 599.
Freshmen, 624.
Friars, 668.
Funerals (City and Univ.), 169.
Gaisford Greek Prose (prize), 823.
   ,,   ,,   Verse   ,,   822.
Gambling, 877.
Games, Puzzles, etc. (see also *Cards, Chess*), 878.
Gardens (College), 452.
Gates of the City, 246.
Gazette (Univ.), 977.
Generals, 708.
Gentry (City), 302.
Geography, Reader in, 570.
Geology of Oxford, 106.
   ,,   Professor of, 571.
Geometry, old study of, 763.
   ,,   Professor of, 359.
German Teacher (Univ.), 598.
Gloucester College, 488.
Godstow (Benedictine Nunnery), 247.

Government (City), 270.
    ,,   (College), 631.
    ,,   (Univ.), 500.
Graces, 717.
Graduates (Univ.), 531.
Grammar, old study, 757.
Grandpont, 225.
Great Go, 738.
Greek Church, 686.
    ,, Professor of, 581.
    ,, Reader in, (Univ.), 582.
    ,, old study of, 766.
    ,, study of, 583.
Green Moral Philosophy Prize, 830.
Grey Friars, 674.
Grinfield Lecturer in the Septuagint, 544.
Group A, Pass, Final Schools (Univ.), 749.
    ,, B, ,,   ,, 750.
    ,, C, ,,   ,, 751.
    ,, D, ,,   ,, 752.
Guides to Oxford, 115.
Gymnastics (Univ.), 879.
Hall and Hall-Houghton Prize (Univ.), 825.
Halls (Univ.), 477.
    ,, (pre-Laudian), 496.
    ,, (private), 482.
    ,, members of, 630.
    ,, Ladies', 175.
    ,, and Offices (College), 450.
Hart Hall, 489.
Heads of Houses (Colleges), 633.
Health, Diseases, etc., 113.
Hebdomadal Board and Council (Univ.), 501.
Hebrew, old study of, 767.
    ,, Regius Professor of, 538.
Hermitages, 248.
Hertford College (new foundation), 464.
    ,,   ,, (old foundation), 491.
    ,, Scholarship, 806.
High School for Boys, 201.

High School for Girls, 202.
High Steward (Univ.), 515.
High Street, 226.
Hincksey, New, 161.
Hindustani Teacher (Univ.), 592.
History, old study of, 773.
History, see *Ancient H., Ecclesiastical H., Indian H., Modern H.*
Hithe Bridge, 227.
Hockey, 880.
Holy Trinity (parish and church), 134.
Holywell (parish and church), 135.
  „   Music Room, 188.
Honorary Degrees, 713.
Honours (Moderations), 733.
  „   (Final Schools), 739.
Honours' Register, Ten Year Book (Univ.), 976.
Horse-racing (Univ.), 881.
Hospitallers, 678.
Hospitals, 172.
  „   old, 249.
Hotels, 174.
Houses, old private (City), 253.
Hundred Rolls (c. 1279), 128.
Hunting, 882.
Illuminations, see *Rejoicings*, public.
In Parviso Disputations, 708.
Inception, 721.
Incidents, in chronological order (City history), 387.
  „   „   (Univ. history), 961.
Incorporation and Constitution (Univ.), 500.
Incorporation from other Universities, 944.
Indian History (Reader), 610.
  „   Institute, 432.
  „   Law, (Reader), 555.
Indulgences, 915.
Inferior Officers (Univ.), 526.
Inns, 174.
Inquests, 273.
Inscriptions, 416.
Insignia (City and Univ.), see *Ancient relics.*

Installation of Chancellor, 514.
Institutions, collegiate, 441.
„   City, 163.
„   old (City), 240.
„   „ (Univ.), 483.
„   Univ., 411.
Intellectual and Literary Life (City), 337.
„   „   (Univ.), 840.
International Law, Professor of, 553.
Interpretation, Theological Professor of, 543.
Inventories, 509.
Ireland Scholarship, 799.
Irish Universities, 941.
Isis, river, 233.
Italian Teacher (Univ.), 600.
Jesuits, 681.
Jesus College, 463.
Jewry, the (City), 326.
Jews (City), 326.
„ (Univ.), 687.
Johnson Essay (prize), 824.
Junior Men (Univ.), 624.
Juraments, 708.
Jurisprudence, Professor of, 554.
Justices, 278.
Keble College, 464.
Keeper of the Archives (Univ.), 524.
Kennicott Hebrew Scholarship, 803.
Laboratories, 433.
Labour, 309.
Ladies' Halls (Lady Margaret's, etc.), 175.
Lanes, old, 254.
Language, University slang, 905.
Latin, Professor of, 584.
„   Reader in (Univ.), 585.
„   study of, 586.
„   Essay (prize), 816.
„   Verse (prize), 814.
Law, honours in, final schools, 742.
„   Professors of, 548.

Law study of, for degree (Univ.), 778.
  „ Courts (City), 273.
  „   „   (Univ.), 507.
Lawn Tennis (Univ.), 883.
Learning, state of (Univ.), 840.
Lecturers (College), 637.
  „   (Univ.), 532.
Lectures (College), 650.
  „   (Univ.), 708.
Lee's Reader in Anatomy, 573.
Legendary History (Univ.), 951.
Lent Disputations, 708.
Letters, see also *Royal Letters*.
  „   official (City), 272.
  „   „   (Univ.), 506.
Libraries, see *Bodleian* (417), *Museum* (433).
  „   old, 422.
  „   (College), 451.
Licenses, formal, 506.
Lieu of Responsions (Examination), 729.
Life and Manners (City), 330.
  „   „   (Univ.), 830.
Lincoln College, 465.
Literae Humaniores, final school, 740.
Literary Life, see *Intellectual and Literary Life*.
Literary Pieces (City), 396.
  „   (Univ.), 978.
Little Go, 728.
Livings (College and Univ.), see *Endowments*.
Local Board, 274.
  „ Divisions (City), 13.
  „   „   (Univ.), 41.
  „ Examinations (Univ.), 919.
Logic, old study of, 758.
  „ Professor of, 605.
Lollards, 688.
Lothian Historical Essay (prize), 826.
Lunatic Asylums, 176.
M.A. Degree, 754.
M.B.   „   786.

M.D. Degree, 787.
Magdalen Bridge, 228.
   ,,   College, 466.
   ,,   Hall, 492.
   ,,   School, 203.
Mandamuses (royal), see *Royal Letters*.
Manners, life and, see *Life*.
Mansfield College, 177.
Manufacturers, 304.
Manuscript Collections, see *Archives*.
Marbles, Arundel, 416.
Market, 178.
   ,,   clerks of, 181.
   ,,   supervisors of, 184.
Martyrs' Memorial, 185.
Mass, 838.
Masters (graduates), 617.
Mathematical Scholarship (Univ.), 802.
Mathematics, honours in (final schools), 741.
   ,,   ,,   (moderations), 735.
   ,,   study of, 562.
Mathurines (Trinitarians) and Trinity House, 675.
Matriculation, 703.
Mayor, 284.
Meadows, 231.
Medicine, Lichfield Lecturers in, 558.
   ,,   Regius Professor of, 557.
   ,,   study of, for degree, 785.
Medley, 159.
Members of Colleges and Halls, 630.
Merton College, 467.
Metaphysical Philosophy, old study of, 771.
   ,,   ,,   Waynflete Professor of, 604.
Meteorology, 105.
Methodists, 323.
Migration of the University, 922.
Military Character of Oxford, 125.
   ,,   Orders (Templars, Hospitallers, etc.), 688.
Mills, 186.
Mineralogy, Professor of, 569.

Minorites, 674.
Mint (tokens and coins), 187.
Missions (City), 335.
   „   (Univ.), 838.
Moderations (Univ. studies), 732.
Modern History, honours in, final schools, 743.
   „   „   Chichele Professor of, 609.
   „   „   Regius Professor of, 608.
   „   Languages and Literature, final school, 744.
Monasteries, 240.
Monks, 662.
Moral and Metaphysical Philosophy, Waynflete Professor of, 604.
Moral Philosophy, old study of, 769.
   „   „   Green Prize, 830.
   „   „   Whyte Professor of, 603.
Morals and Discipline (City), 332.
   „   „   (College), 651.
   „   „   (Univ.), 833.
Motto (City), 129.
   „   (Colleges), 455.
   „   (Univ.), 409.
Mus. Bac. Degree, 793.
Mus. Doc. Degree, 794.
Museum, Laboratories, and Radcliffe Library (Univ.), 433.
Music (City), 348.
   „   (Univ.), 850-1.
   „   (Univ. Study), 792.
   „   (Prof., Choragus and Coryphæus), 613.
Music Room (Holywell), 188.
Mythical History (Univ.), 951.
Name (Oxford), 102.
   „   (Univ.), 402.
Nations, 653.
Natural History, 103.
Natural Philosophy, old study of, 772.
   „   „   Professor of, 563.
Natural Science, Final Schools, 745.
   „   „ (including Medicine and Mathematics), Professors of, 556.
Navigation of Thames, 233.
Neighbourhood (Relations of City to the), 370.

Neighbourhood (Relations of Univ. to the), 937.
New College, 468.
„   School, 204.
New Hincksey, 161.
New Inn Hall, 478.
Newdigate English Verse (prize), 817.
Newspapers (City), 398.
„   (Univ.), 979.
Nixon's School, 205.
Nobility (City), 301.
„   (Univ.), 625.
Non-Collegiate Students, 622.
Non-conformists, see *Dissenters*.
North and South (old disputes), 845.
Novels, see *Literary Pieces*.
Numbers (City), 122.
„   (Univ.), 403.
Nuns, 679.
Oaths (Univ.), 706.
Observatory (Radcliffe), 193.
„   (Univ.), 435.
Officers (City), 28.
„   (Univ.), 513.
Official Literary Pieces (Univ.), 931.
Old Institutions, Buildings, etc. (City), 24.
„   „   (Univ.), 483.
Old Private Houses (City), 253.
Opponency, 708.
Oriel College, 469.
Oriental Studies (in early times), 774.
„   „   , final school, 746.
„   „   , higher, 590.
Oseney Abbey, 255.
Oseney Town, 162.
Oxford, *passim*.
Oxford Historical Society, 118.
Parishes, 131.
Park (University), 436.
Park Town, 229.
Parliament at Oxford, 369.

Parliament (External Relations of City to [including Acts of Parliament]), 368.
„ (External Relations of Univ. to), 933.
„ „ „ Acts of Parliament, 936.
„ (Members of), see *Burgesses*.
Parviso, Disputations in, 708.
Pass (Moderations), 736.
„ (Final Schools), 748.
Pastoral Theology, Professor of, 539.
Pauperism, 311.
Pembroke College, 470.
Penalties (College), 652.
„ (Univ.), 834.
Penance, Friars of, 676.
Penniless Bench, 222.
Periodicals (City), 398.
„ (Univ.), 979.
Persian Teacher (Univ.), 592.
Personal History (City, in order of names, 388.
„ (Univ.) „ 962.
Personal Life (City), 357.
„ (Univ.), 90.
Pestilence, 113.
Petitions, see *Proclamations*, etc. (City and Univ.)
Philology, Professor of Comparative, 602.
Philosophy, old study of, 768.
„ see *Metaphysical Philosophy, Moral Philosophy, Natural Philosophy*.
Physic Garden, 423.
Physics (Lee's Reader), 565.
Physiology, Professor of (Univ.), 574.
Picture Gallery (Bodleian), 419.
Pictures, 442.
„ of Oxford, 115.
Pigeon Shooting (Univ.), 890.
Pigmarket, 421.
Plagues, 113.
Plans of Oxford, 115.
Plants, 111.
Plate (City), 392.

Plate (College), 454.
„ (Univ.), 972.
Play-acting, see *Dramatic Life*.
Plays, see *Literary Pieces*.
Pledges, 484.
Poems, see *Literary Pieces*.
Poetry, Professor of (Univ.), 614.
Police (City), 275.
„ (Univ.), 511.
Political Economy, Professor of, 612.
Political Life (City), 343.
„ (Univ.), 844.
Poll-books, see *Elections*.
Polo (Univ.), 884.
Poor, 311.
Pope (Relations of Univ. to the), 914.
Population (City), 122,
„ (Univ.), 403.
Port Meadow, 231.
Position of Oxford, 104.
Post Office, 189.
Preaching (Univ.), 836.
Preaching Friars, 673.
Preliminaries to Residence, 702.
Presentation to a Degree, 718.
Press, Clarendon, 425.
Presses, old University, 426.
Printing in Oxford (Univ.), 427.
Prisons, 191.
Private Halls, 482.
Private Tutors (Univ.), 619.
Privileged Persons (Univ.), 654.
Privileges (Univ.), 508.
Prizes (College), 650.
„ (Univ.), 813.
Procedure, Public (City), 279.
„ (Univ.), 512.
Proclamations, etc. (City), 272.
„ (Univ.), 506.
Proctors (Univ.), 518.

Professional Men (City), 303.
Professors (Univ.), 532.
Pro-Proctors, 519.
Proscholium, 421.
Protestants (City), 318.
   „   (Univ.), 682.
Pro-Vice-chancellor, 517.
Public Ceremonies (City), 279.
   „   (Univ., see special heads).
Public Houses, 174.
Public Institutions and Buildings (City), 163.
   „   „   (Univ.), 411.
Public Officers and Offices (City), 280.
   „   „   (Univ.), 513.
Public Orator (Univ.), 523.
Puritans, 324.
Pusey and Ellerton Hebrew Scholarship, 804.
Pusey House, 192.
Quadragesimals, 708.
Quadrangles, 452.
Quadrivium, 761.
Quakers (City), 328.
Quarters of the City, 216.
Queen's College, 471.
Questionists, 731.
Quodlibeticae disputationes, 708.
Rabbinical Studies (Reader), 545.
Racquets (Univ.), 885.
Radcliffe Building, 420.
   „   Library, 433.
   „   Observatory, 193.
   „   Travelling Scholarship, 797.
Railways and Stations, 194.
Rates and Taxes, see *Finance*.
Ratting (Univ.), 886.
Readers (Univ.), 532.
Reading in general (Univ.), 841.
Records (City), 390.
   „   (College), 451.
   „   (Univ.), 970.

Regency, Regent Masters, 722.
Registrar (Univ.), 525.
Regius Professors, 533.
Regrators, 183.
Regulations (City), 272.
Rejoicings, Public (City), 387.
 ,, ,, (Univ.), 961.
Religious Life (City), 333.
  ,, (Univ.), 835.
Religious Orders (City), 315.
  ,, ,, (Univ.), 660.
Residence (Univ.), 704.
 ,, preliminaries to, 702.
Resort (City as a), 127.
Responsions (Univ. studies), 728.
  ,, (Examination in lieu of), 729.
Revenues (City), 289.
 ,, (College), 446.
 ,, (Univ.), 414.
Rewley Abbey, 256.
Rhetoric, old study of, 759.
Riding and Driving (Univ.), 887.
Rifle Corps, see *Volunteers*.
Riots (City), 387.
 ,, (Univ.), 961.
Rivers, 217.
Rolleston Prize (Univ.), 829.
Roman Catholic Churches, 195.
Roman Catholics (City and Univ.), 661.
Roman Law (Reader), 551.
Rooms (College), 453.
Rowing, 863.
Royal Charters, see *Charters*, Royal.
Royal Letters, Mandamuses, etc. (City), 362.
  ,,   ,, (Univ.), 929.
Royal Visits (City), 364.
  ,, (Univ.), 930.
Running, 859.
Rural Economy, Professor of, 578.
S.C.L. Degree, 782.

Sac or **Penance**, Friars of (and House), 676.
Sacred Poem (Prize), 819.
Sailing, 888.
St. **Alban Hall**, 479.
St. **Aldate** (parish and church), 136.
St. **Aloysius**, 195.
St. **Andrew** (parish and church), 257.
St. **Barnabas** (parish and church), 137.
St. **Bartholomew's Hospital**, 251.
St. **Benedict** (parish and church), 258.
St. **Bernard's College**, 493.
St. **Budoc** (parish and church), 259.
St. **Clement** (parish and church), 138.
St. **Cross**, 135.
St. **Ebbe** (parish and church), 139.
St. **Edmund Hall**, 480.
St. **Edward** (parish and church), 261.
St. **Frideswide** (Nuns, sec. can., Austin can.), 262.
    ,,   see also the *Cathedral*, 154.
St. **George's College in the Castle**, etc., 491.
    ,,   see also the *Castle*, 167.
St. **Giles** (parish and church), 141.
St. **Giles' Street**, 232.
St. **John Baptist** (parish), 142.
    ,,   (church, see *Merton College*, 467.)
St. **John's College**, 472.
    ,,   Hospital, 252.
St. **Martin** (Carfax) (parish and church), 143.
St. **Mary Hall**, 481.
St. **Mary Magdalen** (parish and church), 144.
St. **Mary the Virgin** (parish and church), 145.
St. **Mary's College**, 495.
St. **Michael** (parish and church), 147.
St. **Michael at South Gate** (church), 263.
St. **Mildred** (parish and church), 264.
St. **Nicholas** (church), 255.
St. **Paul** (parish and church), 148.
St. **Peter le Bailey** (parish and church), 149.
St. **Peter in the East** (parish and church), 151.
St. **Philip and St. James** (parish and church), 152.

St. Scholastica's Day, A.D. 1355, 938.
St. Stephen's House, 196.
St. Thomas (parish and church), 153.
Sanskrit, Professor of, 587.
Sanskrit Scholarship, 801.
Savilian Foundation, 559.
Scholars of Colleges, 642.
Scholars (=students), 62.
Scholarships (Univ.), 795.
School Board, 277.
Schools (City), 197.
Schools (relations of Univ. to), 946.
  ,, New Examination (Univ.), 437.
  ,, Old, 498.
Schools Quadrangle, 421.
Scientific Life (City), 345.
  ,, (Univ.), 847.
Scotch Universities, 941.
Secular Canons, 677.
Clergy, 678.
Select Preachers (Univ.), 546.
Senior Men (Undergraduate), 623.
Septuagint (Grinfield Lecturer), 544.
Sermons (City), 334.
  ,, (Univ.), 836.
Servants (College), 647.
Services, University, 836.
Servitors (College), 646.
Sessions, 273.
Sheldonian Theatre, 438.
Shooting, 889.
Site of Oxford, 104.
Size and bounds (City), 123.
  ,, (Univ.), 404.
Skating, 891.
Sky, 105.
Slang (Univ.), 905.
Smalls, 728.
Smoking (Univ.), 906.
Social Life (City), 352.

Social Life (Univ.), 855.
Socialists (City), 329.
  „ (Univ.), 689.
Societies, see *Clubs and Societies*.
Somerville Hall, 175.
Songs, see *Literary Pieces*.
Sophists, 737.
South, see *North and South*.
Spanish Teacher (Univ.), 601.
Special Studies (Univ.), 726.
Speeches, see *Literary Pieces*.
Stanhope Historical Essay (prize), 821.
Stationers' Company, Relation of, to Bodleian, 418.
  „ „ Clarendon Press, 428.
Stations, 194.
Statutes and Decrees in general (Univ.), 505.
Streets, 215.
  „ old, 265.
Students (Scholares), 62.
Studies, see *Course of Studies* and *Special Studies*.
Study, Ancient Subjects of, 755.
Subscription to the XXXIX Articles, 707.
Suburbs, 155.
Supervisors of the Market, 184.
Surgery, 785.
Swimming (Univ.), 892.
Tales, see *Literary Pieces*.
Taverns, 174.
Taxes, see *Finance*.
Taylor Institution, 440.
Taylor Scholarships, 807.
Teachers (Univ.), 532.
Teas, 872.
Telugu Teacher (Univ.), 594.
Templars, 688.
Tennis (Univ.), 893.
Ten Year Book, 976.
Terms and Vacations, 705.
Terrae filius, 626.
Testimonial Letters, formal, 506.

Tests, Religious, 707.
Thames, or Isis, River, 233.
Theatres, 206.
Theatricals, see *Dramatic Life*.
Theology, honours in, final schools, 747.
,, Professor of, 535.
,, study of, for degree, 788.
Thrift, 312.
Tokens, 187.
Tolls, 232.
Topography, minute, see *Local Divisions*.
Town-Clerk, 288.
Town Council, 271.
Town Councillors, 287.
Town and Gown, 938.
Town Hall, 207.
Trade Guilds (City), 306.
Tradesmen, 305.
Tragedies, see *Literary Pieces*.
Tramways, 208.
Trials (City), 273.
,, (Univ.), 507.
Trinitarians, 675.
Trinity (parish and church), 134.
Trinity College, 473.
Trinity House, 675.
Trivium, 756.
Turl Street, 234.
Tutors (College), 636.
,, (Private), 619.
Unattached Students, 622.
Undergraduate Members (Students, Scholars, Clerks of the Univ.), 62.
Undergraduates (College), 640.
Union (workhouse), 213.
Union Society, 898.
Universities, other than Oxford, 939.
,, (Relations of Oxford Univ. to other), 939.
University of Oxford, 401-999.
,, Chest, 415.

University Church (St. Mary's), 146.
, Exhibitions, 812.
, Galleries, 441.
, Press, 425.
, Prizes, 813.
, Scholarships, 795.
, Sermons and Preaching, 836.
, Services, 836-7.
, Slang, 905.
, Studies, general conditions of course, 701.
, Relations of City to, 938.
University College, 474.
Vacations, 705.
Vehicles, 209.
Vesperies, 719.
Vice-Chancellor (Univ.), 516.
Views of Oxford, 115.
Vinerian Law Professor, 552.
, Scholarship, 798.
Visitations, Parliamentary, 934.
, Royal, 927.
, Heraldic (City), 302.
Visitors (Colleges), 632.
Volunteers (City), 212.
, (Univ.), 894.
Wadham College, 475.
Walking (Univ.), 895.
Walks, 219.
Walls of the City, 266.
Walton Manor, 235.
Wards, 216.
Water, 107.
Water-supply, 109.
Waynflete Professors, see *Moral ... Philosophy* and *Physiology*.
Weather, 105.
Welsh Universities, 941.
Wesleyans, 323.
Whist (Univ.), 866.
White Friars, 671.
Whyte's Professor of Moral Philosophy, 603.

Wills, etc., in Chancellor's Court, 509.
Wines, 872.
Women, Education of, 947.
Worcester College, 476.
Workhouse, 213.
Wrestling, 864.
Wycliffe Hall, 214.
Zoology, Professor of (Univ.), 575.
Zoology of Oxford, 112.

July, 1887.

Clarendon Press, Oxford

A SELECTION OF

BOOKS

PUBLISHED FOR THE UNIVERSITY BY

HENRY FROWDE,

AT THE OXFORD UNIVERSITY PRESS WAREHOUSE,

AMEN CORNER, LONDON.

ALSO TO BE HAD AT THE

CLARENDON PRESS DEPOSITORY, OXFORD.

[*Every book is bound in cloth, unless otherwise described.*]

LEXICONS, GRAMMARS, ORIENTAL WORKS, &c.

ANGLO-SAXON.—*An Anglo-Saxon Dictionary*, based on the MS. Collections of the late Joseph Bosworth, D.D., Professor of Anglo-Saxon, Oxford. Edited and enlarged by Prof. T. N. Toller, M.A. (To be completed in four parts.) Parts I and II. A—HWISTLIAN. 4to. 15*s*. each.

CHINESE.—*A Handbook of the Chinese Language.* By James Summers. 1863. 8vo. half bound, 1*l*. 8*s*.

—— *A Record of Buddhistic Kingdoms*, by the Chinese Monk FÂ-HIEN. Translated and annotated by James Legge, M.A., LL.D. Crown 4to. cloth back, 10*s*. 6*d*.

ENGLISH.—*A New English Dictionary, on Historical Principles:* founded mainly on the materials collected by the Philological Society. Edited by James A. H. Murray, LL.D., with the assistance of many Scholars and men of Science. Part I. A—ANT. Part II. ANT—BATTEN. Part III. BATTER—BOZ. Imperial 4to. 12*s*. 6*d*. each.

—— *An Etymological Dictionary of the English Language.* By W. W. Skeat, Litt.D. *Second Edition*. 1884. 4to. 2*l*. 4*s*.

——Supplement to the First Edition of the above. 4to. 2*s*. 6*d*.

—— *A Concise Etymological Dictionary of the English Language*. By W. W. Skeat, Litt.D. *Second Edition*. 1885. Crown 8vo. 5*s*. 6*d*.

GREEK.—*A Greek-English Lexicon*, by Henry George Liddell, D.D., and Robert Scott, D.D. Seventh Edition, Revised and Augmented throughout. 1883. 4to. 1*l*. 16*s*.

—— *A Greek-English Lexicon*, abridged from Liddell and Scott's 4to. edition, chiefly for the use of Schools. Twenty-first Edition. 1884. Square 12mo. 7*s*. 6*d*.

—— *A copious Greek-English Vocabulary*, compiled from the best authorities. 1850. 24mo. 3*s*.

—— *A Practical Introduction to Greek Accentuation*, by H. W. Chandler, M.A. Second Edition. 1881. 8vo. 10*s*. 6*d*.

HEBREW.—*The Book of Hebrew Roots*, by Abu 'l-Walîd Marwân ibn Janâh, otherwise called Rabbî Yônâh. Now first edited, with an Appendix, by Ad. Neubauer. 1875. 4to. 2*l*. 7*s*. 6*d*.

—— *A Treatise on the use of the Tenses in Hebrew*. By S. R. Driver, D.D. Second Edition. 1881. Extra fcap. 8vo. 7*s*. 6*d*.

—— *Hebrew Accentuation of Psalms, Proverbs, and Job*. By William Wickes, D.D. 1881. Demy 8vo. stiff covers, 5*s*.

—— *A Treatise on the Accentuation of the twenty-one so-called Prose Books of the Old Testament*. By William Wickes, D.D. 1887. Demy 8vo. 10*s*. 6*d*.

ICELANDIC.—*An Icelandic-English Dictionary*, based on the MS. collections of the late Richard Cleasby. Enlarged and completed by G. Vigfússon, M.A. With an Introduction, and Life of Richard Cleasby, by G. Webbe Dasent, D.C.L. 1874. 4to. 3*l*. 7*s*.

—— *A List of English Words the Etymology of which is illustrated by comparison with Icelandic*. Prepared in the form of an APPENDIX to the above. By W. W. Skeat, Litt.D. 1876. stitched, 2*s*.

—— *An Icelandic Primer*, with Grammar, Notes, and Glossary. By Henry Sweet, M.A. Extra fcap. 8vo. 3*s*. 6*d*.

—— *An Icelandic Prose Reader*, with Notes, Grammar and Glossary, by Dr. Gudbrand Vigfússon and F. York Powell, M.A. 1879. Extra fcap. 8vo. 10*s*. 6*d*.

LATIN.—*A Latin Dictionary*, founded on Andrews' edition of Freund's Latin Dictionary, revised, enlarged, and in great part rewritten by Charlton T. Lewis, Ph.D., and Charles Short, LL.D. 1879. 4to. 1*l*. 5*s*.

MELANESIAN.—*The Melanesian Languages*. By R. H. Codrington, D.D., of the Melanesian Mission. 8vo. 18*s*.

SANSKRIT.—*A Practical Grammar of the Sanskrit Language*, arranged with reference to the Classical Languages of Europe, for the use of English Students, by Sir M. Monier-Williams, M.A. Fourth Edition. 8vo. 15*s*.

—— *A Sanskrit-English Dictionary*, Etymologically and Philologically arranged, with special reference to Greek, Latin, German, Anglo-Saxon, English, and other cognate Indo-European Languages. By Sir M. Monier-Williams, M.A. 1872. 4to. 4*l*. 14*s*. 6*d*.

SANSKRIT.—*Nalopákhyánam.* Story of Nala, an Episode of the Mahá-Bhárata: the Sanskrit text, with a copious Vocabulary, and an improved version of Dean Milman's Translation, by Sir M. Monier-Williams, M.A. Second Edition, Revised and Improved. 1879. 8vo. 15*s.*

—— *Sakuntalā.* A Sanskrit Drama, in Seven Acts. Edited by Sir M. Monier-Williams, M.A. Second Edition, 1876. 8vo. 21*s.*

SYRIAC.—*Thesaurus Syriacus:* collegerunt Quatremère, Bernstein, Lorsbach, Arnoldi, Agrell, Field, Roediger: edidit R. Payne Smith, S.T.P. Fasc. I-VI. 1868-83. sm. fol. each, 1*l.* 1*s.* Fasc. VII. 1*l.* 11*s.* 6*d.* Vol. I, containing Fasc. I-V, sm. fol. 5*l.* 5*s.*

—— *The Book of Kalīlah and Dimnah.* Translated from Arabic into Syriac. Edited by W. Wright, LL.D. 1884. 8vo. 21*s.*

GREEK CLASSICS, &c.

Aristophanes: A Complete Concordance to the Comedies and Fragments. By Henry Dunbar, M.D. 4to. 1*l.* 1*s.*

Aristotle: The Politics, with Introduction, Notes, etc., by W. L. Newman, M.A., Fellow of Balliol College, Oxford. Vols. I. and II. *Nearly ready.*

Aristotle: The Politics, translated into English, with Introduction, Marginal Analysis, Notes, and Indices, by B. Jowett, M.A. Medium 8vo. 2 vols. 21*s.*

Catalogus Codicum Graecorum Sinaiticorum. Scripsit V. Gardthausen Lipsiensis. With six pages of Facsimiles. 8vo. *linen,* 25*s.*

Heracliti Ephesii Reliquiae. Recensuit I. Bywater, M.A. Appendicis loco additae sunt Diogenis Laertii Vita Heracliti, Particulae Hippocratei De Diaeta Libri Primi, Epistolae Heracliteae. 1877. 8vo. 6*s.*

Herculanensium Voluminum Partes II. 1824. 8vo. 10*s.*

Fragmenta Herculanensia. A Descriptive Catalogue of the Oxford copies of the Herculanean Rolls, together with the texts of several papyri, accompanied by facsimiles. Edited by Walter Scott, M.A., Fellow of Merton College, Oxford. Royal 8vo. *cloth,* 21*s.*

Homer: A Complete Concordance to the Odyssey and Hymns of Homer; to which is added a Concordance to the Parallel Passages in the Iliad, Odyssey, and Hymns. By Henry Dunbar, M.D. 1880. 4to. 1*l.* 1*s.*

—— *Scholia Graeca in Iliadem.* Edited by Professor W. Dindorf, after a new collation of the Venetian MSS. by D. B. Monro, M.A., Provost of Oriel College. 4 vols. 8vo. 2*l.* 10*s.* Vols. V and VI. *In the Press.*

—— *Scholia Graeca in Odysseam.* Edidit Guil. Dindorfius. Tomi II. 1855. 8vo. 15*s.* 6*d.*

Plato : Apology, with a revised Text and English Notes, and a Digest of Platonic Idioms, by James Riddell, M.A. 1878. 8vo. 8s. 6d.

—— *Philebus*, with a revised Text and English Notes, by Edward Poste, M.A. 1860. 8vo. 7s. 6d.

—— *Sophistes and Politicus*, with a revised Text and English Notes, by L. Campbell, M.A. 1867. 8vo. 18s.

—— *Theaetetus*, with a revised Text and English Notes. by L. Campbell, M.A. Second Edition. 8vo. 10s. 6d.

—— *The Dialogues*, translated into English, with Analyses and Introductions, by B. Jowett, M.A. A new Edition in 5 volumes, medium 8vo. 1875. 3l. 10s.

—— *The Republic*, translated into English, with an Analysis and Introduction, by B. Jowett, M.A. Medium 8vo. 12s. 6d.

Thucydides: Translated into English, with Introduction, Marginal Analysis, Notes, and Indices. By B. Jowett, M.A. 2 vols. 1881. Medium 8vo. 1l. 12s.

THE HOLY SCRIPTURES, &c.

STUDIA BIBLICA.—Essays in Biblical Archæology and Criticism, and kindred subjects. By Members of the University of Oxford. 8vo. 10s. 6d.

ENGLISH.—*The Holy Bible in the earliest English Versions*, made from the Latin Vulgate by John Wycliffe and his followers: edited by the Rev. J. Forshall and Sir F. Madden. 4 vols. 1850. Royal 4to. 3l. 3s.

[Also reprinted from the above, with Introduction and Glossary by W. W. Skeat, M.A.

—— *The Books of Job, Psalms, Proverbs, Ecclesiastes, and the Song of Solomon:* according to the Wycliffite Version made by Nicholas de Hereford, about A.D. 1381, and Revised by John Purvey, about A.D. 1388. Extra fcap. 8vo. 3s. 6d.

—— *The New Testament in English*, according to the Version by John Wycliffe, about A.D. 1380, and Revised by John Purvey, about A.D. 1388. Extra fcap. 8vo. 6s.]

ENGLISH.—*The Holy Bible:* an exact reprint, page for page, of the Authorised Version published in the year 1611. Demy 4to. half bound, 1*l*. 1*s*.

—— *The Psalter, or Psalms of David, and certain Canticles,* with a Translation and Exposition in English, by Richard Rolle of Hampole. Edited by H. R. Bramley, M.A., Fellow of S. M. Magdalen College, Oxford. With an Introduction and Glossary. Demy 8vo. 1*l*. 1*s*.

—— *Lectures on Ecclesiastes.* Delivered in Westminster Abbey by the Very Rev. George Granville Bradley, D.D., Dean of Westminster. Crown 8vo. 4*s*. 6*d*.

GOTHIC.—*The Gospel of St. Mark in Gothic,* according to the translation made by Wulfila in the Fourth Century. Edited with a Grammatical Introduction and Glossarial Index by W. W. Skeat, M.A. Extra fcap. 8vo. 4*s*.

GREEK.—*Vetus Testamentum* ex Versione Septuaginta Interpretum secundum exemplar Vaticanum Romae editum. Accedit potior varietas Codicis Alexandrini. Tomi III. Editio Altera. 18mo. 18*s*.

—— *Origenis Hexaplorum* quae supersunt; sive, Veterum Interpretum Graecorum in totum Vetus Testamentum Fragmenta. Edidit Fridericus Field, A.M. 2 vols. 1875. 4to. 5*l*. 5*s*.

—— *The Book of Wisdom:* the Greek Text, the Latin Vulgate, and the Authorised English Version; with an Introduction, Critical Apparatus, and a Commentary. By William J. Deane, M.A. Small 4to. 12*s*. 6*d*.

—— *Novum Testamentum Graece.* Antiquissimorum Codicum Textus in ordine parallelo dispositi. Accedit collatio Codicis Sinaitici. Edidit E. H. Hansell, S.T.B. Tomi III. 1864. 8vo. half morocco. Price reduced to 24*s*.

—— *Novum Testamentum Graece.* Accedunt parallela S. Scripturae loca, etc. Edidit Carolus Lloyd, S.T.P.R. 18mo. 3*s*.

On writing paper, with wide margin, 10*s*.

—— *Novum Testamentum Graece* juxta Exemplar Millianum. 18mo. 2*s*. 6*d*. On writing paper, with wide margin, 9*s*.

—— *Evangelia Sacra Graece.* Fcap. 8vo. limp, 1*s*. 6*d*.

—— *The Greek Testament,* with the Readings adopted by the Revisers of the Authorised Version:—
(1) Pica type, with Marginal References. Demy 8vo. 10*s*. 6*d*.
(2) Long Primer type. Fcap. 8vo. 4*s*. 6*d*.
(3) The same, on writing paper, with wide margin, 15*s*.

—— *The Parallel New Testament,* Greek and English; being the Authorised Version, 1611; the Revised Version, 1881; and the Greek Text followed in the Revised Version. 8vo. 12*s*. 6*d*.

The Revised Version is the joint property of the Universities of Oxford and Cambridge.

GREEK.—*Canon Muratorianus*: the earliest Catalogue of the Books of the New Testament. Edited with Notes and a Facsimile of the MS. in the Ambrosian Library at Milan, by S. P. Tregelles, LL.D. 1867. 4to. 10s. 6d.

—— *Outlines of Textual Criticism applied to the New Testament.* By C. E. Hammond, M.A. Fourth Edition. Extra fcap. 8vo. 3s. 6d.

HEBREW, etc.—*The Psalms in Hebrew without points.* 1879. Crown 8vo. Price reduced to 2s., in stiff cover.

—— *A Commentary on the Book of Proverbs.* Attributed to Abraham Ibn Ezra. Edited from a MS. in the Bodleian Library by S. R. Driver, M.A. Crown 8vo. paper covers, 3s. 6d.

—— *The Book of Tobit.* A Chaldee Text, from a unique MS. in the Bodleian Library; with other Rabbinical Texts, English Translations, and the Itala. Edited by Ad. Neubauer, M.A. 1878. Crown 8vo. 6s.

—— *Horae Hebraicae et Talmudicae*, a J. Lightfoot. A new Edition, by R. Gandell, M.A. 4 vols. 1859. 8vo. 1l. 1s.

LATIN.—*Libri Psalmorum* Versio antiqua Latina, cum Paraphrasi Anglo-Saxonica. Edidit B. Thorpe, F.A.S. 1835. 8vo. 10s. 6d.

—— *Old-Latin Biblical Texts: No. I.* The Gospel according to St. Matthew from the St. Germain MS. (g₁). Edited with Introduction and Appendices by John Wordsworth, D.D. Small 4to., stiff covers, 6s.

—— *Old-Latin Biblical Texts: No. II.* Portions of the Gospels according to St. Mark and St. Matthew, from the Bobbio MS. (k), &c. Edited by John Wordsworth, D.D., W. Sanday, M.A., D.D., and H. J. White, M.A. Small 4to., stiff covers, 21s.

OLD-FRENCH.—*Libri Psalmorum* Versio antiqua Gallica e Cod. MS. in Bibl. Bodleiana adservato, una cum Versione Metrica aliisque Monumentis pervetustis. Nunc primum descripsit et edidit Franciscus Michel, Phil. Doc. 1860. 8vo. 10s. 6d.

FATHERS OF THE CHURCH, &c.

St. Athanasius: Historical Writings, according to the Benedictine Text. With an Introduction by William Bright, D.D. 1881. Crown 8vo. 10s. 6d.

—— *Orations against the Arians.* With an Account of his Life by William Bright, D.D. 1873. Crown 8vo. 9s.

St. Augustine: Select Anti-Pelagian Treatises, and the Acts of the Second Council of Orange. With an Introduction by William Bright, D.D. Crown 8vo. 9s.

Canons of the First Four General Councils of Nicaea, Constantinople, Ephesus, and Chalcedon. 1877. Crown 8vo. 2s. 6d.

—— *Notes on the Canons of the First Four General Councils.* By William Bright, D.D. 1882. Crown 8vo. 5s. 6d.

Cyrilli Archiepiscopi Alexandrini in XII Prophetas. Edidit P. E. Pusey, A.M. Tomi II. 1868. 8vo. cloth. 2l. 2s.

—— *in D. Joannis Evangelium.* Accedunt Fragmenta varia necnon Tractatus ad Tiberium Diaconum duo. Edidit post Aubertum P. E. Pusey, A.M. Tomi III. 1872. 8vo. 2l. 5s.

—— *Commentarii in Lucae Evangelium* quae supersunt Syriace. E MSS. apud Mus. Britan. edidit R. Payne Smith, A.M. 1858. 4to. 1l. 2s.

—— Translated by R. Payne Smith, M.A. 2 vols. 1859. 8vo. 14s.

Ephraemi Syri, Rabulae Episcopi Edesseni, Balaei, aliorumque Opera Selecta. E Codd. Syriacis MSS. in Museo Britannico et Bibliotheca Bodleiana asservatis primus edidit J. J. Overbeck. 1865. 8vo. 1l. 1s.

Eusebius' Ecclesiastical History, according to the text of Burton, with an Introduction by William Bright, D.D. 1881. Crown 8vo. 8s. 6d.

Irenaeus: The Third Book of St. Irenaeus, Bishop of Lyons, against Heresies. With short Notes and a Glossary by H. Deane, B.D. 1874. Crown 8vo. 5s. 6d.

Patrum Apostolicorum, S. Clementis Romani, S. Ignatii, S. Polycarpi, quae supersunt. Edidit Guil. Jacobson, S.T.P.R. Tomi II. Fourth Edition, 1863. 8vo. 1l. 1s.

Socrates' Ecclesiastical History, according to the Text of Hussey, with an Introduction by William Bright, D.D. 1878. Crown 8vo. 7s. 6d.

ECCLESIASTICAL HISTORY, BIOGRAPHY, &c.

Ancient Liturgy of the Church of England, according to the uses of Sarum, York, Hereford, and Bangor, and the Roman Liturgy arranged in parallel columns, with preface and notes. By William Maskell, M.A. Third Edition. 1882. 8vo. 15s.

Baedae Historia Ecclesiastica. Edited, with English Notes, by G. H. Moberly, M.A. 1881. Crown 8vo. 10s. 6d.

Bright (W.). Chapters of Early English Church History.
1878. 8vo. 12*s*.

Burnet's History of the Reformation of the Church of England.
A new Edition. Carefully revised, and the Records collated with the originals, by N. Pocock, M.A. 7 vols. 1865. 8vo. *Price reduced to* 1*l*. 10*s*.

Councils and Ecclesiastical Documents relating to Great Britain and Ireland. Edited, after Spelman and Wilkins, by A. W. Haddan, B.D., and W. Stubbs, M.A. Vols. I. and III. 1869–71. Medium 8vo. each 1*l*. 1*s*.

> Vol. II. Part I. 1873. Medium 8vo. 10*s*. 6*d*.

> Vol. II. Part II. 1878. Church of Ireland; Memorials of St. Patrick. Stiff covers, 3*s*. 6*d*.

Hamilton (John, Archbishop of St. Andrews), The Catechism of. Edited, with Introduction and Glossary, by Thomas Graves Law. With a Preface by the Right Hon. W. E. Gladstone. 8vo. 12*s*. 6*d*.

Hammond (C. E.). Liturgies, Eastern and Western. Edited, with Introduction, Notes, and Liturgical Glossary. 1878. Crown 8vo. 10*s*. 6*d*.

> An Appendix to the above. 1879. Crown 8vo. paper covers, 1*s*. 6*d*.

John, Bishop of Ephesus. The Third Part of his Ecclesiastical History. [In Syriac.] Now first edited by William Cureton, M.A. 1853. 4to. 1*l*. 12*s*.

—— Translated by R. Payne Smith, M.A. 1860. 8vo. 10*s*.

Leofric Missal, The, as used in the Cathedral of Exeter during the Episcopate of its first Bishop, A.D. 1050–1072; together with some Account of the Red Book of Derby, the Missal of Robert of Jumièges, and a few other early MS. Service Books of the English Church. Edited, with Introduction and Notes, by F. E. Warren, B.D. 4to. half morocco, 35*s*.

Monumenta Ritualia Ecclesiae Anglicanae. The occasional Offices of the Church of England according to the old use of Salisbury, the Prymer in English, and other prayers and forms, with dissertations and notes. By William Maskell, M.A. Second Edition. 1882. 3 vols. 8vo. 2*l*. 10*s*.

Records of the Reformation. The Divorce, 1527–1533. Mostly now for the first time printed from MSS. in the British Museum and other libraries. Collected and arranged by N. Pocock, M.A. 1870. 2 vols. 8vo. 1*l*. 16*s*.

Shirley (W. W.). Some Account of the Church in the Apostolic Age. Second Edition, 1874. Fcap. 8vo. 3*s*. 6*d*.

Stubbs (W.). Registrum Sacrum Anglicanum. An attempt to exhibit the course of Episcopal Succession in England. 1858. Small 4to. 8*s*. 6*d*.

Warren (F. E.). Liturgy and Ritual of the Celtic Church.
1881. 8vo. 14*s*.

ENGLISH THEOLOGY.

Bampton Lectures, 1886. *The Christian Platonists of Alexandria.* By Charles Bigg, D.D. 8vo. 10s. 6d.

Butler's Works, with an Index to the Analogy. 2 vols. 1874. 8vo. 11s.

Also separately,

Sermons, 5s. 6d.   *Analogy of Religion*, 5s. 6d

Greswell's Harmonia Evangelica. Fifth Edition. 8vo. 1855. 9s. 6d.

Heurtley's Harmonia Symbolica: Creeds of the Western Church. 1858. 8vo. 6s. 6d.

Homilies appointed to be read in Churches. Edited by J. Griffiths, M.A. 1859. 8vo. 7s. 6d.

Hooker's Works, with his life by Walton, arranged by John Keble, M.A. Sixth Edition, 1874. 3 vols. 8vo. 1l. 11s. 6d.

—— the text as arranged by John Keble, M.A. 2 vols. 1875. 8vo. 11s.

Jewel's Works. Edited by R. W. Jelf, D.D. 8 vols. 1848. 8vo. 1l. 10s.

Pearson's Exposition of the Creed. Revised and corrected by E. Burton, D.D. Sixth Edition, 1877. 8vo. 10s. 6d.

Waterland's Review of the Doctrine of the Eucharist, with a Preface by the late Bishop of London. Crown 8vo. 6s. 6d.

—— *Works*, with Life, by Bp. Van Mildert. A new Edition, with copious Indexes. 6 vols. 1856. 8vo. 2l. 11s.

Wheatly's Illustration of the Book of Common Prayer. A new Edition, 1846. 8vo. 5s.

Wyclif. A Catalogue of the Original Works of John Wyclif, by W. W. Shirley, D.D. 1865. 8vo. 3s. 6d.

—— *Select English Works.* By T. Arnold, M.A. 3 vols. 1869-1871. 8vo. 1l. 1s.

—— *Trialogus.* With the Supplement now first edited. By Gotthard Lechler. 1869. 8vo. 7s.

HISTORICAL AND DOCUMENTARY WORKS.

British Barrows, a Record of the Examination of Sepulchral Mounds in various parts of England. By William Greenwell, M.A., F.S.A. Together with Description of Figures of Skulls, General Remarks on Prehistoric Crania, and an Appendix by George Rolleston, M.D., F.R.S. 1877. Medium 8vo. 25*s*.

Clarendon's History of the Rebellion and Civil Wars in England. 7 vols. 1839. 18mo. 1*l*. 1*s*.

Clarendon's History of the Rebellion and Civil Wars in England. Also his Life, written by himself, in which is included a Continuation of his History of the Grand Rebellion. With copious Indexes. In one volume, royal 8vo. 1842. 1*l*. 2*s*.

Clinton's Epitome of the Fasti Hellenici. 1851. 8vo. 6*s*. 6*d*.

—— *Epitome of the Fasti Romani.* 1854. 8vo. 7*s*.

Corpvs Poeticvm Boreale. The Poetry of the Old Northern Tongue, from the Earliest Times to the Thirteenth Century. Edited, classified, and translated, with Introduction, Excursus, and Notes, by Gudbrand Vigfússon, M.A., and F. York Powell, M.A. 2 vols. 1883. 8vo. 42*s*.

Freeman (E. A.). History of the Norman Conquest of England; its Causes and Results. In Six Volumes. 8vo. 5*l*. 9*s*. 6*d*.

—— *The Reign of William Rufus and the Accession of* Henry the First. 2 vols. 8vo. 1*l*. 16*s*.

Gascoigne's Theological Dictionary ("Liber Veritatum"): Selected Passages, illustrating the condition of Church and State, 1403-1458. With an Introduction by James E. Thorold Rogers, M.A. Small 4to. 10*s*. 6*d*.

Johnson (Samuel, LL.D.), Boswell's Life of; including Boswell's Journal of a Tour to the Hebrides, and Johnson's Diary of a Journey into North Wales. Edited by G. Birkbeck Hill, D.C.L. In six volumes, medium 8vo. With Portraits and Facsimiles of Handwriting. Half bound, 3*l*. 3*s*. *Just Published.*

Magna Carta, a careful Reprint. Edited by W. Stubbs, D.D. 1879. 4to. stitched, 1*s*.

Passio et Miracula Beati Olaui. Edited from a Twelfth-Century MS. in the Library of Corpus Christi College, Oxford, with an Introduction and Notes, by Frederick Metcalfe, M.A. Small 4to. stiff covers, 6*s*.

Protests of the Lords, including those which have been expunged, from 1624 to 1874; with Historical Introductions. Edited by James E. Thorold Rogers, M.A. 1875. 3 vols. 8vo. 2*l.* 2*s.*

Rogers (J. E. T.). History of Agriculture and Prices in England, A.D. 1259-1793.
    Vols. I and II (1259-1400). 1866. 8vo. 2*l.* 2*s.*
    Vols. III and IV (1401-1582). 1882. 8vo. 2*l.* 10*s.*

Saxon Chronicles (Two of the) parallel, with Supplementary Extracts from the Others. Edited, with Introduction, Notes, and a Glossarial Index, by J. Earle, M.A. 1865. 8vo. 16*s.*

Stubbs (W., D.D.). Seventeen Lectures on the Study of Medieval and Modern History, &c., delivered at Oxford 1867-1884. Demy 8vo. half-bound, 10*s.* 6*d.*

Sturlunga Saga, including the Islendinga Saga of Lawman Sturla Thordsson and other works. Edited by Dr. Gudbrand Vigfússon. In 2 vols. 1878. 8vo. 2*l.* 2*s.*

York Plays. The Plays performed by the Crafts or Mysteries of York on the day of Corpus Christi in the 14th, 15th, and 16th centuries. Now first printed from the unique MS. in the Library of Lord Ashburnham. Edited with Introduction and Glossary by Lucy Toulmin Smith. 8vo. 21*s.*

Statutes made for the University of Oxford, and for the Colleges and Halls therein, by the University of Oxford Commissioners. 1882. 8vo. 12*s.* 6*d.*

Statuta Universitatis Oxoniensis. 1886. 8vo. 5*s.*

The Examination Statutes for the Degrees of B.A., B. Mus., B.C.L., and B.M. Revised to Trinity Term, 1887. 8vo. sewed, 1*s.*

The Student's Handbook to the University and Colleges of Oxford. Extra fcap. 8vo. 2*s.* 6*d.*

The Oxford University Calendar for the year 1887. Crown 8vo. 4*s.* 6*d.*
    The present Edition includes all Class Lists and other University distinctions for the seven years ending with 1886.

    Also, supplementary to the above, price 5s. (pp. 606),

The Honours Register of the University of Oxford. A complete Record of University Honours, Officers, Distinctions, and Class Lists; of the Heads of Colleges, &c., &c., from the Thirteenth Century to 1883.

MATHEMATICS, PHYSICAL SCIENCE, &c.

Acland (H. W., M.D., F.R.S.). Synopsis of the Pathological
Series in the Oxford Museum. 1867. 8vo. 2s. 6d.

De Bary (Dr. A.). Comparative Anatomy of the Vegetative
Organs of the Phanerogams and Ferns. Translated and Annotated by F. O. Bower, M.A., F.L.S., and D. H. Scott, M.A., Ph.D., F.L.S. With 241 woodcuts and an Index. Royal 8vo., half morocco, 1l. 2s. 6d.

Goebel (Dr. K.). Outlines of Classification and Special Morphology of Plants. A New Edition of Sachs' Text-Book of Botany, Book II. English Translation by H. E. F. Garnsey, M.A. Revised by I. Bayley Balfour, M.A., M.D., F.R.S. With 407 Woodcuts. Royal 8vo. half morocco, 21s.

Sachs (Julius von). Lectures on the Physiology of Plants.
Translated by H. Marshall Ward, M.A. With 445 Woodcuts. Royal 8vo. half morocco, 1l. 11s. 6d. *Just Published.*

De Bary (Dr. A). Comparative Morphology and Biology of
the Fungi, Mycetozoa and Bacteria. Authorised English Translation by Henry E. F. Garnsey, M.A. Revised by Isaac Bayley Balfour, M.A., M.D., F.R.S. With 198 Woodcuts. Royal 8vo., half morocco, 1l. 2s. 6d.

Müller (J.). On certain Variations in the Vocal Organs of
the Passeres that have hitherto escaped notice. Translated by F. J. Bell, B.A., and edited, with an Appendix, by A. H. Garrod, M.A., F.R.S. With Plates. 1878. 4to. paper covers, 7s. 6d.

Price (Bartholomew, M.A., F.R.S.). Treatise on Infinitesimal
Calculus.

> Vol. I. Differential Calculus. Second Edition. 8vo. 14s. 6d.
>
> Vol. II. Integral Calculus, Calculus of Variations, and Differential Equations. Second Edition, 1865. 8vo. 18s.
>
> Vol. III. Statics, including Attractions; Dynamics of a Material Particle. Second Edition, 1868. 8vo. 16s.
>
> Vol. IV. Dynamics of Material Systems; together with a chapter on Theoretical Dynamics, by W. F. Donkin, M.A., F.R.S. 1862. 8vo. 16s.

Pritchard (C., D.D., F.R.S.). Uranometria Nova Oxoniensis.
A Photometric determination of the magnitudes of all Stars visible to the naked eye, from the Pole to ten degrees south of the Equator. 1885. Royal 8vo. 8s. 6d.

—— *Astronomical Observations* made at the University
Observatory, Oxford, under the direction of C. Pritchard, D.D. No. 1. 1878. Royal 8vo. paper covers, 3s. 6d.

Rigaud's Correspondence of Scientific Men of the 17th Century,
with Table of Contents by A. de Morgan, and Index by the Rev. J. Rigaud,
M.A. 2 vols. 1841–1862. 8vo. 18*s*. 6*d*.

Rolleston (George, M.D., F.R.S.). Scientific Papers and Addresses. Arranged and Edited by William Turner, M.B., F.R.S. With a Biographical Sketch by Edward Tylor, F.R.S. With Portrait, Plates, and Woodcuts. 2 vols. 8vo. 1*l*. 4*s*.

Westwood (J. O., M.A., F.R.S.). Thesaurus Entomologicus Hopeianus, or a Description of the rarest Insects in the Collection given to the University by the Rev. William Hope. With 40 Plates. 1874. Small folio, half morocco, 7*l*. 10*s*.

The Sacred Books of the East.

TRANSLATED BY VARIOUS ORIENTAL SCHOLARS, AND EDITED BY
F. MAX MÜLLER.

[Demy 8vo. cloth.]

Vol. I. The Upanishads. Translated by F. Max Müller.
Part I. The *Kh*ândogya-upanishad, The Talavakâra-upanishad, The Aitareya-âra*n*yaka, The Kaushîtaki-brâhma*n*a-upanishad, and The Vâ*g*asaneyi-sa*m*hitâ-upanishad. 10*s*. 6*d*.

Vol. II. The Sacred Laws of the Âryas, as taught in the Schools of Âpastamba, Gautama, Vâsish*th*a, and Baudhâyana. Translated by Prof. Georg Bühler. Part I. Âpastamba and Gautama. 10*s*. 6*d*.

Vol. III. The Sacred Books of China. The Texts of Confucianism. Translated by James Legge. Part I. The Shû King, The Religious portions of the Shih King, and The Hsiâo King. 12*s*. 6*d*.

Vol. IV. The Zend-Avesta. Translated by James Darmesteter. Part I. The Vendîdâd. 10*s*. 6*d*.

Vol. V. The Pahlavi Texts. Translated by E. W. West.
Part I. The Bundahi*s*, Bahman Ya*s*t, and Shâyast lâ-shâyast. 12*s*. 6*d*.

Vols. VI and IX. The Qur'ân. Parts I and II. Translated by E. H. Palmer. 21*s*.

Vol. VII. The Institutes of Vish*n*u. Translated by Julius Jolly. 10*s*. 6*d*.

Vol. VIII. The Bhagavadgîtâ, with The Sanatsugâtîya, and
The Anugîtâ. Translated by Kâshinâth Trimbak Telang. 10s. 6d.

Vol. X. The Dhammapada, translated from Pâli by F. Max
Müller; and The Sutta-Nipâta, translated from Pâli by V. Fausböll; being Canonical Books of the Buddhists. 10s. 6d.

Vol. XI. Buddhist Suttas. Translated from Pâli by T. W.
Rhys Davids. 1. The Mahâparinibbâna Suttanta ; 2. The Dhamma-*k*akka-ppavattana Sutta; 3. The Tevi*gg*a Suttanta; 4. The Akankheyya Sutta; 5. The *K*etokhila Sutta; 6. The Mahâ-sudassana Suttanta; 7. The Sabbâsava Sutta. 10s. 6d.

Vol. XII. The *S*atapatha-Brâhma*n*a, according to the Text
of the Mâdhyandina School. Translated by Julius Eggeling. Part I. Books I and II. 12s. 6d.

Vol. XIII. Vinaya Texts. Translated from the Pâli by
T. W. Rhys Davids and Hermann Oldenberg. Part I. The Pâtimokkha. The Mahâvagga, I-IV. 10s. 6d.

Vol. XIV. The Sacred Laws of the Âryas, as taught in the
Schools of Apastamba, Gautama, Vâsish*th*a and Baudhâyana. Translated by Georg Bühler. Part II. Vâsish*th*a and Baudhâyana. 10s. 6d.

Vol. XV. The Upanishads. Translated by F. Max Müller.
Part II. The Ka*th*a-upanishad, The Mu*nd*aka-upanishad, The Taittirîyaka-upanishad, The B*ri*hadâra*n*yaka-upanishad, The *S*veta*s*vatara-upanishad, The Pra*sn*a-upanishad, and The Maitrâya*n*a-Brâhma*n*a-upanishad. 10s. 6d.

Vol. XVI. The Sacred Books of China. The Texts of Confucianism. Translated by James Legge. Part II. The Yî King. 10s. 6d.

Vol. XVII. Vinaya Texts. Translated from the Pâli by
T. W. Rhys Davids and Hermann Oldenberg. Part II. The Mahâvagga, V-X. The *K*ullavagga, I-III. 10s. 6d.

Vol. XVIII. Pahlavi Texts. Translated by E. W. West.
Part II. The Dâ*d*istân-î Dînîk and The Epistles of Mânû*sk*îhar. 12s. 6d.

Vol. XIX. The Fo-sho-hing-tsan-king. A Life of Buddha
by A*s*vaghosha Bodhisattva, translated from Sanskrit into Chinese by Dharmaraksha, A.D. 420, and from Chinese into English by Samuel Beal. 10s. 6d.

Vol. XX. Vinaya Texts. Translated from the Pâli by T. W.
Rhys Davids and Hermann Oldenberg. Part III. The *K*ullavagga, IV-XII. 10s. 6d.

Vol. XXI. The Saddharma-pu*nd*arîka; or, the Lotus of the
True Law. Translated by H. Kern. 12s. 6d.

Vol. XXII. *G*aina-Sûtras. Translated from Prâkrit by Hermann Jacobi. Part I. The Â*kâ*râṅga-Sûtra. The Kalpa-Sûtra. 10s. 6d.

Vol. XXIII. The Zend-Avesta. Translated by James Darmesteter. Part II. The Sîrôzahs, Ya*s*ts, and Nyâyi*s*. 10s. 6d.

Vol. XXIV. Pahlavi Texts. Translated by E. W. West.
Part III. Dînâ-î Maînôg-î Khirad, *S*ikand-gûmânîk, and Sad-Dar. 10s. 6d.

Second Series.

Vol. XXV. Manu. Translated by Georg Bühler. 21s.

Vol. XXVI. The *S*atapatha-Brâhma*n*a. Translated by Julius Eggeling. Part II. 12s. 6d.

Vols. XXVII and XXVIII. The Sacred Books of China.
The Texts of Confucianism. Translated by James Legge. Parts III and IV. The Lî *K*î, or Collection of Treatises on the Rules of Propriety, or Ceremonial Usages. 25s.

Vols. XXIX and XXX. The G*ri*hya-Sûtras, Rules of Vedic Domestic Ceremonies. Translated by Hermann Oldenberg.

Part I (Vol. XXIX), 12s. 6d. *Just Published.*
Part II (Vol. XXX). *In the Press.*

Vol. XXXI. The Zend-Avesta. Part III. The Yasna, Visparad, Âfrînagân, and Gâhs. Translated by L. H. Mills. 12s. 6d.

The following Volumes are in the Press:—

Vol. XXXII. Vedic Hymns. Translated by F. Max Müller.
Part I.

Vol. XXXIII. Nârada, and some Minor Law-books.
Translated by Julius Jolly. [*Preparing.*]

Vol. XXXIV. The Vedânta-Sûtras, with *S*aṅkara's Commentary. Translated by G. Thibaut. [*Preparing.*]

*** *The Second Series will consist of Twenty-Four Volumes.*

Clarendon Press Series

I. ENGLISH, &c.

A First Reading Book. By Marie Eichens of Berlin; and edited by Anne J. Clough. Extra fcap. 8vo. stiff covers, 4*d.*

Oxford Reading Book, Part I. For Little Children. Extra fcap. 8vo. stiff covers, 6*d.*

Oxford Reading Book, Part II. For Junior Classes. Extra fcap. 8vo. stiff covers, 6*d.*

An Elementary English Grammar and Exercise Book. By O. W. Tancock, M.A. Second Edition. Extra fcap. 8vo. 1*s.* 6*d.*

An English Grammar and Reading Book, for Lower Forms in Classical Schools. By O. W. Tancock, M.A. Fourth Edition. Extra fcap. 8vo. 3*s.* 6*d.*

Typical Selections from the best English Writers, with Introductory Notices. Second Edition. In 2 vols. Extra fcap. 8vo. 3*s.* 6*d.* each.
    Vol. I. Latimer to Berkeley.   Vol. II. Pope to Macaulay.

Shairp (J. C., LL.D.). Aspects of Poetry; being Lectures delivered at Oxford. Crown 8vo. 10*s.* 6*d.*

A Book for the Beginner in Anglo-Saxon. By John Earle, M.A. Third Edition. Extra fcap. 8vo. 2*s.* 6*d.*

An Anglo-Saxon Reader. In Prose and Verse. With Grammatical Introduction, Notes, and Glossary. By Henry Sweet, M.A. Fourth Edition, Revised and Enlarged. Extra fcap. 8vo. 8*s.* 6*d.*

A Second Anglo-Saxon Reader. By the same Author. Extra fcap. 8vo. *Nearly ready.*

An Anglo-Saxon Primer, with Grammar, Notes, and Glossary. By the same Author. Second Edition. Extra fcap. 8vo. 2*s.* 6*d.*

Old English Reading Primers; edited by Henry Sweet, M.A.
    I. Selected Homilies of Ælfric. Extra fcap. 8vo., stiff covers, 1*s.* 6*d.*
    II. Extracts from Alfred's Orosius. Extra fcap. 8vo., stiff covers, 1*s.* 6*d.*

First Middle English Primer, with Grammar and Glossary. By the same Author. Extra fcap. 8vo. 2*s.*

Second Middle English Primer. Extracts from Chaucer, with Grammar and Glossary. By the same Author. Extra fcap. 8vo. 2*s.*

Principles of English Etymology. First Series. *The Native Element.* By W. W. Skeat, Litt.D. Crown 8vo. 9*s. Just Published.*

The Philology of the English Tongue. By J. Earle, M.A.
Third Edition. Extra fcap. 8vo. 7s. 6d.

An Icelandic Primer, with Grammar, Notes, and Glossary.
By the same Author. Extra fcap. 8vo. 3s. 6d.

An Icelandic Prose Reader, with Notes, Grammar, and Glossary.
By G. Vigfússon, M.A., and F. York Powell, M.A. Ext. fcap. 8vo. 10s. 6d.

A Handbook of Phonetics, including a Popular Exposition of
the Principles of Spelling Reform. By H. Sweet, M.A. Extra fcap. 8vo. 4s. 6d.

Elementarbuch des Gesprochenen Englisch. Grammatik,
Texte und Glossar. Von Henry Sweet. Extra fcap. 8vo., stiff covers, 2s. 6d.

The Ormulum; with the Notes and Glossary of Dr. R. M.
White. Edited by R. Holt, M.A. 1878. 2 vols. Extra fcap. 8vo. 21s.

Specimens of Early English. A New and Revised Edition.
With Introduction, Notes, and Glossarial Index. By R. Morris, LL.D., and
W. W. Skeat, Litt.D.
> Part I. From Old English Homilies to King Horn (A.D. 1150 to A.D. 1300).
> Second Edition. Extra fcap. 8vo. 9s.
>
> Part II. From Robert of Gloucester to Gower (A.D. 1298 to A.D. 1393).
> Second Edition. Extra fcap. 8vo. 7s. 6d.

Specimens of English Literature, from the 'Ploughmans
Crede' to the 'Shepheardes Calender' (A.D. 1394 to A.D. 1579). With Introduction, Notes, and Glossarial Index. By W. W. Skeat, Litt.D. Extra fcap.
8vo. 7s. 6d.

The Vision of William concerning Piers the Plowman, in three
Parallel Texts; together with *Richard the Redeless*. By William Langland
(about 1362–1399 A.D.). Edited from numerous Manuscripts, with Preface,
Notes, and a Glossary, by W. W. Skeat, Litt.D. 2 vols. 8vo. 31s. 6d.

The Vision of William concerning Piers the Plowman, by
William Langland. Edited, with Notes, by W. W. Skeat, Litt.D. Third
Edition. Extra fcap. 8vo. 4s. 6d.

Chaucer. I. *The Prologue to the Canterbury Tales;* the
Knightes Tale; The Nonne Prestes Tale. Edited by R. Morris, Editor of
Specimens of Early English, &c., &c. Extra fcap. 8vo. 2s. 6d.

—— II. *The Prioresses Tale; Sir Thopas;* The Monkes
Tale; The Clerkes Tale; The Squieres Tale, &c. Edited by W. W. Skeat,
Litt.D. Third Edition. Extra fcap. 8vo. 4s. 6d.

—— III. *The Tale of the Man of Lawe;* The Pardoneres
Tale; The Second Nonnes Tale; The Chanouns Yemannes Tale. By the
same Editor. Second Edition. Extra fcap. 8vo. 4s. 6d.

Gamelyn, The Tale of. Edited with Notes, Glossary, &c., by
W. W. Skeat, Litt.D. Extra fcap. 8vo. Stiff covers, 1s. 6d.

Minot (Laurence). Poems. Edited, with Introduction and
Notes, by Joseph Hall, M.A., Head Master of the Hulme Grammar School,
Manchester. Extra fcap. 8vo. 4s. 6d. *Just Published.*

Spenser's Faery Queene. Books I and II. Designed chiefly for the use of Schools. With Introduction, Notes, and Glossary. By G. W. Kitchin, D.D. Extra fcap. 8vo. 2*s.* 6*d*. each.

Hooker. Ecclesiastical Polity, Book I. Edited by R. W. Church, M.A. Second Edition. Extra fcap. 8vo. 2*s.*

OLD ENGLISH DRAMA.

The Pilgrimage to Parnassus with *The Two Parts of the Return from Parnassus.* Three Comedies performed in St. John's College, Cambridge, A.D. MDXCVII–MDCI. Edited from MSS. by the Rev. W. D. Macray, M.A., F.S.A. Medium 8vo. Bevelled Boards, Gilt top, 8*s.* 6*d.*

Marlowe and Greene. Marlowe's Tragical History of Dr. Faustus, and *Greene's Honourable History of Friar Bacon and Friar Bungay.* Edited by A. W. Ward, M.A. *New and Enlarged Edition.* Extra fcap. 8vo. 6*s.* 6*d.*

Marlowe. Edward II. With Introduction, Notes, &c. By O. W. Tancock, M.A. Extra fcap. 8vo. 3*s.*

SHAKESPEARE.

Shakespeare. Select Plays. Edited by W. G. Clark, M.A., and W. Aldis Wright, M.A. Extra fcap. 8vo. stiff covers.

The Merchant of Venice. 1*s.*   Macbeth. 1*s.* 6*d.*
Richard the Second. 1*s.* 6*d.*   Hamlet. 2*s.*

Edited by W. Aldis Wright, M.A.

The Tempest. 1*s.* 6*d.*   Midsummer Night's Dream. 1*s.* 6*d.*
As You Like It. 1*s.* 6*d.*   Coriolanus. 2*s.* 6*d.*
Julius Cæsar. 2*s.*   Henry the Fifth. 2*s.*
Richard the Third. 2*s.* 6*d.*   Twelfth Night. 1*s.* 6*d.*
King Lear. 1*s.* 6*d.*   King John. 1*s.* 6*d.*

Shakespeare as a Dramatic Artist; a popular Illustration of the Principles of Scientific Criticism. By R. G. Moulton, M.A. Crown 8vo. 5*s.*

Bacon. I. *Advancement of Learning.* Edited by W. Aldis Wright, M.A. Second Edition. Extra fcap. 8vo. 4*s.* 6*d.*

—— II. *The Essays.* With Introduction and Notes. By S. H. Reynolds, M.A., late Fellow of Brasenose College. *In Preparation.*

Milton. I. *Areopagitica.* With Introduction and Notes. By John W. Hales, M.A. Third Edition. Extra fcap. 8vo. 3*s.*

—— II. *Poems.* Edited by R. C. Browne, M.A. 2 vols. Fifth Edition. Extra fcap. 8vo. 6*s.* 6*d.* Sold separately, Vol. I. 4*s.*; Vol. II. 3*s.*

In paper covers:—
Lycidas, 3*d.*   L'Allegro, 3*d.*   Il Penseroso, 4*d.*   Comus, 6*d.*
Samson Agonistes, 6*d.*

—— III. *Samson Agonistes.* Edited with Introduction and Notes by John Churton Collins. Extra fcap. 8vo. stiff covers, 1*s.*

Bunyan. I. *The Pilgrim's Progress, Grace Abounding, Relation of the Imprisonment of Mr. John Bunyan.* Edited, with Biographical Introduction and Notes, by E. Venables, M.A. 1879. Extra fcap. 8vo. 5*s.* In ornamental Parchment, 6*s.*

—— II. *Holy War, &c.* Edited by E. Venables, M.A. In the Press.

Clarendon. History of the Rebellion. Book VI. Edited by T. Arnold, M.A. Extra fcap. 8vo. 4*s.* 6*d.*

Dryden. Select Poems. Stanzas on the Death of Oliver Cromwell; Astræa Redux; Annus Mirabilis; Absalom and Achitophel; Religio Laici; The Hind and the Panther. Edited by W. D. Christie, M.A. Second Edition. Extra fcap. 8vo. 3*s.* 6*d.*

Locke's Conduct of the Understanding. Edited, with Introduction, Notes, &c., by T. Fowler, D.D. Second Edition. Extra fcap. 8vo. 2*s.*

Addison. Selections from Papers in the Spectator. With Notes. By T. Arnold, M.A. Extra fcap. 8vo. 4*s.* 6*d.* In ornamental Parchment, 6*s.*

Steele. Selections from the Tatler, Spectator, and Guardian. Edited by Austin Dobson. Extra fcap. 8vo. 4*s.* 6*d.* In white Parchment, 7*s.* 6*d.*

Pope. With Introduction and Notes. By Mark Pattison, B.D.

—— I. *Essay on Man.* Extra fcap. 8vo. 1*s.* 6*d.*

—— II. *Satires and Epistles.* Extra fcap. 8vo. 2*s.*

Parnell. The Hermit. Paper covers, 2*d.*

Gray. Selected Poems. Edited by Edmund Gosse. Extra fcap. 8vo. Stiff covers, 1*s.* 6*d.* In white Parchment, 3*s.*

—— *Elegy and Ode on Eton College.* Paper covers, 2*d.*

Goldsmith. The Deserted Village. Paper covers, 2*d.*

Johnson. I. *Rasselas; Lives of Dryden and Pope.* Edited by Alfred Milnes, M.A. (London). Extra fcap. 8vo. 4*s.* 6*d.*, or *Lives of Dryden and Pope* only, stiff covers, 2*s.* 6*d.*

—— II. *Vanity of Human Wishes.* With Notes, by E. J. Payne, M.A. Paper covers, 4*d.*

Boswell's Life of Johnson. With the Journal of a Tour to the Hebrides. Edited, with copious Notes, Appendices, and Index, by G. Birkbeck Hill, D.C.L., Pembroke College. With Portraits and Facsimiles. 6 vols. Medium 8vo. *Half bound*, 3*l.* 3*s.* *Just Published.*

Cowper. Edited, with Life, Introductions, and Notes, by H. T. Griffith, B.A.

—— I. *The Didactic Poems of* 1782, with Selections from the Minor Pieces, A.D. 1779-1783. Extra fcap. 8vo. 3*s.*

—— II. *The Task, with Tirocinium,* and Selections from the Minor Poems, A.D. 1784-1799. Second Edition. Extra fcap. 8vo. 3*s.*

Burke. Select Works. Edited, with Introduction and Notes, by E. J. Payne, M.A.

—— I. *Thoughts on the Present Discontents ; the two Speeches on America.* Second Edition. Extra fcap. 8vo. 4s. 6d.

—— II. *Reflections on the French Revolution.* Second Edition. Extra fcap. 8vo. 5s.

—— III. *Four Letters on the Proposals for Peace with the* Regicide Directory of France. Second Edition. Extra fcap. 8vo. 5s.

Keats. Hyperion, Book I. With Notes by W. T. Arnold, B.A. Paper covers, 4d.

Byron. Childe Harold. Edited, with Introduction and Notes, by H. F. Tozer, M.A. Extra fcap. 8vo. 3s. 6d. In white Parchment, 5s.

Scott. Lay of the Last Minstrel. Edited with Preface and Notes by W. Minto, M.A. With Map. Extra fcap. 8vo. Stiff covers, 2s. Ornamental Parchment, 3s. 6d.

—— *Lay of the Last Minstrel.* Introduction and Canto I, with Preface and Notes, by the same Editor. 6d.

II. LATIN.

Rudimenta Latina. Comprising Accidence, and Exercises of a very Elementary Character, for the use of Beginners. By John Barrow Allen, M.A. Extra fcap. 8vo. 2s.

An Elementary Latin Grammar. By the same Author. Forty-second Thousand. Extra fcap. 8vo. 2s. 6d.

A First Latin Exercise Book. By the same Author. Fourth Edition. Extra fcap. 8vo. 2s. 6d.

A Second Latin Exercise Book. By the same Author. Extra fcap. 8vo. 3s. 6d.

Reddenda Minora, or Easy Passages, Latin and Greek, for Unseen Translation. For the use of Lower Forms. Composed and selected by C. S. Jerram, M.A. Extra fcap. 8vo. 1s. 6d.

Anglice Reddenda, or Easy Extracts, Latin and Greek, for Unseen Translation. By C. S. Jerram, M.A. Third Edition, Revised and Enlarged. Extra fcap. 8vo. 2s. 6d.

Anglice Reddenda. Second Series. By the same Author. Extra fcap. 8vo. 3s. *Just Published.*

Passages for Translation into Latin. For the use of Passmen and others. Selected by J. Y. Sargent, M.A. Sixth Edition. Extra fcap. 8vo. 2s. 6d.

Exercises in Latin Prose Composition; with Introduction, Notes, and Passages of Graduated Difficulty for Translation into Latin. By G. G. Ramsay, M.A., LL.D. Second Edition. Extra fcap. 8vo. 4s. 6d.

Hints and Helps for Latin Elegiacs. By H. Lee-Warner, M.A.
Extra fcap. 8vo. 3s. 6d.

First Latin Reader. By T. J. Nunns, M.A. Third Edition.
Extra fcap. 8vo. 2s.

Caesar. The Commentaries (for Schools). With Notes and
Maps. By Charles E. Moberly, M.A.
    Part I. *The Gallic War.* Second Edition. Extra fcap. 8vo. 4s. 6d.
    Part II. *The Civil War.* Extra fcap. 8vo. 3s. 6d.
    The Civil War. Book I. Second Edition. Extra fcap. 8vo. 2s.

Cicero. Speeches against Catilina. By E. A. Upcott, M.A.,
Assistant Master in Wellington College. *In the Press.*

Cicero. Selection of interesting and descriptive passages. With
Notes. By Henry Walford, M.A. In three Parts. Extra fcap. 8vo. 4s. 6d.
    Each Part separately, limp, 1s. 6d.
    Part I. Anecdotes from Grecian and Roman History. Third Edition.
    Part II. Omens and Dreams: Beauties of Nature. Third Edition.
    Part III. Rome's Rule of her Provinces. Third Edition.

Cicero. De Senectute. Edited, with Introduction and Notes,
by L. Huxley, M.A. In one or two Parts. Extra fcap. 8vo. 2s.

Cicero. Selected Letters (for Schools). With Notes. By the
late C. E. Prichard, M.A., and E. R. Bernard, M.A. Second Edition.
Extra fcap. 8vo. 3s.

Cicero. Select Orations (for Schools). In Verrem I. De
Imperio Gn. Pompeii. Pro Archia. Philippica IX. With Introduction and
Notes by J. R. King, M.A. Second Edition. Extra fcap. 8vo. 2s. 6d.

Cornelius Nepos. With Notes. By Oscar Browning, M.A.
Second Edition. Extra fcap. 8vo. 2s. 6d.

Horace. Selected Odes. With Notes for the use of a Fifth
Form. By E. C. Wickham, M.A. In one or two Parts. Extra fcap. 8vo.
cloth, 2s.

Livy. Selections (for Schools). With Notes and Maps. By
H. Lee-Warner, M.A. Extra fcap. 8vo. In Parts, limp, each 1s. 6d.
    Part I. The Caudine Disaster. Part II. Hannibal's Campaign
    in Italy. Part III. The Macedonian War.

Livy. Books V–VII. With Introduction and Notes. By
A. R. Cluer, B.A. Second Edition. Revised by P. E. Matheson, M.A.
(In one or two vols.) Extra fcap. 8vo. 5s.

Livy. Books XXI, XXII, and XXIII. With Introduction
and Notes. By M. T. Tatham, M.A. Extra fcap. 8vo. 4s. 6d.

Ovid. Selections for the use of Schools. With Introductions
and Notes, and an Appendix on the Roman Calendar. By W. Ramsay, M.A.
Edited by G. G. Ramsay, M.A. Third Edition. Extra fcap. 8vo. 5s. 6d.

Ovid. Tristia. Book I. The Text revised, with an Introduction and Notes. By S. G. Owen, B.A. Extra fcap. 8vo. 3*s.* 6*d.*

Plautus. Captivi. Edited by W. M. Lindsay, M.A. Extra fcap. 8vo. (In one or two Parts). 2*s.* 6*d. Just Published.*

Plautus. The Trinummus. With Notes and Introductions. (Intended for the Higher Forms of Public Schools.) By C. E. Freeman, M.A., and A. Sloman, M.A. Extra fcap. 8vo. 3*s.*

Pliny. Selected Letters (for Schools). With Notes. By the late C. E. Prichard, M.A., and E. R. Bernard, M.A. Extra fcap. 8vo. 3*s.*

Sallust. With Introduction and Notes. By W. W. Capes, M.A. Extra fcap. 8vo. 4*s.* 6*d.*

Tacitus. The Annals. Books I–IV. Edited, with Introduction and Notes (for the use of Schools and Junior Students), by H. Furneaux, M.A. Extra fcap. 8vo. 5*s.*

Terence. Andria. With Notes and Introductions. By C. E. Freeman, M.A., and A. Sloman, M.A. Extra fcap. 8vo. 3*s.*

—— *Adelphi.* With Notes and Introductions. (Intended for the Higher Forms of Public Schools.) By A. Sloman, M.A. Extra fcap. 8vo. 3*s.*

Tibullus and Propertius. Selections. Edited by G. G. Ramsay, M.A. Extra fcap. 8vo. (In one or two vols.) 6*s.*

Virgil. With Introduction and Notes. By T. L. Papillon, M.A. Two vols. Crown 8vo. 10*s.* 6*d.* The Text separately, 4*s.* 6*d.*

Virgil. The Eclogues. Edited by C. S. Jerram, M.A. In two Parts. Crown 8vo. *Nearly ready.*

Avianus, The Fables of. Edited, with Prolegomena, Critical Apparatus, Commentary, etc. By Robinson Ellis, M.A., LL.D. Demy 8vo. 8*s.* 6*d.*

Catulli Veronensis Liber. Iterum recognovit, apparatum criticum prolegomena appendices addidit, Robinson Ellis, A.M. 1878. Demy 8vo. 16*s.*

—— *A Commentary on Catullus.* By Robinson Ellis, M.A. 1876. Demy 8vo. 16*s.*

Catulli Veronensis Carmina Selecta, secundum recognitionem Robinson Ellis, A.M. Extra fcap. 8vo. 3*s.* 6*d.*

Cicero de Oratore. With Introduction and Notes. By A. S. Wilkins, M.A.
        Book I. 1879. 8vo. 6*s.*   Book II. 1881. 8vo. 5*s.*

—— *Philippic Orations.* With Notes. By J. R. King, M.A. Second Edition. 1879. 8vo. 10*s.* 6*d.*

Cicero. Select Letters. With English Introductions, Notes, and Appendices. By Albert Watson, M.A. Third Edition. Demy 8vo. 18*s*.

—— *Select Letters.* Text. By the same Editor. Second Edition. Extra fcap. 8vo. 4*s*.

—— *pro Cluentio.* With Introduction and Notes. By W. Ramsay, M.A. Edited by G. G. Ramsay, M.A. 2nd Ed. Ext. fcap. 8vo. 3*s*. 6*d*.

Horace. With a Commentary. Volume I. The Odes, Carmen Seculare, and Epodes. By Edward C. Wickham, M.A. Second Edition. 1877. Demy 8vo. 12*s*.

—— A reprint of the above, in a size suitable for the use of Schools. In one or two Parts. Extra fcap. 8vo. 6*s*.

Livy, Book I. With Introduction, Historical Examination, and Notes. By J. R. Seeley, M.A. Second Edition. 1881. 8vo. 6*s*.

Ovid. P. Ovidii Nasonis Ibis. Ex Novis Codicibus edidit, Scholia Vetera Commentarium cum Prolegomenis Appendice Indice addidit, R. Ellis, A.M. 8vo. 10*s*. 6*d*.

Persius. The Satires. With a Translation and Commentary. By John Conington, M.A. Edited by Henry Nettleship, M.A. Second Edition. 1874. 8vo. 7*s*. 6*d*.

Juvenal. XIII Satires. Edited, with Introduction and Notes, by C. H. Pearson, M.A., and Herbert A. Strong, M.A., LL.D., Professor of Latin in Liverpool University College, Victoria University. In two Parts. Crown 8vo. Complete, 6*s*.

Also separately, Part I. Introduction, Text, etc., 3*s*. Part II. Notes, 3*s*. 6*d*.

Tacitus. The Annals. Books I-VI. Edited, with Introduction and Notes, by H. Furneaux, M.A. 8vo. 18*s*.

Nettleship (H., M.A.). Lectures and Essays on Subjects connected with Latin Scholarship and Literature. Crown 8vo. 7*s*. 6*d*.

—— *The Roman Satura:* its original form in connection with its literary development. 8vo. sewed, 1*s*.

—— *Ancient Lives of Vergil.* With an Essay on the Poems of Vergil, in connection with his Life and Times. 8vo. sewed, 2*s*.

Papillon (T. L., M.A.). A Manual of Comparative Philology. Third Edition, Revised and Corrected. 1882. Crown 8vo. 6*s*.

Pinder (North, M.A.). Selections from the less known Latin Poets. 1869. 8vo. 15*s*.

Sellar (W. Y., M.A.). Roman Poets of the Augustan Age. VIRGIL. New Edition. 1883. Crown 8vo. 9*s*.

—— *Roman Poets of the Republic.* New Edition, Revised and Enlarged. 1881. 8vo. 14*s*.

Wordsworth (J., M.A.). Fragments and Specimens of Early Latin. With Introductions and Notes. 1874. 8vo. 18*s*.

III. GREEK.

A Greek Primer, for the use of beginners in that Language.
By the Right Rev. Charles Wordsworth, D.C.L. Seventh Edition. Extra fcap. 8vo. 1s. 6d.

Easy Greek Reader. By Evelyn Abbott, M.A. In one or two Parts. Extra fcap. 8vo. 3s.

Graecae Grammaticae Rudimenta in usum Scholarum. Auctore Carolo Wordsworth, D.C.L. Nineteenth Edition, 1882. 12mo. 4s.

A Greek-English Lexicon, abridged from Liddell and Scott's 4to. edition, chiefly for the use of Schools. Twenty-first Edition. 1886. Square 12mo. 7s. 6d.

Greek Verbs, Irregular and Defective; their forms, meaning, and quantity; embracing all the Tenses used by Greek writers, with references to the passages in which they are found. By W. Veitch. Fourth Edition. Crown 8vo. 10s. 6d.

The Elements of Greek Accentuation (for Schools): abridged from his larger work by H. W. Chandler, M.A. Extra fcap. 8vo. 2s. 6d.

A SERIES OF GRADUATED GREEK READERS:—

First Greek Reader. By W. G. Rushbrooke, M.L. Second Edition. Extra fcap. 8vo. 2s. 6d.

Second Greek Reader. By A. M. Bell, M.A. Extra fcap. 8vo. 3s. 6d.

Fourth Greek Reader; being Specimens of Greek Dialects. With Introductions, etc. By W. W. Merry, D.D. Extra fcap. 8vo. 4s. 6d.

Fifth Greek Reader. Selections from Greek Epic and Dramatic Poetry, with Introductions and Notes. By Evelyn Abbott, M.A. Extra fcap. 8vo. 4s. 6d.

The Golden Treasury of Ancient Greek Poetry: being a Collection of the finest passages in the Greek Classic Poets, with Introductory Notices and Notes. By R. S. Wright. M.A. Extra fcap. 8vo. 8s. 6d.

A Golden Treasury of Greek Prose, being a Collection of the finest passages in the principal Greek Prose Writers, with Introductory Notices and Notes. By R. S. Wright, M.A., and J. E. L. Shadwell, M.A. Extra fcap. 8vo. 4s. 6d.

Aeschylus. Prometheus Bound (for Schools). With Introduction and Notes, by A. O. Prickard, M.A. Second Edition. Extra fcap. 8vo. 2s.

—— **Agamemnon.** With Introduction and Notes, by Arthur Sidgwick, M.A. Second Edition. Extra fcap. 8vo. 3s.

—— **Choephoroi.** With Introduction and Notes by the same Editor. Extra fcap. 8vo. 3s.

Aristophanes. In Single Plays. Edited, with English Notes, Introductions, &c., by W. W. Merry, M.A. Extra fcap. 8vo.
    I. The Clouds, Second Edition, 2*s.*
    II. The Acharnians, Third Edition. In one or two parts, 3*s.*
    III. The Frogs, Second Edition. In one or two parts, 3*s.*

Cebes. Tabula. With Introduction and Notes. By C. S. Jerram, M.A. Extra fcap. 8vo. 2*s.* 6*d.*

Demosthenes. Olynthiacs and Philippics. Edited by Evelyn Abbott, M.A. Extra fcap. 8vo. In two Parts. *In the Press.*

Euripides. Alcestis (for Schools). By C. S. Jerram, M.A. Extra fcap. 8vo. 2*s.* 6*d.*

—— *Helena.* Edited, with Introduction, Notes, etc., for Upper and Middle Forms. By C. S. Jerram, M.A. Extra fcap. 8vo. 3*s.*

—— *Iphigenia in Tauris.* Edited, with Introduction, Notes, etc., for Upper and Middle Forms. By C. S. Jerram, M.A. Extra fcap. 8vo. cloth, 3*s.*

—— *Medea.* By C. B. Heberden, M.A. In one or two Parts. Extra fcap. 8vo. 2*s.*

Herodotus, Selections from. Edited, with Introduction, Notes, and a Map, by W. W. Merry, D.D. Extra fcap. 8vo. 2*s.* 6*d.*

Homer. Odyssey, Books I–XII (for Schools). By W. W. Merry, D.D. Thirty-second Thousand. Extra fcap. 8vo. 4*s.* 6*d.*
    Book II, separately, 1*s.* 6*d.*

—— *Odyssey,* Books XIII–XXIV (for Schools). By the same Editor. Second Edition. Extra fcap. 8vo. 5*s.*

—— *Iliad,* Book I (for Schools). By D. B. Monro, M.A. Second Edition. Extra fcap. 8vo. 2*s.*

—— *Iliad,* Books I–XII (for Schools). With an Introduction, a brief Homeric Grammar, and Notes. By D. B. Monro, M.A. Second Edition. Extra fcap. 8vo. 6*s.*

—— *Iliad,* Books VI and XXI. With Introduction and Notes. By Herbert Hailstone, M.A. Extra fcap. 8vo. 1*s.* 6*d.* each.

Lucian. Vera Historia (for Schools). By C. S. Jerram, M.A. Second Edition. Extra fcap. 8vo. 1*s.* 6*d.*

Plato. Meno. With Introduction and Notes. By St. George Stock, M.A., Pembroke College. Extra fcap. 8vo. (In one or two Parts.) 2*s.* 6*d. Just Published.*

Plato. Selections from the Dialogues [including the whole of the *Apology* and *Crito*]. With Introduction and Notes by John Purves, M.A., and a Preface by the Rev. B. Jowett, M.A. Extra fcap. 8vo. 6*s.* 6*d.*

C 3

Sophocles. For the use of Schools. Edited with Introductions and English Notes By Lewis Campbell, M.A., and Evelyn Abbott, M.A. *New and Revised Edition.* 2 Vols. Extra fcap. 8vo. 10s. 6d.

Sold separately, Vol. I, Text, 4s. 6d.; Vol. II, Explanatory Notes, 6s.

Sophocles. In Single Plays, with English Notes, &c. By Lewis Campbell, M.A., and Evelyn Abbott, M.A. Extra fcap. 8vo. limp.

Oedipus Tyrannus, Philoctetes. New and Revised Edition, 2s. each.
Oedipus Coloneus,   Antigone, 1s. 9d. each.
Ajax,   Electra,   Trachiniae, 2s. each.

—— *Oedipus Rex:* Dindorf's Text, with Notes by the present Bishop of St. David's. Extra fcap. 8vo. limp, 1s. 6d.

Theocritus (for Schools). With Notes. By H. Kynaston, D.D. (late Snow). Third Edition. Extra fcap. 8vo. 4s. 6d.

Xenophon. Easy Selections (for Junior Classes). With a Vocabulary, Notes, and Map. By J. S. Phillpotts, B.C.L., and C. S. Jerram, M.A. Third Edition. Extra fcap. 8vo. 3s. 6d.

—— *Selections* (for Schools). With Notes and Maps. By J. S. Phillpotts, B.C.L. Fourth Edition. Extra fcap. 8vo. 3s. 6d.

—— *Anabasis,* Book I. Edited for the use of Junior Classes and Private Students. With Introduction, Notes, etc. By J. Marshall, M.A., Rector of the Royal High School, Edinburgh. Extra fcap. 8vo. 2s. 6d.

—— *Anabasis,* Book II. With Notes and Map. By C. S. Jerram, M.A. Extra fcap. 8vo. 2s.

—— *Cyropaedia,* Books IV and V. With Introduction and Notes by C. Bigg, D.D. Extra fcap. 8vo. 2s. 6d.

Aristotle's Politics. By W. L. Newman, M.A. [*In the Press.*]

Aristotelian Studies. I. On the Structure of the Seventh Book of the Nicomachean Ethics. By J. C. Wilson, M.A. 8vo. stiff, 5s.

Aristotelis Ethica Nicomachea, ex recensione Immanuelis Bekkeri. Crown 8vo. 5s.

Demosthenes and Aeschines. The Orations of Demosthenes and Æschines on the Crown. With Introductory Essays and Notes. By G. A. Simcox, M.A., and W. H. Simcox, M.A. 1872. 8vo. 12s.

Head (Barclay V.). Historia Numorum: A Manual of Greek Numismatics. Royal 8vo. half-bound. 2l. 2s.

Hicks (E. L., M.A.). A Manual of Greek Historical Inscriptions. Demy 8vo. 10s. 6d.

Homer. Odyssey, Books I-XII. Edited with English Notes, Appendices, etc. By W. W. Merry, D.D., and the late James Riddell, M.A. 1886. Second Edition. Demy 8vo. 16s.

Homer. A Grammar of the Homeric Dialect. By D. B. Monro, M.A. Demy 8vo. 10s. 6d.

Sophocles. The Plays and Fragments. With English Notes and Introductions, by Lewis Campbell, M.A. 2 vols.
    Vol. I. Oedipus Tyrannus. Oedipus Coloneus. Antigone. 8vo. 16s.
    Vol. II. Ajax. Electra. Trachiniae. Philoctetes. Fragments. 8vo. 16s.

IV. FRENCH AND ITALIAN.

Brachet's Etymological Dictionary of the French Language, with a Preface on the Principles of French Etymology. Translated into English by G. W. Kitchin, D.D. Third Edition. Crown 8vo. 7s. 6d.

—— *Historical Grammar of the French Language.* Translated into English by G. W. Kitchin, D.D. Fourth Edition. Extra fcap. 8vo. 3s. 6d.

Works by GEORGE SAINTSBURY, M.A.

Primer of French Literature. Extra fcap. 8vo. 2s.

Short History of French Literature. Crown 8vo. 10s. 6d.

Specimens of French Literature, from Villon to Hugo. Crown 8vo. 9s.

MASTERPIECES OF THE FRENCH DRAMA.

Corneille's Horace. Edited, with Introduction and Notes, by George Saintsbury, M.A. Extra fcap. 8vo. 2s. 6d.

Molière's Les Précieuses Ridicules. Edited, with Introduction and Notes, by Andrew Lang, M.A. Extra fcap. 8vo. 1s. 6d.

Racine's Esther. Edited, with Introduction and Notes, by George Saintsbury, M.A. Extra fcap. 8vo. 2s.

Beaumarchais' Le Barbier de Séville. Edited, with Introduction and Notes, by Austin Dobson. Extra fcap. 8vo. 2s. 6d.

Voltaire's Mérope. Edited, with Introduction and Notes, by George Saintsbury. Extra fcap. 8vo. cloth, 2s.

Musset's On ne badine pas avec l'Amour, and *Fantasio.* Edited, with Prolegomena, Notes, etc., by Walter Herries Pollock. Extra fcap. 8vo. 2s.

    The above six Plays may be had in ornamental case, and bound in Imitation Parchment, price 12s. 6d.

Sainte-Beuve. Selections from the Causeries du Lundi. Edited by George Saintsbury. Extra fcap. 8vo. 2*s.*

Quinet's Lettres à sa Mère. Selected and edited by George Saintsbury. Extra fcap. 8vo. 2*s.*

Gautier, Théophile. Scenes of Travel. Selected and Edited by George Saintsbury. Extra fcap. 8vo. 2*s.*

L'Éloquence de la Chaire et de la Tribune Françaises. Edited by Paul Blouët, B.A. (Univ. Gallic.). Vol. I. French Sacred Oratory. Extra fcap. 8vo. 2*s.* 6*d.*

Edited by GUSTAVE MASSON, B.A.

Corneille's Cinna. With Notes, Glossary, etc. Extra fcap. 8vo. *cloth*, 2*s.* Stiff covers, 1*s.* 6*d.*

Louis XIV and his Contemporaries; as described in Extracts from the best Memoirs of the Seventeenth Century. With English Notes, Genealogical Tables, &c. Extra fcap. 8vo. 2*s.* 6*d.*

Maistre, Xavier de. Voyage autour de ma Chambre. Ourika, by *Madame de Duras;* Le Vieux Tailleur, by *MM. Erckmann-Chatrian;* La Veillée de Vincennes, by *Alfred de Vigny;* Les Jumeaux de l'Hôtel Corneille, by *Edmond About;* Mésaventures d'un Écolier, by *Rodolphe Töpffer.* Third Edition, Revised and Corrected. Extra fcap. 8vo. 2*s.* 6*d.*

Molière's Les Fourberies de Scapin, and *Racine's Athalie.* With Voltaire's Life of Molière. Extra fcap. 8vo. 2*s.* 6*d.*

Molière's Les Fourberies de Scapin. With Voltaire's Life of Molière. Extra fcap. 8vo. stiff covers, 1*s.* 6*d.*

Molière's Les Femmes Savantes. With Notes, Glossary, etc. Extra fcap. 8vo. *cloth*, 2*s.* Stiff covers, 1*s.* 6*d.*

Racine's Andromaque, and *Corneille's Le Menteur.* With Louis Racine's Life of his Father. Extra fcap. 8vo. 2*s.* 6*d.*

Regnard's Le Joueur, and *Brueys and Palaprat's Le Grondeur.* Extra fcap. 8vo. 2*s.* 6*d.*

Sévigné, Madame de, and her chief Contemporaries, Selections from the Correspondence of. Intended more especially for Girls' Schools. Extra fcap. 8vo. 3*s.*

Dante. Selections from the Inferno. With Introduction and Notes. By H. B. Cotterill, B.A. Extra fcap. 8vo. 4*s.* 6*d.*

Tasso. La Gerusalemme Liberata. Cantos i, ii. With Introduction and Notes. By the same Editor. Extra fcap. 8vo. 2*s.* 6*d.*

V. GERMAN.

Scherer (W.). A History of German Literature. Translated from the Third German Edition by Mrs. F. Conybeare. Edited by F. Max Müller. 2 vols. 8vo. 21s.

Max Müller. The German Classics, from the Fourth to the Nineteenth Century. With Biographical Notices, Translations into Modern German, and Notes. By F. Max Müller, M.A. A New Edition, Revised, Enlarged, and Adapted to Wilhelm Scherer's 'History of German Literature,' by F. Lichtenstein. 2 vols. crown 8vo. 21s.

GERMAN COURSE. By HERMANN LANGE.

The Germans at Home; a Practical Introduction to German Conversation, with an Appendix containing the Essentials of German Grammar. Third Edition. 8vo. 2s. 6d.

The German Manual; a German Grammar, Reading Book, and a Handbook of German Conversation. 8vo. 7s. 6d.

Grammar of the German Language. 8vo. 3s. 6d.

German Composition; A Theoretical and Practical Guide to the Art of Translating English Prose into German. 8vo. 4s. 6d.

German Spelling; A Synopsis of the Changes which it has undergone through the Government Regulations of 1880. Paper covers, 6d.

Lessing's Laokoon. With Introduction, English Notes, etc. By A. Hamann, Phil. Doc., M.A. Extra fcap. 8vo. 4s. 6d.

Schiller's Wilhelm Tell. Translated into English Verse by E. Massie, M.A. Extra fcap. 8vo. 5s.

Also, Edited by C. A. BUCHHEIM, Phil. Doc.

Becker's Friedrich der Grosse. Extra fcap. 8vo. *In the Press.*

Goethe's Egmont. With a Life of Goethe, &c. Third Edition. Extra fcap. 8vo. 3s.

—— *Iphigenie auf Tauris.* A Drama. With a Critical Introduction and Notes. Second Edition. Extra fcap. 8vo. 3s.

Heine's Prosa, being Selections from his Prose Works. With English Notes, etc. Extra fcap. 8vo. 4s. 6d.

Heine's Harzreise. With Life of Heine, Descriptive Sketch of the Harz, and Index. Extra fcap. 8vo. paper covers, 1s. 6d.; cloth, 2s. 6d.

Lessing's Minna von Barnhelm. A Comedy. With a Life of Lessing, Critical Analysis, etc. Extra fcap. 8vo. 3s. 6d.

—— *Nathan der Weise.* With Introduction, Notes, etc. Extra fcap. 8vo. 4s. 6d.

Schiller's Historische Skizzen; Egmont's Leben und Tod, and
Belagerung von Antwerpen. With a Map. Extra fcap. 8vo. 2s. 6d.

—— *Wilhelm Tell.* With a Life of Schiller; an historical and critical Introduction, Arguments, and a complete Commentary, and Map. Sixth Edition. Extra fcap. 8vo. 3s. 6d.

—— *Wilhelm Tell.* School Edition. With Map. 2s.

Modern German Reader. A Graduated Collection of Extracts in Prose and Poetry from Modern German writers:—
Part I. With English Notes, a Grammatical Appendix, and a complete Vocabulary. Fourth Edition. Extra fcap. 8vo. 2s. 6d.
Part II. With English Notes and an Index. Extra fcap. 8vo. 2s. 6d.

Niebuhr's Griechische Heroen-Geschichten. Tales of Greek Heroes. Edited with English Notes and a Vocabulary, by Emma S. Buchheim. School Edition. Extra fcap. 8vo., *cloth,* 2s. *Stiff covers,* 1s. 6d.

VI. MATHEMATICS, PHYSICAL SCIENCE, &c.
By LEWIS HENSLEY, M.A.

Figures made Easy: a first Arithmetic Book. Crown 8vo. 6d.

Answers to the Examples in Figures made Easy, together with two thousand additional Examples, with Answers. Crown 8vo. 1s.

The Scholar's Arithmetic. Crown 8vo. 2s. 6d.

Answers to the Examples in the Scholar's Arithmetic. Crown 8vo. 1s. 6d.

The Scholar's Algebra. Crown 8vo. 2s. 6d.

Aldis (W. S., M.A.). A Text-Book of Algebra. Crown 8vo. Nearly ready.

Baynes (R. E., M.A.). Lessons on Thermodynamics. 1878. Crown 8vo. 7s. 6d.

Chambers (G. F., F.R.A.S.). A Handbook of Descriptive Astronomy. Third Edition. 1877. Demy 8vo. 28s.

Clarke (Col. A. R., C.B., R.E.). Geodesy. 1880. 8vo. 12s. 6d.

Cremona (Luigi). Elements of Projective Geometry. Translated by C. Leudesdorf, M.A. 8vo. 12s. 6d.

Donkin. Acoustics. Second Edition. Crown 8vo. 7s. 6d.

Euclid Revised. Containing the Essentials of the Elements of Plane Geometry as given by Euclid in his first Six Books. Edited by R. C. J. Nixon, M.A. Crown 8vo. 7s. 6d.

Sold separately as follows,
Books I–IV. 3s. 6d. Books I, II. 1s. 6d.
Book I. 1s.

Galton (Douglas, C.B., F.R.S.). The Construction of Healthy Dwellings. Demy 8vo. 10s. 6d.

Hamilton (Sir R. G. C.), and J. Ball. Book-keeping. New and enlarged Edition. Extra fcap. 8vo. limp cloth, 2s.
  Ruled Exercise books adapted to the above may be had, price 2s.

Harcourt (A. G. Vernon, M.A.), and *H. G. Madan, M.A. Exercises in Practical Chemistry.* Vol. I. Elementary Exercises. Fourth Edition. Crown 8vo. 10s. 6d.

Maclaren (Archibald). A System of Physical Education: Theoretical and Practical. Extra fcap. 8vo. 7s. 6d.

Madan (H. G., M.A.). Tables of Qualitative Analysis. Large 4to. paper, 4s. 6d.

Maxwell (J. Clerk, M.A., F.R.S.). A Treatise on Electricity and Magnetism. Second Edition. 2 vols. Demy 8vo. 1l. 11s. 6d.

—— *An Elementary Treatise on Electricity.* Edited by William Garnett, M.A. Demy 8vo. 7s. 6d.

Minchin (G. M., M.A.). A Treatise on Statics with Applications to Physics. Third Edition, Corrected and Enlarged. Vol. I. *Equilibrium of Coplanar Forces.* 8vo. 9s. Vol. II. *Statics.* 8vo. 16s.

—— *Uniplanar Kinematics of Solids and Fluids.* Crown 8vo. 7s. 6d.

Phillips (John, M.A., F.R.S.). Geology of Oxford and the Valley of the Thames. 1871. 8vo. 21s.

—— *Vesuvius.* 1869. Crown 8vo. 10s. 6d.

Prestwich (Joseph, M.A., F.R.S.). Geology, Chemical, Physical, and Stratigraphical. Vol. I. Chemical and Physical. Royal 8vo. 25s.

Roach (T., M.A.). Elementary Trigonometry. Crown 8vo. 4s. 6d. *Just Published.*

Rolleston's Forms of Animal Life. Illustrated by Descriptions and Drawings of Dissections. New Edition. (*Nearly ready.*)

Smyth. A Cycle of Celestial Objects. Observed, Reduced, and Discussed by Admiral W. H. Smyth, R.N. Revised, condensed, and greatly enlarged by G. F. Chambers, F.R.A.S. 1881. 8vo. *Price reduced to* 12s.

Stewart (Balfour, LL.D., F.R.S.). A Treatise on Heat, with numerous Woodcuts and Diagrams. Fourth Edition. Extra fcap. 8vo. 7s. 6d.

Vernon-Harcourt (L. F., M.A.). A Treatise on Rivers and Canals, relating to the Control and Improvement of Rivers, and the Design, Construction, and Development of Canals. 2 vols. (Vol. I, Text. Vol. II, Plates.) 8vo. 21*s*.

—— *Harbours and Docks;* their Physical Features, History, Construction, Equipment, and Maintenance; with Statistics as to their Commercial Development. 2 vols. 8vo. 25*s*.

Watson (H. W., M.A.). A Treatise on the Kinetic Theory of Gases. 1876. 8vo. 3*s*. 6*d*.

Watson (H. W., D. Sc., F.R.S.), and S. H. Burbury, M.A.
I. *A Treatise on the Application of Generalised Coordinates to the Kinetics of a Material System.* 1879. 8vo. 6*s*.
II. *The Mathematical Theory of Electricity and Magnetism.* Vol. I. Electrostatics. 8vo. 10*s*. 6*d*.

Williamson (A. W., Phil. Doc., F.R.S.). Chemistry for Students. A new Edition, with Solutions. 1873. Extra fcap. 8vo. 8*s*. 6*d*.

VII. HISTORY.

Bluntschli (J. K.). The Theory of the State. By J. K. Bluntschli, late Professor of Political Sciences in the University of Heidelberg. Authorised English Translation from the Sixth German Edition. Demy 8vo. half bound, 12*s*. 6*d*.

Finlay (George, LL.D.). A History of Greece from its Conquest by the Romans to the present time, B.C. 146 to A.D. 1864. A new Edition, revised throughout, and in part re-written, with considerable additions, by the Author, and edited by H. F. Tozer, M.A. 7 vols. 8vo. 3*l*. 10*s*.

Fortescue (Sir John, Kt.). The Governance of England: otherwise called The Difference between an Absolute and a Limited Monarchy. A Revised Text. Edited, with Introduction, Notes, and Appendices, by Charles Plummer, M.A. 8vo. half bound, 12*s*. 6*d*.

Freeman (E.A., D.C.L.). A Short History of the Norman Conquest of England. Second Edition. Extra fcap. 8vo. 2*s*. 6*d*.

George (H. B., M.A.). Genealogical Tables illustrative of Modern History. Third Edition, Revised and Enlarged. Small 4to. 12*s*.

Hodgkin (T.). Italy and her Invaders. Illustrated with Plates and Maps. Vols. I—IV., A.D. 376-553. 8vo. 3*l*. 8*s*.

Kitchin (G. W., D.D.). A History of France. With numerous Maps, Plans, and Tables. In Three Volumes. *Second Edition.* Crown 8vo. each 10*s*. 6*d*.
    Vol. I. Down to the Year 1453.
    Vol. II. From 1453-1624.   Vol. III. From 1624-1793.

Payne (E. J., M.A.). A History of the United States of America. In the Press.

Ranke (L. von). A History of England, principally in the Seventeenth Century. Translated by Resident Members of the University of Oxford, under the superintendence of G. W. Kitchin, D.D., and C. W. Boase, M.A. 1875. 6 vols. 8vo. 3*l*. 3*s*.

Rawlinson (George, M.A.). A Manual of Ancient History. Second Edition. Demy 8vo. 14*s*.

Rogers (J. E. Thorold, M.A.). The First Nine Years of the Bank of England. 8vo. 8*s*. 6*d*.

Select Charters and other Illustrations of English Constitutional History, from the Earliest Times to the Reign of Edward I. Arranged and edited by W. Stubbs, D.D. Fifth Edition. 1883. Crown 8vo. 8*s*. 6*d*.

Stubbs (W., D.D.). The Constitutional History of England, in its Origin and Development. Library Edition. 3 vols. demy 8vo. 2*l*. 8*s*.

Also in 3 vols. crown 8vo. price 12*s*. each.

—— *Seventeen Lectures on the Study of Medieval and Modern History,* &c., delivered at Oxford 1867–1884. Demy 8vo. half-bound, 10*s*. 6*d*.

Wellesley. A Selection from the Despatches, Treaties, and other Papers of the Marquess Wellesley, K.G., during his Government of India. Edited by S. J. Owen, M.A. 1877. 8vo. 1*l*. 4*s*.

Wellington. A Selection from the Despatches, Treaties, and other Papers relating to India of Field-Marshal the Duke of Wellington, K.G. Edited by S. J. Owen, M.A. 1880. 8vo. 24*s*.

A History of British India. By S. J. Owen, M.A., Reader in Indian History in the University of Oxford. In preparation.

VIII. LAW.

Alberici Gentilis, I.C.D., I.C., De Iure Belli Libri Tres. Edidit T. E. Holland, I.C.D. 1877. Small 4to. half morocco, 21*s*.

Anson (Sir William R., Bart., D.C.L.). Principles of the English Law of Contract, and of Agency in its Relation to Contract. Fourth Edition. Demy 8vo. 10*s*. 6*d*.

—— *Law and Custom of the Constitution.* Part I. Parliament. Demy 8vo. 10*s*. 6*d*.

Bentham (Jeremy). An Introduction to the Principles of Morals and Legislation. Crown 8vo. 6*s*. 6*d*.

Digby (Kenelm E., M.A.). An Introduction to the History of the Law of Real Property. Third Edition. Demy 8vo. 10*s*. 6*d*.

Gaii Institutionum Juris Civilis Commentarii Quattuor; or, Elements of Roman Law by Gaius. With a Translation and Commentary by Edward Poste, M.A. Second Edition. 1875. 8vo. 18*s*.

Hall (W. E., M.A.). International Law. Second Ed. 8vo. 21*s*.

Holland (T. E., D.C.L.). The Elements of Jurisprudence. Third Edition. Demy 8vo. 10*s*. 6*d*.

—— *The European Concert in the Eastern Question*, a Collection of Treaties and other Public Acts. Edited, with Introductions and Notes, by Thomas Erskine Holland, D.C.L. 8vo. 12*s*. 6*d*.

Imperatoris Iustiniani Institutionum Libri Quattuor; with Introductions, Commentary, Excursus and Translation. By J. B. Moyle, B.C.L., M.A. 2 vols. Demy 8vo. 21*s*.

Justinian, The Institutes of, edited as a recension of the Institutes of Gaius, by Thomas Erskine Holland, D.C.L. Second Edition, 1881. Extra fcap. 8vo. 5*s*.

Justinian, Select Titles from the Digest of. By T. E. Holland, D.C.L., and C. L. Shadwell, B.C.L. 8vo. 14*s*.

Also sold in Parts, in paper covers, as follows:—
Part I. Introductory Titles. 2*s*. 6*d*. Part II. Family Law. 1*s*.
Part III. Property Law. 2*s*. 6*d*. Part IV. Law of Obligations (No. 1). 3*s*. 6*d*.
Part IV. Law of Obligations (No. 2). 4*s*. 6*d*.

Lex Aquilia. The Roman Law of Damage to Property: being a Commentary on the Title of the Digest 'Ad Legem Aquiliam' (ix. 2). With an Introduction to the Study of the Corpus Iuris Civilis. By Erwin Grueber, Dr. Jur., M.A. Demy 8vo. 10*s*. 6*d*.

Markby (W., D.C.L.). Elements of Law considered with reference to Principles of General Jurisprudence. Third Edition. Demy 8vo. 12*s*.6*d*.

Stokes (Whitley, D.C.L.). The Anglo-Indian Codes.
Vol. I. *Substantive Law.* 8vo. 30*s*. *Just Published.*
Vol. II. *Adjective Law.* In the Press.

Twiss (Sir Travers, D.C.L.). The Law of Nations considered as Independent Political Communities.
Part I. On the Rights and Duties of Nations in time of Peace. A new Edition, Revised and Enlarged. 1884. Demy 8vo. 15*s*.
Part II. On the Rights and Duties of Nations in Time of War. Second Edition, Revised. 1875. Demy 8vo. 21*s*.

IX. MENTAL AND MORAL PHILOSOPHY, &c.

Bacon's Novum Organum. Edited, with English Notes, by G. W. Kitchin, D.D. 1855. 8vo. 9*s*. 6*d*.

—— Translated by G. W. Kitchin, D.D. 1855. 8vo. 9*s*. 6*d*.

Berkeley. The Works of George Berkeley, D.D., formerly Bishop of Cloyne; including many of his writings hitherto unpublished. With Prefaces, Annotations, and an Account of his Life and Philosophy, by Alexander Campbell Fraser, M.A. 4 vols. 1871. 8vo. 2*l*. 18*s*.
The Life, Letters, &c. 1 vol. 16*s*.

Berkeley. Selections from. With an Introduction and Notes. For the use of Students in the Universities. By Alexander Campbell Fraser, LL.D. Second Edition. Crown 8vo. 7*s.* 6*d.*

Fowler (T., D.D.). The Elements of Deductive Logic, designed mainly for the use of Junior Students in the Universities. Eighth Edition, with a Collection of Examples. Extra fcap. 8vo. 3*s.* 6*d.*

—— *The Elements of Inductive Logic,* designed mainly for the use of Students in the Universities. Fourth Edition. Extra fcap. 8vo. 6*s.*

—— *and Wilson (J. M., B.D.). The Principles of Morals* (Introductory Chapters). 8vo. *boards,* 3*s.* 6*d.*

—— *The Principles of Morals.* Part II. (Being the Body of the Work.) 8vo. 10*s.* 6*d.*

Edited by T. FOWLER, D.D.

Bacon. Novum Organum. With Introduction, Notes, &c. 1878. 8vo. 14*s.*

Locke's Conduct of the Understanding. Second Edition. Extra fcap. 8vo. 2*s.*

Danson (J. T.). The Wealth of Households. Crown 8vo. 5*s.*

Green (T. H., M.A.). Prolegomena to Ethics. Edited by A. C. Bradley, M.A. Demy 8vo. 12*s.* 6*d.*

Hegel. The Logic of Hegel; translated from the Encyclopaedia of the Philosophical Sciences. With Prolegomena by William Wallace, M.A. 1874. 8vo. 14*s.*

Lotze's Logic, in Three Books; of Thought, of Investigation, and of Knowledge. English Translation; Edited by B. Bosanquet, M.A. Fellow of University College, Oxford. 8vo. *cloth,* 12*s.* 6*d.*

—— *Metaphysic,* in Three Books; Ontology, Cosmology, and Psychology. English Translation; Edited by B. Bosanquet, M.A. 8vo. *cloth,* 12*s.* 6*d.*

Martineau (James, D.D.). Types of Ethical Theory. Second Edition. 2 vols. Crown 8vo. 15*s.*

Rogers (J. E. Thorold, M.A.). A Manual of Political Economy, for the use of Schools. Third Edition. Extra fcap. 8vo. 4*s.* 6*d.*

Smith's Wealth of Nations. A new Edition, with Notes, by J. E. Thorold Rogers, M.A. 2 vols. 8vo. 1880. 21*s.*

X. FINE ART.

Butler (A. J., M.A., F.S.A.) The Ancient Coptic Churches of *Egypt.* 2 vols. 8vo. 30s.

Head (Barclay V.). Historia Numorum. A Manual of Greek Numismatics. Royal 8vo. *half morocco,* 42s.

Hullah (John). The Cultivation of the Speaking Voice. Second Edition. Extra fcap. 8vo. 2s. 6d.

Jackson (T. G., M.A.). Dalmatia, the Quarnero and Istria; with Cettigne in Montenegro and the Island of Grado. By T. G. Jackson, M.A., Author of 'Modern Gothic Architecture.' In 3 vols. 8vo. With many Plates and Illustrations. *Half bound,* 42s.

Ouseley (Sir F. A. Gore, Bart.). A Treatise on Harmony. Third Edition. 4to. 10s.

—— A Treatise on Counterpoint, Canon, and Fugue, based upon that of Cherubini. Second Edition. 4to. 16s.

—— A Treatise on Musical Form and General Composition. Second Edition. 4to. 10s.

Robinson (J. C., F.S.A.). A Critical Account of the Drawings by Michel Angelo and Raffaello in the University Galleries, Oxford. 1870. Crown 8vo. 4s.

Troutbeck (J., M.A.) and R. F. Dale, M.A. A Music Primer (for Schools). Second Edition. Crown 8vo. 1s. 6d.

Tyrwhitt (R. St. J., M.A.). A Handbook of Pictorial Art. With coloured Illustrations, Photographs, and a chapter on Perspective by A. Macdonald. Second Edition. 1875. 8vo. half morocco, 18s.

Upcott (L. E., M.A.). An Introduction to Greek Sculpture. Crown 8vo. 4s. 6d.

LONDON: HENRY FROWDE,
OXFORD UNIVERSITY PRESS WAREHOUSE, AMEN CORNER,

OXFORD: CLARENDON PRESS DEPOSITORY,
116 HIGH STREET.

☞ The DELEGATES OF THE PRESS *invite suggestions and advice from all persons interested in education; and will be thankful for hints, &c. addressed to* the SECRETARY TO THE DELEGATES, *Clarendon Press, Oxford.*

www.ingramcontent.com/pod-product-compliance
Lightning Source LLC
Chambersburg PA
CBHW020857230426
43666CB00008B/1219